HOW TO HEAR
GOD's
VOICE

An INTERACTIVE *Learning Experience*

HOW TO HEAR
GOD's
VOICE

An **INTERACTIVE** *Learning Experience*

Mark & Patti
VIRKLER

Mark and Patti have been writing books together for nearly 30 years. Sometimes Mark is the main author and researcher, and sometimes Patti is. Whichever of them does the actual writing, they are both wholly involved in each project, discussing, analyzing, adjusting, confirming, correcting, and editing. They therefore consider all of their books as joint ventures, and list themselves both as authors.

Destiny Image® Publishers, Inc.
P.O. Box 310
Shippensburg, PA 17257-0310

"Speaking to the Purposes of God for This Generation
and for the Generations to Come"

ISBN-13: 978-0-7684-2318-1

ISBN-10: 0-7684-2318-X

For Worldwide Distribution
Printed in the U.S.A.

4 5 6 7 8 9 / 09 08 07

This book and all other Destiny Image, Revival Press, MercyPlace, Fresh Bread, Destiny Image Fiction, and Treasure House books are available at Christian bookstores and distributors worldwide.

For a U.S. bookstore nearest you, call
1-800-722-6774.

For more information on foreign distributors, call
717-532-3040.

Or reach us on the Internet:
www.destinyimage.com

ENDORSEMENTS

Practical yet inspirational, the Virklers have combined the best of the school of the Word and the school of the Spirit to bring us this landmark work about *How to Hear God's Voice*. This book will help guide and ground multitudes in their adventure to discern the voice of God. Great job!

James W. Goll
Co-founder, Encounters Network
Author of *The Seer*, *The Lost Art of Intercession*, and *Praying for Israel's Destiny*

Mark Virkler's seminar, *How to Hear God's Voice*, was a tremendous blessing to me and our church. Through the discipline of interactive journaling it seems as if the eyes and ears of our hearts have popped open. I highly recommend his book and seminar.

Bill Dwyer, Pastor
Valley Vineyard, Reseda, California

When I heard Mark's material in the early 1980s, it quadrupled my ability to hear God's voice—removing a lot of the guess work.

Rev. Dale Bolton, Senior Pastor
Thornhill Vineyard, Ontario, Canada

How to Hear God's Voice is very, very rich and wonderful. I am going to study personally with it. I praise God for your ministry and important contribution to the Body of Christ. If you have written other study manuals, would you kindly send a copy of each one of them to me?

Dr. Paul Yonggi Cho
Founder, Yoido Full Gospel Church of Korea

I was introduced to a course of study called *How to Hear God's Voice* containing a real anointed teaching on drawing closer to God. It is the favorite of all our students and I don't think I will ever have a school without it.

Dr. Harold Reents, Former Academic Dean
Christ for the Nations

How to Hear God's Voice by Mark and Patti Virkler has dramatically changed my prayer life. I have found that I can will to dialogue with Christ on a daily basis, and I do. I believe this inspired approach to be absolutely essential to the growth of every serious Christian. I further believe Communion With God is an excellent example of the uniquely powerful way God is reaching out to His people today.

Dr. Richard Watson, Former Professor
Oral Roberts University

I believe How to *Hear God's Voice* is a practical and powerful biblical technique to help anyone hear the voice of God. Dr. Mark Virkler's course and his book have greatly enriched the level of intimacy with God that our church members and I experience. Dr. Virkler's methods have helped our church step into greater openness to the supernatural and to a more immediate expectancy for the presence of God. I highly recommend *How to Hear God's Voice* to the Body of Christ.

Rev. Dr. Ronald V. Burgio
Senior Pastor, Love Joy Gospel Church, Buffalo, New York
President, Elim Fellowship, Lima, New York

I have an awareness of God I've never had before. I received great insight that I've never before known.

Betty Bowen

Worship has been enhanced so very much since attending the *How to Hear God's Voice* class. God has seemingly released the prophetic in song and word in me.

Betsy Braun

Praise the Lord for the *How to Hear God's Voice* course! Through the adventure into the practices of journaling, vision, and unabashed praise I feel closer to God than in all my years of one-sided prayer and self-righteous appearances in church on Sunday. Admittedly, I was at first quite skeptical of the validity and worth of journaling and awakening the visual capacity to hear rhema from God. I feared that by accepting spontaneous thoughts and feelings as the communication of the Almighty I might in some way offend the Lord by supposing my own feelings and desires to be His, thereby elevating myself to divine status and offering praise and worship to myself.

However, after honest consideration and attentive prayer over the matter, my heart and mind were opened and I knew undoubtedly that God was communicating with me and I ran greater risk of offending Him by rejecting His counsel as false rather than by accepting it in faith. Safely I can say that God has spoken to me.

As a result of this course I have drawn infinitely closer to the Lord and continue to move closer still. Communion with Him is indescribably more rewarding than lopsided prayer directed to a far-away God. For my entire life I lived outside of communion with Him; I stood in the Holy Place and never entered the Holy of Holies. The most amazing thing is that I never knew that I was missing the most wonderful experience in life. I could have lived out my time here quite content in never truly knowing God and believed myself to be taking full advantage of the invitation to be His child. How thankful I am that I have been shown that there is more available! How truly awesome to have full knowledge that the veil has been rent and we as lowly creations may spend a lifetime communing with the Lord! Hallelujah!

Jessica Burton

The guys from the federal prison camp, as well as the mentors, just couldn't say enough about the materials and what they've learned through *How to Hear God's Voice*.

Steve Cronk, South Florida Area Director
Prison Fellowship

An audiotape of the *Four Keys to Hearing God's Voice* by Mark Virkler convinced me to go further. The teaching on this tape was sound, but the most important thing to me was hearing Mark instruct. I became convinced that he spoke about what he knew and not about something he had merely read or heard…I just got back from a full two-day silent retreat as I did visioning for our parish. It was wonderful. I realized while I was on retreat that I no longer have any nagging doubts about journaling. I simply journal and see what the Lord says when I need to. I certainly thank you for your ministry.

Rev. Ronald G. Horst, M.Div.
Rector of The Anglican Parish of Lansdowne Front Ontario, Canada

I have been an active Baptist pastor for 37 years. As far as I am personally concerned, seminars like Counseled by God and *How to Hear God's Voice* and Naturally Supernatural are absolutely fundamental to the building up of the inner life. At this present time we have six ongoing classes in *How to Hear God's Voice* using Mark's video series and another class on Counseled by God.

Rev. Peter Lord
Park Avenue Baptist Church

THIS BOOK IS DEDICATED WITH GRATITUDE

To our spiritual advisors, Roger Miller, Maurice Fuller, and Gary Greig, who have encouraged us greatly as we have walked this road of spiritual intimacy with Almighty God.

And to all who have proven this message in their own lives and have begun to hear God's voice, see vision, and journal.

CONTENTS

RECOMMENDATION FOR GROUP USE

We recommend that those who want to learn these principles do so with at least one other spiritually mature person. It is even better for a group to study together in the context of a local church. See if your pastor will oversee this group and help you by offering this course to your entire church.

The path of Christian spirituality should not be traveled alone. There is too much room for deception. Commitment to a group and to mature shepherds in the Body of Christ gives you the protection necessary to safely enter the spirit world.

Additional Materials Available for This Course

Audio cassettes, CDs, and video tapes of Mark Virkler teaching this course are available, as well as a Teacher's Guide and PowerPoint presentation. Please visit our website at www.cwgministries.org for details and ordering information.

Memory Verses

Each week share with the group a memory verse that strengthens you in your prayer life.

It is always extremely valuable to write out Scripture verses, for it helps you see things in the Word that you may otherwise overlook. God commanded that every incoming king of Israel "write for himself a copy of this law on a scroll in the presence of the Levitical priests" (Deut. 17:18). That is how important God feels it is to write the Scriptures. So we encourage you to write out at least one verse per week on a small card and carry it with you throughout this course. Memorize the verses weekly, and review them regularly.

The Prayer Life of Your Group

We encourage you to journal daily, and your group to journal together weekly, writing down what God is speaking to you, and sharing with one another in your group meetings. This will inspire faith among all.

Beginning to Hear God's Voice

You really learn to hear God's voice **when you begin listening, using vision, and recording what is coming to you by way of flowing thoughts and flowing pictures.** Your prayer life is the proof of the pudding, where the rubber meets the road. Whether or not you have excelled in hearing God's voice will be determined by your prayer life and the results that flow from it.

INTRODUCTION

Many years ago in the mid '80s I had a very vivid dream from the Lord. I was to go to a 'dairy' in Buffalo, New York and get the very richest of cream. Carol and I prayed about it and decided to drive over.

The only person I knew living in Buffalo at that time was Tommy Reid, pastor of Orchard Park Tabernacle. We went to visit him and as a result met one of the professors in his Bible school named Mark Virkler. We came home from that meeting with our 'cream'—Mark's study course on "Communion With God." [Note: *Communion With God* is the previous title of *How to Hear God's Voice*.]

Reflecting on that day, I was completely unaware of the impact this book would have. I did not realize that I would so easily begin to hear the voice of the Lord speaking to me, and I had no idea of the long-term effect that hearing His voice would have upon my life and ministry.

The course itself was well-presented, quickly pointing out how the Bible is full of visions, dreams and revelations as the Lord was continually speaking to biblical personalities. It was clearly the will of the Lord to speak also to me. At the time I did not know that. I thought I would perhaps hear the Lord speak to me two or three times throughout my entire life. But no, Jesus said, "My sheep hear My voice, and I know them and they follow Me" (Jn. 10:27).

Additionally, the 'fear of deception' issues were thoroughly addressed, pointing out the differences between occult, New Age teachings, and biblical truth. I really needed to hear and understand that clearly at the time as well.

Hearing the voice of God is one of my foundational values today and has been for many years. It is one of the core courses and values at Toronto Airport Christian Fellowship and Catch the Fire Ministries. Hundreds of our School of Ministry graduates have had their lives revolutionized by this teaching. Our church pastors and cell leaders have likewise been launched into prophetic and intimate ministry for the Lord, because they now regularly hear the voice of the Lord speaking love, affirmation, and direction into their lives.

It is astounding to me to realize that the very thing that our wonderful, personal, loving God wants to do is foreign and far removed from so many in the Church. But all that is changing.

Please know that God loves you. Your Heavenly Daddy is very, very interested in everything about you. Ephesians chapter 1 tells us that He chose you before the foundation of the world. He purposed for you to be His son or daughter, being adopted through Jesus Christ. Christ bought you and redeemed you through His own blood, He loves you and He even counts the number of hairs on your head (Matt. 10:30). Of course He wants to speak to you; Joel 2:28 makes that abundantly clear. God is a loving, caring, speaking, and communicating God and Father.

This book has potential to change the world. It will certainly change your life. It did mine; it did Carol's, along with hundreds of our friends. It will bring you into a place of hearing and knowing the heart of your loving Heavenly Father. Your inner being will learn experientially that He is a very personal God, wanting to commune with you and share His heart with you. Hearing His loving affirmation and direction will strengthen your relationship and build intimacy with Him. Lasting fruit will grow in your ministry.

Fasten your seatbelt; you are about to take the adventure of your life.

John Arnott, Sr. Pastor
Toronto Airport Christian Fellowship
and Catch the Fire Ministries

GOD WANTS TO BE YOUR FRIEND

Hungering for God

When I accepted Jesus Christ into my heart at age 15, an immediate hunger to know God sprang up within my spirit. I first attempted to satisfy this desire by devouring the Bible. Within weeks, it was obvious to me that the people in the Bible knew God through hearing Him speak to them and seeing visions of Him. God was their Friend. They walked and talked with Him. Every day, Adam and Eve were hearing God's voice and living out of it. What an astounding lifestyle! From Genesis to Revelation people heard God's voice and saw visions. I wanted that, too! What I didn't know at the time was that this hunger to know God had actually been placed in my heart by the Holy Spirit, and that God fully intended to satisfy this passion.

Eternal Life Is Intimacy with Almighty God!

Jesus said, "This is eternal life, that they might **know** Thee, the only true God and Jesus Christ whom Thou hast sent" (Jn. 17:3, emphasis added). What a dynamic statement: eternal life is **knowing** God! But this is not the simple, casual "knowing" of an acquaintance, or even a close friend. The word used here for "know" is *ginosko*, and it means "to be involved in an intimate, growing relationship." In the Greek version of the Old Testament, this is the word used in Genesis 4:1, where it says, "Adam **knew** Eve and she bore a son" (emphasis added). This is the most intimate relationship possible. Jesus makes the fantastic statement that this is what eternal life is all about! This is the essence of eternal life: to be involved in an intimate, growing relationship with the God of all creation and His only Son, Jesus. What a magnificent destiny!

Paul grasped this precious truth. In Philippians 3:10,11, he said that his great desire was, "that I might **know** Him, and the power of His [inner] resurrection and the fellowship of His sufferings, being conformed to His death; in order that I may attain to the [outer] resurrection from the dead" (emphasis added). Can you hear the yearning of Paul's heart? "That I might **know** Him!" Out of that precious love relationship, we will sense His life flowing within us, putting the flesh to death and flowing out through us to others. This is the reason for our salvation! This is why we were born again!

The Hebrew counterpart of the Greek *ginosko* is *yada*[1], and we like to use that word to characterize our time of loving fellowship in prayer. Prayer is so much more than presenting our petitions to God. It is our "*yada* time." Prayer is the link between lovers. It is communing with our Lover, Jesus — being intimate, quietly sensing each other's presence, being totally available to one another. It is a treasuring of one another so much that we desire to be together constantly, to share everything with one another, and to walk through life together. It is a feasting on one another's love. It is communion between two lovers: a relationship, not rules. Lovers come together whenever they can to share what is on their hearts. Their relationship is characterized by joy and spontaneity, not legalistic bondage.

Romance With the King of Kings

It is so important that we learn to seek the Lord for Himself alone, and not for the things He can give us. He longs for us to abide in Him, to feast on His love. He wants us to enjoy fellowship with Him as our dearest Friend. His heart yearns to be ministered to by our love.

We hurt Him so when we become too busy with our daily tasks to spend time enjoying His love or when we carelessly let sin slip into our lives, destroying our close communion. We must seek Him as our greatest treasure, seeing our time of sharing with Him as the highest priority in our lives.

As a result of our relationship with Him, we will begin to see His power flowing out from us, touching hearts, renewing life and strength, and working miracles. For out of relationship will come faith — simple faith, which is simply being close enough to Jesus to know what He wants to do in a situation and then doing whatever He instructs. But the only way we will ever be able to know exactly what Jesus is thinking and saying is by spending much time with Him — living in His presence every moment of our lives. There are no shortcuts to this! But, oh, the fullness of joy we find in His presence!

"Come Wholly Unto Me"

The Lord speaks of coming wholeheartedly to Him so we can fully experience Him. The following are five aspects of the wholeheartedness that God requires in our approach to Him:

- Make Me your **greatest treasure** so I can give Myself to you (Mark 12:30).

- **Search** for Me with your whole heart so I can reveal Myself to you (Jer. 29:13).

- **Trust** Me with your whole heart so I can guide your steps (Prov. 3:5).

- **Praise** Me with your whole heart so I can gift you with My presence (Ps. 9:1).

- **Return** to Me with your whole heart so I can be compassionate and bless you (Joel 2:12).

Communion: The Desire of God's Heart

God created us for the supreme purpose of having a love relationship with Him. Let's look throughout the covenants at the unchanging desire of God's heart.

We have already talked about the lifestyle of communion Adam and Eve enjoyed in the Garden of Eden before the fall. In the cool of the day, perhaps in the morning and in the evening, God would seek out man for fellowship. How amazing! The Creator of all actively sought the companionship of His creation, walking and talking with them, sharing their life together. Was it for this that we were created?

Because of sin, man lost that close relationship. But God found a man who recognized His voice, believed His words, and obeyed His instructions. His name was Abraham, and he was honored with the title "the Friend of God" (James 2:23). Abraham is the father of all those who believe, and as Abraham's children we, too, can be known as God's friends.

In the fullness of time, God called Abraham's physical descendents, the nation of Israel, out of Egyptian bondage into a life and a land set apart unto Him. God led them with a pillar of fire by night and a cloud by day until they came to Mount Sinai. The people prepared and purified themselves to finally meet directly with their Deliverer. The mountain was covered with fire, with cloud, and with a thick darkness, and out of the midst of the darkness and fire, they heard the voice of God (Deut. 5:22-31)!

How wonderful! How amazing! How frightening! They didn't expect that the voice of God would come with the fire of God, and they decided they would rather not have a relationship with Him if He was going to be that way!

Instead they chose to send Moses to God as their representative, to let him have the relationship and find out what God wanted them to do. God agreed to their request but warned that, first, He was not going to stop talking. If they didn't want to hear Him, they would have to leave. And second, if they did not want to hear Him, they would instead have to live under laws, commandments, statutes, and judgments.

The only alternative to relationship is law. But that was not what He wanted for His children.

The years passed, and God's people lived under the Law, not expecting that anyone but the occasional prophet or seer would hear from God. Eventually there grew up a young man whose heart longed for his God. As he tended his father's flocks, he understood the heart of the Shepherd of Israel. He contemplated the wonders of creation and learned to love the Creator. He meditated on the Law and perceived the mercy and justice of the great Judge. His heart overflowed with extravagant worship for his King, and God was pleased, saying, "I have found David…a man after Mine own heart." (Acts 13:22) "At last there is someone who 'gets it' — this is what I have always wanted — to love and to be loved!"

Near the end of Jesus' earthly life, He took the time to pray for His disciples. Not just those who had walked with Him along the Galilee countryside but for those of us who would believe because of their testimony. Jesus said that the Father had given Him authority over all people so that He might give eternal life to those whom He had been given. In John 17:3, Jesus defined what that eternal life was that He wanted to give to those who believed in Him: "Now this is eternal life: that they may know you, the only true God, and Jesus Christ, whom you have sent." Jesus lived and died so that we might have an intimate, growing, personal relationship with God the Father and His Son Jesus Christ.

We all know the story of Mary and Martha (Luke 10:38-42). Though Jesus loved Martha and no doubt appreciated her acts of service, it was Mary's decision to leave her work and simply sit at Jesus' feet that won His words of praise. It is not our works that will last forever, but our loving relationship with Him that will never be taken away from us.

The writer of Hebrews reminds us of the foolishness of the Hebrew children at the mountain of God (Heb. 12:18-26). But he also gives us great hope, telling us that God is giving us another chance! We, the Church of Jesus Christ, have come to another mountain and God is still speaking! We again have the opportunity to choose — will we welcome God's voice and the purifying fire that must accompany it, or will we again refuse Him Who is speaking? Will we finally embrace the loving personal communion our God is offering, or will we be content to let someone represent us in God's presence and just tell us what He is saying? Will we live in relationship or under law?

Finally we come to John's vision on the Isle of Patmos. He has seen so many amazing things, and suddenly he "heard what sounded like a great multitude, like the roar of rushing waters and like loud peals of thunder, shouting, 'Hallelujah! For our Lord God Almighty reigns! Let us rejoice and be glad and give him glory! For the wedding of the Lamb has come and his bride has made herself ready.'"

The culmination of all of history is a wedding! How wonderful! And we — the Church, the body of believers — we have been chosen to be the Bride of Christ, the Eternal Son of God! Can we comprehend such an amazing thing? Jesus wants to spend eternity sharing His Life with us! And He wants to start today.

From My Journal

Allow me to share two entries from my journal. Notice how the *rhema* is grounded in Logos, and though not really anything new to me, is still what I need to hear over and over so that I can believe it for each moment of each day.

(We will explore *Logos* and *rhema* in future chapters, but for now let us define *Logos* as the written Word of God — the Bible — and *rhema* as the voice of God in your heart.)

*"I am the Alpha and Omega, the beginning and the end. I am the first and the last, the light and the power. I am able to do exceedingly abundantly above all that you are able to think and ask. **Just come to Me**, and I will be your strength. I will be your lover. **You must simply come to Me**. It cannot be accomplished without time together, **so, come to Me often, continuously**. I am always here. I am always ready to listen and respond. I am a great and loving God, slow to anger and abounding in lovingkindness. I do forgive your sins. I do clothe you with righteousness. You must only seek Me with all your heart and turn from your ways, and **come to Me. Will you do that?"***

"I enjoy just being with you, not doing anything special together, just being together. I enjoy the fragrance of your worship. Times of solitude are peaceful to Me. It is like a quiet brook, flowing on the mountainside. I desire your presence. It is refreshing to Me. It is the fulfillment of My purposes when you choose to be with Me. It brings Me great pleasure. Do it often. Do not think every time we come together it must be to accomplish something. Simply being together is the greatest accomplishment, just being with one another. Come let us enjoy one another."

Prayer Is a Dialogue, Not a Monologue

Prayer is our link to God, and therefore, the most important activity we can engage in. Prayer is supposed to be powerful, effective and meaningful in our lives. Yet many times it is nothing more than a dutiful recitation of the items on our prayer list. We need to learn how to make prayer what it should be — a dynamic dialogue with the Lover of our souls.

Of paramount importance is learning to break free from the prison of rationalism in which Western culture is locked and relearning how to have spiritual experiences — experiences that come from God's Spirit to my spirit and only secondarily to my brain. We must return to the balance that was so beautifully expressed in

Jesus' life Who did nothing on His own initiative, but only what He heard and saw the Father doing (John 5:19,20,30).

The following are the things I needed to learn for prayer to become purposeful in my life:

✓ I can have a relationship with God through spiritual experiences rather than the dry monologue of simple mental prayer.

✓ The essence of prayer is my love relationship with the King of Kings, not simply going to Him to get things.

✓ The main purpose for learning to hear God's voice is so that I might really know Him — His heart, His joys, His desires, His hurts, His character, His will.

✓ The principles from the Bible that relate to prayer and the spiritual realm provide direction and understanding as I travel the road of spiritual experiences.

✓ The Holy Spirit will mold my prayer life, instead of me taking the principles of prayer God has shown me and reducing them to legalistic bondage.

✓ Spirit-born specific action and power flow as a natural result of my love relationship, causing the activities of my life to be of the Spirit and not the flesh. This keeps my relationship with the King of Kings from being simply self-indulgent on my part and helps me to realize that many others need to be touched by His love also.

Christianity Is More Than a Religion

One basic distinction between Christianity and the many other religions is that Christianity goes beyond a simple code of ethics, a list of rules and laws that one must follow, and offers direct, spiritual experiences with a loving God. We not only know about God, we experience Him. We not only say the sinner's prayer, and accept by faith that we are saved, but we experience His Spirit bearing witness with our spirits that we are the children of God (Rom. 8:16). We not only seek guidance from the laws of the Bible, we also find guidance through the Spirit granting peace in our hearts.

We do not simply read the Bible as a lifeless book with black print on white pages, but we experience it as alive (Heb. 4:12). God "illumines" or quickens it to our hearts as we pray for a spirit of revelation (Eph. 1:17). We do not just pray according to our own desires; rather, God "burdens" our hearts to pray in harmony with His will. God has sent His Holy Spirit into our hearts, crying "Abba Father" (Rom. 8:15), so that we can have a direct on-going love experience with Him. It is a major provision of the New Testament period that God has come to dwell within the hearts of men. This is taught in many places throughout the Bible. For instance:

> *And I will ask the Father, and He will give you another Helper, that He may be with you forever; that is the Spirit of truth, whom the world cannot receive, because it does not behold Him or know Him, but you know Him because He abides with you, and will be in you. I will not leave you as orphans; I will come to you.* (John 14:16-18)

> *Or do you not know that your body is a temple of the Holy Spirit who is in you, whom you have from God, and that you are not your own?* (1 Corinthians 6:19)

> *But we have this treasure in earthen vessels, that the surpassing greatness of the power may be of God and not from ourselves....* (2 Corinthians 4:7)

I am sure all Christians have experienced the truth of Philippians 4:13, "I can do all things through Him [Christ] Who strengthens me [fuses His strength to mine, literal Greek]." Being too weak to handle a problem, we have called upon the indwelling Spirit to help us and have found His strength overcoming our weakness, His joy overcoming our sorrow, or His peace overcoming our anxiety.

Christianity is much more than a code of ethics; it is much more than a religion. It is a love relationship with the King of Kings. It is a direct encounter with Him through the indwelling work of His Holy Spirit, which we freely receive as His gift to us. This, then, causes Christianity to ascend far beyond rationalism into the world of direct spiritual experiences. First Corinthians 2:9,10 tells us:

> *Things which eye has not seen and ear has not heard, and which have not entered the heart of man, all that God has prepared for those who love Him. For to us God revealed them through the Spirit; for the Spirit searches all things, even the depths of God.*

Divine Revelation Within Our Spirits

We come to know truth with our hearts or spirits, rather than with our minds. God reveals things that our natural eyes and ears could never sense through His Spirit speaking directly to our spirits. It is not that our natural eyes, ears and mind have no place in God's glorious revelation, for they are wonders of His creation as much as our hearts and spirits are. However, each part of man (his body, soul, and spirit) has a special function in God's plan.

God says that there are some things that He can only "reveal through the Spirit." Through the indwelling Holy Spirit, God has given us direct communion with Himself. We hear His voice within our hearts. We are led by the Spirit (Rom. 8:14). We have inner subjective experiences. Through insight, we receive revelation from Him, and He illumines Scripture to us. Through intuition, we sense the promptings of the Holy Spirit and the voice of God. So, our life in the spirit, our relationship with God, is an inner, intuitive, spiritual, heart experience.

The Use and Abuse of Doctrine and Technique

We must receive the caution Jesus gave in John 5:39,40. "You search the Scriptures, because you think that in them you have eternal life; and it is these that bear witness to Me; and you are unwilling to come to Me, that you may have eternal life." It is quite easy to acquire correct doctrine and head knowledge from Scripture. We can learn what the Word says about Christ and become satisfied with that information. But such intellectual exercise does not profit our spirits at all. We must take a further step of loving trust in Jesus as a Person Who is alive right now and yearns to be a part of our lives. Only through heart faith can we experience the things that the Scriptures testify about Him.

Finney Spoke of Three Classes of People

Many, understanding the "Confession of Faith" as summarizing the doctrines of the Bible, very much neglect the Bible and rest in a belief of the articles of faith. Others, more cautious and more in earnest, search the Scriptures to see what they say about Christ, but stop short and rest in the formation of correct theological opinions; while others, and they are the only saved class, love the Scriptures intensely because they testify of Jesus. They search and devour the Scriptures because they tell them who Jesus is and what they may trust Him for.

They do not stop short and rest in this testimony; but by an act of loving trust [they] go directly to Him, to His person, thus joining their souls to Him in a union that receives from Him, by a direct divine communication, the things for which they are led to trust Him. This is certainly Christian experience. This is receiving from Christ the eternal life which God has given us in Him. This is saving faith…The error to which I call attention does not consist in laying too much stress in teaching and believing the facts and doctrines of the Gospel: but consists in stopping short of trusting the personal Christ for what those facts and doctrines teach us to trust Him, and satisfying ourselves with believing the testimony about Him, instead of committing our souls to Him by an act of loving trust.

(Taken from protected material used by permission of the Christian Literature Crusade, Fort Washington, PA 10934.)

Do not stop with the doctrine and techniques taught in this manual or trust in them. Life and power flow only from Jesus. On the other hand, do not discard doctrines or techniques. Recognize that they have been given as channels through which the grace of God flows. Let them lead you into a full encounter with our Lord Jesus Christ, allowing you to wholly experience His life.

Experiencing Scripture, Not Just Codifying It

I can study the Bible rationally, simply with the mind, and learn many facts about God. For instance, I can learn that God loves me. But since love is an inner heart experience, I cannot fully experience God's love until He touches my heart, heals my hurts, and breaks my hardness. When He fills me to overflowing and brings tears of joy to my eyes, then through an intuitive, spiritual experience, I have fully experienced the love I read about.

However, spirit-to-Spirit encounters with God have become much too rare among Western Christians. Since rationalism has taken over the Western world in the past few hundred years, the Church has also come under its influence and has not given the attention it should to the work of the Spirit in our lives. Therefore, we are often bound by rationalism and miss the fullness of relationship with our Father that the early Church enjoyed.

Forty-nine percent of the New Testament contains references to spiritual (non-rational) experiences. To be bound by rationalism will effectively cut off half of New Testament Christianity. If you are not relating intuitively to God, but only intellectually, you will lose your opportunity to flow in the nine gifts of the Holy Spirit; to receive guidance through dreams and visions; to have a fully meaningful and effective prayer life; to commune with the Lord in a dialogue, to build an extremely intimate relationship with Him; and to wholly experience the inward benefits of true worship.

Through rationalism (an over-emphasis on reason), Christianity and the Western world have ceased to know how to deal with their inner lives (commonly called heart, spirit, subconscious, or unconscious). Because this entire area of our lives has been cut off and ignored, not only by Western culture but also by the Church, people have not been able to deal successfully with the forces within them (repressed hurts, fears, anxieties, forces of darkness — demons) and have been left more and more to seek escapes such as drinking, drugs, sensual fulfillment and suicide. Others become neurotic and psychotic; still others go to the occult and Eastern religions to satisfy the inner desires of the spirit which are not being met in "rational Christianity."

We must rediscover direct contact with God and once again become open to intuitive, spiritual experiences. We must rediscover our spiritual senses and reinstate them in our lives, allowing the power of the Father, of Jesus Christ, and of the Holy Spirit to heal, strengthen and guide us from within. Therein lies the work of the

Notes

Church. Direct inner experiences with the Lord bring healing to the spirit, soul and body.

Take your Bible and **prayerfully read and meditate on** First Corinthians 1:18–2:16, asking God to grant you understanding and revelation concerning these verses. In your journal, please record the thoughts and insights you receive.

The following, Figure 1.1 and Figure 1.2, is a brief comparison of rationalism and Spirit-to-spirit encounters. Take time to consider its truth and your own life in regard to these two philosophies. Where do you stand?

A Brief Examination of the Two Approaches

True reality is the physical world.	True reality is the spiritual world.
Reality is perceived through the mind.	Reality is perceived through the spirit.
My goal is to develop my mind.	My goal is to develop my spirit.
I live out of what my mind is telling me.	I live out of what my spirit is telling me.
My mind directs me through calculated, cognitive, and analytical thoughts.	My spirit directs me through spontaneous, flowing thoughts that are placed in it by the Spirit of God.
My mind is cultivated by using it in academic study.	My spirit is cultivated by using it in communication with God.
Direction is received from my mind's analysis of stored knowledge.	Direction is received from my spirit by waiting quietly upon the Lord allowing Him to spontaneously inject into my heart His thoughts, burdens, and visions.
Out of the mind flows *Logos* —the written, recorded Word of God.	Out of the spirit flows *rhema* — what God is speaking to me at that moment.
A Christian who has **only** developed his mind flows with a knowledge of the *Logos*.	A Christian with a developed spirit flows with the power of the Spirit and is grounded in a knowledge of the *Logos*.

Figure 1.1

A Theological Backdrop for Experiencing Spiritual Intimacy
The Mind and the Spirit (1 Cor. 1:18–2:16)

To experience spiritual communication, most
Westerners will have to do the following:

Dethrone the Mind
(Rationalism)

Enthrone the Spirit
(Spirit Control)

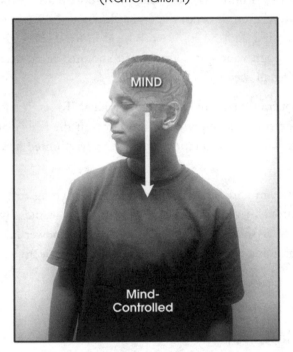

Rationalism Defined: "Reliance on reason as the basis for establishment of religious truth: a theory that reason is in itself a source of knowledge superior to and independent of sense perceptions."
(*Webster's New Collegiate Dictionary*)

Realize that knowledge can be transmitted Spirit-to-spirit.

"Things which eye has not seen and ear has not heard, and which have not entered the heart of man, all that God has prepared for those who love Him. For to us God revealed them through the Spirit; for the Spirit searches all things, even the depths of God. (1 Cor. 2:9,10)

God is calling us to present our minds and our hearts to Him to fill and to flow through. Biblical meditation incorporates both Spirit-led reasoning and heart revelation.

Jesus allowed divine initative to guide both His heart and His mind (Jn. 5:19). Let us seek to do the same. Our lives will be fully restored and balanced when they match the lives of New Testament Christians.

Figure 1.2

God is not calling us to use the mind **OR** the spirit, but the mind **AND** the spirit. Biblical meditation **combines the analysis of the mind with the spontaneity of the heart,** or both left and right brain functions. (We will explore this in detail in the next chapter.) Jesus joined rationalism and spiritual communion in perfect balance in His own personal life. Let us seek to do the same. Our lives will be fully restored and balanced when they match the lives of New Testament Christians.

Being a Christian does not mean throwing your mind away. Your mind is used as you approach God, but your mind has now found its **proper place.** Although it is the organ that **processes** revelation, it is not the organ through which revelation is **received.** The spirit is. The mind and the spirit work hand-in-hand. Direction in your walk comes by *rhema* through your spirit. Your Spirit-anointed mind acts as a check and safeguard, comparing all *rhema* to *Logos.*

Revelation itself is not irrational, but rather superrational. To say it another way, revelation is not foolishness; it has simply taken into account the reality of the spiritual world, and this appears irrational to rationalism, which has limited its scope merely to the physical world.

For example, for Abraham and Sarah to believe they were going to have a baby at 90 years of age is irrational if your framework is limited only to the physical laws. However, if you believe in a God Who injects His supernatural power into the natural, and Who said He was going to give them a child, then it is perfectly rational (or super-rational) to believe for a child.

Contrasting Two Worldviews

The following are two worldviews that you might embrace. Only one of them is true, but let me show you both so you can carefully examine your life and determine your position, and then decide if that is where you want to stand.

One Worldview — Rationalism

In this worldview you believe that man lives in a box — a space/time/energy/mass box. This is the totality of the real world. You contact this world through your five outer senses: touch, taste, sight, hearing, and smell. If you were to leave this box and travel toward the spiritual world, you would find that it is either non-existent or, if it does exist, it is unknowable.

This is the worldview my religious leaders taught me when I was first saved. They did admit to a spiritual world, but they said it was unknowable in this dispensation. I was told not to expect any direct contact with God during this age because we had been given the Bible and there was no longer a need to encounter God directly. I was also taught not to expect dreams or visions or God's voice or tongues or healing or miracles or any of the gifts of the Holy Spirit to operate. Even though my mind

FIRST WORLDVIEW — RATIONALISM

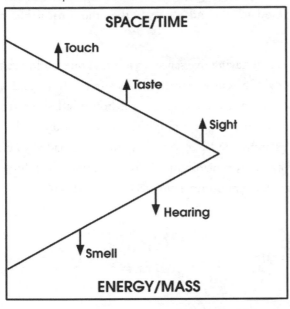

Figure 1.3

SECOND WORLDVIEW — RATIONALISM/MYSTICISM COMBINED

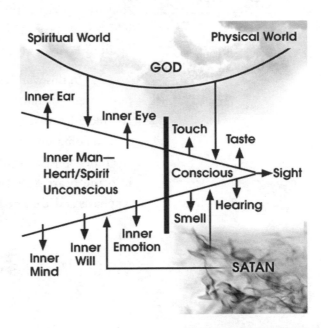

Figure 1.4

accepted this teaching, my heart hungered for direct spirit encounter with Almighty God, and it would not be satisfied with anything less.

A Second Worldview — Rationalism/Mysticism Combined

Mysticism is not a word I use very often because of some people's fears and inability to separate Eastern mysticism from Christian mysticism. However, here I am using it to mean **a belief in direct spirit encounter**. Surely Christianity as it is portrayed in the Bible involves a lot of direct spirit encounter as God meets with mankind through angels, dreams, visions, His voice and supernatural occurrences of many kinds.

In this worldview you believe that there is both a physical world and a spiritual world. You are a conscious individual with five senses that interact with the outer world: touch, taste, sight, hearing and smell. However, in this worldview you recognize that you have a heart or a spirit also. Paul called this the "inner man" in Romans 7:22 and this part of you also has five senses. These five senses are designed to touch the spiritual world. They are: the eyes of the heart, which see dream and vision; the ears of the heart, which hear God's spoken words (as well as the words of satan, angels and demons); the inner mind, which is able to ponder and meditate deep within (for example, the Bible says in Luke 2:19 that "Mary pondered these things in her heart"); the inner will, where man can make commitments as Paul did when he "purposed in

Notes

his spirit to go to Jerusalem" (Acts 19:21); and the emotion of his heart, where man is able to sense and experience the emotions of Almighty God flowing through him. For example, love, joy and peace are all emotions of God that are grown within us as the fruit of the Holy Spirit. The Holy Spirit is joined to our spirits (1 Cor. 6:17), and thus we experience the feelings of God through the emotional capacity of our spirits, which have been designed by God to feel and incubate the emotions of His Holy Spirit Who lives within us.

In this worldview, instead of having five senses that touch one world, we have ten senses that touch two worlds. Obviously this results in a much fuller and more complete life than living rationally only. We recognize that both God and satan are able to communicate with man on both levels, through the outer world and through the inner spiritual world. For example the Bible says that "the devil had already **put into the heart** of Judas Iscariot, the son of Simon, to betray Him…" (John 13:2, emphasis added). The following diagram outlines this second worldview.

Which Worldview Is Yours?

In which worldview do you live more comfortably? Are you more at ease responding to your outer senses, or are you equally comfortable with your inner senses, such as vision and intuition? If you are not living as you want to, you can change. First, acknowledge you are not what you want to be and ask the Lord's forgiveness for allowing yourself to be led astray by the rationalism of our culture. Second, ask the Lord to change you, to heal you, and to restore the eyes and ears of your heart. Then continue reading, and we will give you more specific help in making this transition. I had to make this change, so I can promise you that it is possible.

The person who has decided that the spiritual experiences found within the Bible are no longer available today will probably relegate any and all spiritual experiences to satan. I, however, believe the Bible is for today and is to be lived in all its fullness. Even though for many years I was taught to dispensationalize many parts of it away, I have now rejected that teaching and am a Bible-believing Christian — one who believes the Bible is to be lived in these days!

I used to scorn liberals who had demythalized away the supernatural parts of the Bible. I was glad I was an evangelical, a Bible-believing Christian. However, one day the Lord pointed out to me that I did not believe the whole Bible was for me, either. He reminded me that I believed the Old Testament was for the Jews; the Gospels were about the supernatural lifestyle of Jesus and not a way of life I could experience myself; the book of Acts was transitional and not for today; and the book of Revelation was for the future. All I had left to me was the teaching portions of the Epistles that did not speak about the supernatural, such as the gifts of the Holy Spirit.

I was appalled! I repented for my dispensationalism and told God I wanted my Bible back, so I could live it from cover to cover. If you don't have your whole Bible to live, I suggest you, too, may want to take a moment right now in prayer and repent for allowing it to be stolen from you and tell God you want it all back for you to live today.

Notes

Going Beyond Rational Christianity

As I began moving away from rational Christianity toward spiritual Christianity, the Lord gave me the following focuses to help me see the moves I needed to make.

Then the Lord spoke to me a verse of Scripture from John 5:39,40. He said, "Mark, 'you search the Scriptures, because you think that in them you have eternal life; and it is these that bear witness of Me; and you are unwilling to COME TO ME, THAT YOU MAY HAVE LIFE.'" It was as if a sword went through me. Of course! I had idolized the Bible! In my love for the Scriptures, I had made them God rather than a book that God had written to me about other people's experiences with Him. I had been willing to live out of the Bible, rather than out of God Himself.

I was pierced within when I realized that Jesus had initially spoken this verse to the Pharisees of His day. I began to argue with God that I wasn't a Pharisee! But as I told Him everything I did, the Lord replied that the Pharisees also had done those things. I became frightened, realizing that it was very likely I might indeed be a pharisee.

God Is Calling Us to Go Beyond Rational Christianity

Rational Christianity	Spiritual Christianity
1. Code of ethics	1. The power that works within
2. Laws	2. Intimacy (Abba Father)
3. Works	3. Romance (marriage of the Bride)
4. Head knowledge	4. Illumined truth
5. Theology	5. Spiritual encounter
6. External guidance	6. Inner witness
7. Self effort	7. Fused witness
8. Conscious level only	8. Dreams, visions, communion

Figure 1.5

I noted that the thing the Pharisees loved most was the Law. They memorized it, spoke it, lived it, and taught it to others. That was a perfect description of me. I lived out of biblical law rather than out of an intimacy with the Holy Spirit. I had not learned how to live out of the truth that Christ had died so we could continuously experience the life of the Holy Spirit within us, and live in Him, rather than a set of rules.

"And I will ask the Father, and He will give you another Helper, that He may be with you forever; that is the Spirit of truth, whom the world cannot receive, because it does not behold Him or know Him, but you know Him because He abides with you, and will be in you." (John 14:16,17)

Offering a Prayer of Repentance

I repented, asking the Lord's forgiveness for living like a pharisee and idolizing the Bible. I made a commitment to **come to Him** and to begin trusting the moving of the Holy Spirit within my heart. **It was a new beginning for me!**

If you need to offer a similar prayer, please stop now and spend time with God before continuing. You can use the test in Appendix I to allow the Holy Spirit to search your heart for any pharisaical characteristics.

Very Different From the New Age Movement!

Sometimes people ask me what the difference is between what the New Age teaches and what I am teaching here in *How to Hear God's Voice*. As I demonstrate below, we begin and build from a totally different foundation than the New Age movement.

Therefore, the differences are immense. And these are just a few. As we go along I will point out more. I believe it is ludicrous to suggest that people beginning from such totally opposite foundations could end up in the same place. The New Ager will find himself contacting demons, familiar spirits, and evil spirits. The Christian who is covered by the blood of Jesus and guided by the Holy Spirit will be led into the throne room of God as John was in Revelation.

Guardrails for the Spiritual Path

It is understandable that there would be caution in the hearts of some people about exploring the spiritual realm. If the only supernatural people you have heard of were operating from satan's kingdom, and there has been nothing supernatural about your Christianity, of course you will want to be careful. But do not allow satan to plant fear in your heart and prevent you from experiencing all that God has provided for you. You do not need to be afraid because God has laid out some very clear protective guidelines that will keep you safe as you enter the spiritual world. Stated succinctly they are:

1. You are a born-again Christian, having accepted Jesus Christ into your heart as your Lord and Savior, and having had your sins washed away by His cleansing blood.*

2. You accept the Bible as the inerrant Word of God.

3. You demonstrate your love and respect for God by your commitment to knowing His Word. You follow a plan for reading through the entire Bible regularly (such as once each year), as well as enjoying more in-depth meditation on books, characters, or topics.

4. You have an attitude of submission to what God has shown you from the Bible.

We believe:	The New Ager believes:
The God of the Bible is the God of this universe.	The God of the Bible is not the God of this universe.
Salvation is by the blood of Jesus.	There is no need of salvation.
The Bible is the inerrant Word of God.	The Bible is not the inerrant Word of God.
We should be students of the Bible.	There is no need to be a student of the Bible.
All Spirit encounter must be tested against the Bible.	Spirit encounter need not be tested against the Bible.
We should be linked to the Body of Christ.	There is no need whatsoever to be linked to the Body of Christ.

Figure 1.6

* If you have not yet asked Jesus Christ into your life as your Lord and Savior, then please turn to Appendix A now for more information on why you would want to take this step, and a prayer you can pray so that you can be born again.

5. You have two or three spiritual advisors to whom you go for input on a regular basis.

A fairly young Christian can meet all these requirements. In fact, new Christians should begin communing with God immediately as they begin their walk with Him. There they will find the rest and peace their souls so eagerly long for.

Establishing Spiritual Advisors

I believe it is absolutely imperative that everyone recognize the people God has placed as spiritual advisors in their lives. The Bible says we are to submit ourselves to one another (Eph. 5:21). Hebrews 13:17 specifically states, "Obey your leaders, and submit to them; for they watch over your soul, as those who will give an account. Let them do this with joy and not grief, for this would be unprofitable for you."

What does "obey" mean? The Greek word *peitho* which is used in Hebrews 13:17 (above) means "to allow yourself to be persuaded by." Obedience is the posture of your heart. It is an attitude that says, "I am open and listening to what God is saying to me through you."

Submission is an openness to the Spirit-led counsel and correction of several others, while keeping a sense of personal responsibility for our own discernment of God's voice within us.

We note several key points in this definition:

1) You are going to several (at least two or three) people.

2) You are not asking for their opinions. You are asking them to seek God and tell you what they sense in their hearts from Him.

3) You are going to maintain personal responsibility for the final decision, since on judgment day you will ultimately be the one responsible for your life's actions (Rom. 14:12).

If the counsel of your advisors disagrees with what you believe the Lord has told you, you will go back to God in prayer, asking Him to show you the truth in what these three have offered to you, and how He wants you to act upon it.

Using the above approach prevents petty dictators from running your life and protects you from man's wisdom (which is not God's wisdom) and your own foolishness, while keeping you from violating your own conscience. This is all priceless. Adopt this as a lifestyle in all you do. We have!

What is the purpose of such submission or openness to the input of others? "In the multitude of counselors there is safety" (Prov. 11:14). God has established spiritual advisors as a loving means of protecting us from self-deception within our own hearts, as well as from the trickery of satan. This becomes particularly important as you begin to walk in the spirit realm, becoming open to visions and God's intuitive voice within. The role of the spiritual advisor is to provide much needed confirmation for you as a learner just beginning to hear God's voice, offering you encouragement to go on and assuring you that it truly is the voice of God you are hearing. He also helps catch any error in your journaling and, when necessary, cautions you to wait a bit before proceeding with any action.

The center of this relationship is not authority but *friendship*. The one who can serve effectively as a spiritual advisor in your life is:

- One who is a *close friend* — one who knows you, and whose voice and heart you recognize.

- One who has a *solid biblical orientation*.

- One who is *sensitive to the voice of the Spirit* of God in his own heart.

- One who is *willing to commit himself to you*, who will invest his time and energy, and is willing to lay down his life for you.

- One who is himself *relating to spiritual advisors on a regular basis*.

- One who is *"equal to"* or *"ahead of you"* in the area you are asking him (or her) about.

For your part, you are willing to honor the voice of your advisors. You take your initial journaling and prophecy to them for confirmation, in order to help you gain confidence in discerning the voice of God within your heart. I especially like to have confirmation from my spiritual advisors when making a major decision, one that calls for a major change in the direction of my life, my ministry, or my job, or a major investment that will commit me financially for an extended period.

You also recognize that God is the authority over all (Rom. 13:1), and that the heart of the king is in the Lord's hand (Prov. 21:1). Therefore, you pray for God to grant wisdom to those who counsel you (1 Tim. 2:1-4).

When asked, the spiritual advisor will seek God for confirmation or adjustment concerning the things you bring before him. He will share with you what the Lord says to him. If there is a discrepancy, you will go back to the Lord to find out what He has to say to help clear up the disagreement. You will again present to your spiritual advisor what you sense God is saying, in an effort to resolve the difficulty.

How Many Spiritual Advisors Should I Have?

"Every fact is to be confirmed by the testimony of two or three witnesses" (2 Cor. 13:1).

I recommend that everyone have two or three spiritual advisors. When major directional moves are being made, I prefer a consensus of all three. I have consistently received spiritual counsel from at least three individuals since 1976. They have effectively kept me from making major mistakes in my life, which is why I love promoting God's concept that "in the multitude of counselors there is safety" (Prov. 11:14).

Who Should Be My Spiritual Advisors?

Some people have a hard time finding spiritual counselors. Let me suggest a few helpful hints: First, recognize that there are no perfect people. Therefore you might as well plan to receive spiritual counsel through an imperfect person and trust that God can work His perfection through imperfect people.

Also, you will most likely find your spiritual advisors among the people God has already placed around you. Some of these relationships are already in place. For instance, parents, spouses, employers, home cell group leaders, pastors, elders, etc. all have spheres of influence in your life. Married couples will obviously want to honor and seek out each other's advice. Each may also want a second person to whom they look for spiritual input concerning some of their journaling. They should talk it over with their spouse and agree together so they are both comfortable with the choices of spiritual advisors outside the marriage. Each should choose someone of the same sex since it is not wise to build close spiritual relationships with the opposite sex. There is too much danger that they will evolve into physical relationships and cause destructive explosions.

Isn't This Like the Shepherding Movement of the 1970s?

Not really. Those involved in the shepherding movement were trying to restore the concept of spiritual covering and spiritual authority, however, in some cases it turned into domination, legalism, and a spirit of control. Jesus said that we do not rule over others as the heathen do with the use of force, but **in love we serve one another**. The use of domination, intimidation, and control is strictly forbidden in the way of love (1 Pet. 5:1-6). Love draws, domination forces.

The picture of church leadership given in the Bible is of a shepherd and his sheep. Shepherds must lead sheep. Sheep cannot be driven. Therefore I will repeat, the center of these relationships must be friendship and spiritual kinship, not control. Any authority **is in a *rhema* word from God**, which can come through your spiritual advisor. However, it is the *rhema* that has the authority, not any position or title. (See www.cbeinternational.org.)

Again I will emphasize that after you have received the input and counsel of your advisors, and have prayerfully considered all that they have said, **you** maintain final responsibility before God for your response to what you believe is His *rhema* word to you. In Paul's discussion concerning believers having different understandings of God's will in Romans 14, he does not insist that everyone must do as he says or as the elders say, despite what they believe they have heard from God.

On the contrary, in verse 12 he reminds them of their personal accountability before God, and in verse 23 he declares, "he that doubts is damned if he eat, because he eats not of faith: for whatsoever is not of faith is sin." If you do something that you believe is against what God has told you, *even if you are wrong*, it is sin for you because you are acting in disobedience and outside of faith.

The Bible declares: "For we must all appear before the judgment seat of Christ; that every one may receive the things done in his body, according to that he hath done, whether it be good or bad" (2 Cor. 5:10). I am not aware of anyplace in Scripture where God accepted "the Nuremburg defense:" "I'm not guilty of the sinful thing I did because I was just following orders." You will stand alone before God to give an account of your obedience to His *Logos* and His *rhema* to you.

First Kings 13 relates a sobering story that strongly emphasizes this point. A man of God came out of Judah by the word of the Lord with a prophetic message for King Jeroboam. Though the king initially rejected the prophet's words, the Lord confirmed them with supernatural manifestations. Seeing the power of God, the king changed his tune and invited the prophet to stay, eat and be refreshed at his house. But the prophet refused, saying, "For so it was commanded me by the word of the LORD, saying, 'You shall eat no bread, nor drink water, nor return by the way which you came.'" (1 Kings 13:9,10 NASB).

So far this is a fairly standard Bible story, unfolding as you would expect. But then something unforeseen happens. An "old prophet" went out to meet this new guy in the neighborhood who was also hearing from God. He, too, invited the man of God to stop by his house for a bite to eat. The young prophet gave him the same answer as he had given the king, "No, God told me not to." But the old prophet replied, "I am also a prophet like you and God told me it was okay for you to eat with me." And so he did.

According to most of the teaching on submission given in the Church today, the younger prophet did the right thing by obeying his elder. The older man had a recognized office of prophet in the community, and he said that he was giving the word of the Lord. The younger man was not only *justified* in setting aside what he believed the Lord had told him; he was actually *obligated* to do so, according to contemporary teaching.

Unfortunately for him, the Lord didn't see it that way. Through the lying older prophet, the Lord spoke His judgment on the young man: "Thus says the LORD, 'Because you have disobeyed the command of the LORD, and have not observed the commandment which the LORD your God commanded you, but have returned and eaten bread and drunk water in the place of which He said to you, 'Eat no bread and drink no water'; your body shall not come to the grave of your fathers....'" Now when he had gone, a lion met him on the way and killed him, and his body was thrown on the road, with the donkey standing beside it; the lion also was standing beside the body" (1 Kings 13:21-25 NASB).

He paid for his "submission" to man over his obedience to the *rhema* of God to him with his life. Wisdom demands that you humbly seek the advice of spiritual counselors and listen to them with an open spirit (recognizing that you could be mistaken), but you carry final responsibility for what you do with God's word to you.

Changing Advisors

I believe we are free to change spiritual mentors as we grow and develop. If you change spiritual advisors every six months, this most likely indicates a problem in your life. However, if every five years or so you are replacing your advisors, it may be an indication that growth and change are taking place in your life, which is necessitating new people to mentor you. The important thing is that when you leave one mentoring relationship you enter another; you should not live without adequate counsel.

Since one of my criteria for a spiritual advisor is that he must be equal to or ahead of me in the area I am asking him about, I usually have several sets of spiritual advisors. One group is knowledgeable in the area of health, so I take my health issues to them. Another set are financial leaders, so I take my financial issues to them. Others have experience in working in universities, so I take questions about my building of Christian Leadership University to them. Another group is biblically and spiritually mature individuals, so I take questions about my spiritual life to them. I expect you will also grow from one set of two or three spiritual advisors to several sets of counselors.

Prayer: "God, we trust You to work through the principle of spiritual counsel as laid out in Your Word, and to work Your perfection through our imperfection. Lord, who have You placed around me that You want me to draw upon as a spiritual mentor?"

Now fix your eyes upon the Lord as you wait before Him. See whose names pop into your mind, and jot them down on a piece of paper. Contact these individuals and briefly explain the concept of a spiritual advisor as given above, and why you are being encouraged to seek counselors as you explore this methodology for hearing God's voice. If they express a willingness to seek confirmation from the Lord about assuming this service to you, make copies of the page entitled "To Be Signed by One's

Spiritual Advisor" and give them each a copy. Be sure to get the signed copies back from them.

Do Not Skip Over This Step of Establishing and Using Spiritual Advisors!

It is absolutely essential that you not miss this step of recognizing two or three spiritual advisors in your life, and that you go to them on a regular basis to confirm that what you felt you heard from God actually came from God. The Lord has created us to live in relationship with one another. It is satan who seeks to destroy relationships, and who offers us the spirit of pride which says, "I know more than…." Pride is the first sin in the Bible ("You will be like God, knowing good and evil" — Gen. 3:5), and it is the most prevalent sin in the Bible. It is the center of satan's heart. You do not want his arrogance in your heart. "God is opposed to the proud, but gives grace to the humble" (James 4:6).

First Thessalonians 5:20,21 exhorts us to "examine everything carefully; hold fast to that which is good; … do not despise prophetic utterances." It is clear from this that there may be errors in the prophetic words we receive (which is essentially what "hearing God's voice" is), or there would be no need to examine everything carefully and only hold on to the good part.

We must accept that mistakes are part of every learning process, and not despise prophetic utterances or reject the goal of clearly discerning God's voice. Your spiritual advisors will help you recognize any flaws in what you believe you hear, and guide you in understanding why they happened and how to prevent them in the future. With their assistance even your mistakes can be growing and learning experiences rather than cause for doubt and retreat. Examining everything carefully with the help of two or three spiritual advisors and only holding fast to what is good will allow you to move forward much more quickly in God and in fulfilling His purposes for your life. For your sake, do this!

Usually, however, when you share your words from the Lord to your spiritual advisors, they will confirm that it indeed is Him. What an encouragement to you this will be! Your faith will be empowered and you will press on with even greater excitement. Who among us does not need his faith strengthened from time to time? So establish these three spiritual advisors NOW in your life, before you continue with this book.

How to Succeed When Living Out of God's Voice

I have found that people who do not **establish and draw on** spiritual advisors are generally unsuccessful in maintaining a lifestyle of living out of the voice of

Notes

God over the long term. Some never get started, because they are never certain whether what they are hearing is God or not and they allow doubt to block the flow. Others begin with confidence, but when they make a mistake in hearing God's voice, or **think** they have made a mistake, their faith is damaged so badly they quit.

During the first few days and weeks of journaling, I strongly recommend that you share all your journaling with at least one of your spiritual advisors for confirmation that you are on the right track. Once you both have confidence in your discernment, you can cut back to only sharing those things that a) you are uncertain about whether they came from God, or b) are big decisions.

Spiritual Advisor's Understanding

"In the multitude of counselors there is safety" (Prov. 11:14).

Submission is openness to the Spirit-led counsel and correction of several others, while keeping a sense of personal responsibility for our own discernment of God's voice within us.

Having understood the role of a spiritual advisor as defined above, I am willing to seek God for spiritual wisdom when asked by _____ and report back to them in a timely manner. I will not give my opinion; I will share what I feel God is speaking into my heart concerning the situation.

I myself choose to also walk in relationship to two or more spiritual advisors in the Body of Christ.

I understand that to offer spiritual counsel does not involve the use of force, domination, manipulation or control (1 Pet. 5:1-6), and I will never use any of these in our relationship.

When asked for counsel in an area in which I do not feel fully qualified and anointed, I will recommend other spiritual advisors who I know are strong in the area in question.

I will never encourage this person to do anything contrary to the spirit or the letter of Scripture.

If I do not follow these principles, the person indicated above is encouraged to find another spiritual advisor to whom they can relate.

Date _____   Name _____

Please provide a copy of this understanding to each party in the relationship. This page may be photocopied.

Left and Right Hemisphere Brain Functions

You may think it strange to explore how the brain works in the middle of a discussion on spirituality and hearing the voice of God. I enjoy learning about studies in disciplines other than Christianity that relate to the steps of growth that I am

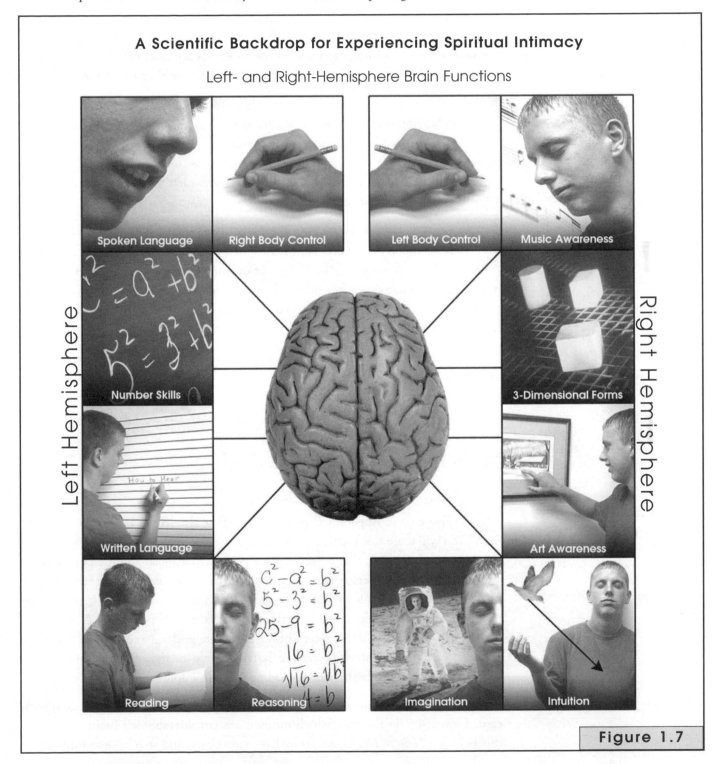

Figure 1.7

taking in my Christian walk. The discussion on left and right hemisphere brain functions is one of these studies.

Some people refuse to learn how left and right brain functions can apply to their spiritual lives because they are not taught in the Bible. My response is that while all of the Bible is truth, not all truth is in the Bible. To reject scientific discoveries because they were not first stated in the Scriptures would be ignorant and narrow-minded in the extreme. None of us would knowingly choose that position. Just because something is not taught in the Bible does not mean it is not true. God never claimed to put everything He knew in the Bible. As a matter of fact, Jesus said He knew things He wasn't going to tell the disciples because they could not yet bear it (John 16:12).

Therefore, my standard for affirming truth is not limited to clear statements of Scripture. Instead I require that what I embrace must be compatible with principles in the Bible. Left and right brain understanding is compatible with biblical principles, particularly the doctrine that God has given each of us unique gifts (Rom. 12:6-8; Gal. 4:11; 1 Cor. 12:1-12).

In 1981, Roger Sperry won the Nobel Prize in Physiology or Medicine for his experimentation on left and right hemisphere brain functions. It has been discovered that although we do use both sides of our brains, most of us tend to rely a bit more heavily on one side or the other. The chart on the preceding page provides a pictorial overview of the functions carried on by each hemisphere of the brain. Please take a moment and examine it now.

You will note that the left hemisphere of the brain works primarily with analytical functions, while the right hemisphere processes intuitive and visionary functions.

"Brain Preference Indicator Test"

Please go to Appendix B now and complete the "Brain Preference Indicator Test." You will score this yourself using the scoring key at the end of the Appendix. If you have a score of 5.0, that means you are perfectly balanced and use both sides of your brain equally. A person with a score of 5.0 can move very easily from one side to the other. There is a large bell curve near the center of the scoring key, meaning that 80 percent of the scores will be between 4 and 6, and 98 percent of all scores will be between 3 and 7. Only 1 percent of the scores are under 3 and another 1 percent above 7, which means these people are extremely left- or right-brain. This indicates that most of us do use both sides of our brains a fair amount.

The scale is exponential, with small moves out from 5.0 being quite significant. I am a 4.5 on the scale which means I am **considerably** left-brain. Therefore, this book on *How to Hear God's Voice* has many charts and step-by-step formulas in it. That is what left-brain people need and what they are all about. Right-brain individuals simply say, "Oh, hearing God's voice is easy: you just know that you know that you know!" Well, that doesn't help a left-brain person at all. I am writing as a left-brainer and for left-brainers. Not that this won't help right-brainers, also. It will. It will confirm to them that what they are doing naturally is good and is right, and it will give them a detailed vocabulary to communicate the way they live inwardly to others who do not naturally live that same way.

My wife, Patti, (a 5.01) has rewritten this book into a right-brain version called *Dialogue With God* which skips all the charts and things that left-brainers demand and need. If you are a right-brainer, you will probably enjoy *Dialogue With God*. (Note: We put both our names on all the books we have written, but Patti is the primary author of *Dialogue With God* and Mark is the primary author of *How to Hear God's Voice*.)

When I began to journal, God told me to love my wife exactly as she was and to not try to change her into a 4.5. Honoring her intuition (as well as my intuition) has helped me make much wiser decisions in my life. Honoring the right-brain strengths of my wife has greatly improved my marriage. Testing our children and helping them find jobs that are consistent with their brain preference has blessed and established them in the workplace. Our left-brain daughter is an editor and phone consultant. Our right-brain son is a typesetter, webmaster, and marketer. Let journaling and an understanding of left- and right-brain functions bring success to your marriage, your life, and your family.

In surveying groups of people in America, I have found that approximately 60 percent lean toward left-brain functions and about 40 percent toward right-brain functions. Only a few indicate that they have a balance between the two. This imbalance probably exists because our educational system considers reading, writing and arithmetic (required courses which deal with left-brain functions) to be more central to effective living than art, music and drama (elective courses which deal with right-brain functions). This idolatry of the left-brain functions is so complete in our culture that scientists have discovered that the left half of the brain actually grows slightly heavier than the right side of the brain during the schooling years.

Psychologists tell us that they consider the majority of people in our culture to be neurotic. I suspect that a large contributing factor to this widespread neurosis is the failure to cultivate both sides of our brains in a balanced way.

Corresponding to this idolization of logic is the demise of creativity, which is a more right-brain function involving vision, intuition and visualization. Statistics show that almost all children rank high in creativity before they enter school at age five. By age seven, only 10 percent still have high creativity, and by the time we are adults, only 2 percent score high in creativity tests.

Therefore, what we are doing in our current educational system is essentially destroying the creative ability God has placed within man. I believe it is because we train the left side of the brain — the logical, analytical part — and stifle the right side of the brain — the intuitive, imaginative side. Where in Scripture do we see God suggesting we do this? I suspect God gave us two sides of our brains so we could offer both sides to Him to use.

Understanding right and left brain functions can help us understand and respect those with gifts different from ours. For instance, when a husband and wife are involved in making a decision, the husband may reason it out (a left-brain function) while the wife may intuit the decision (a right-brain function). If they have learned to honor the strengths in one another, they will not cut off the other's gift simply because it does not line up with their own decision-making process, but will instead value it as a complement to their own abilities.

Those who function more strongly in the left brain will find the revelation process flowing most naturally in conjunction with their analytical thoughts. As an example, Luke (Luke 1:1-4) investigated everything carefully, then wrote it out in consecutive order (obviously left-brain activity). May I suggest that he allowed the Holy Spirit's intuitive, spontaneous impressions to flow into his reasoning process, and the end product was pure revelation that stands to this day.

On the other hand, when John wrote Revelation he said, "I was in the Spirit on the Lord's day, and I heard behind me a loud voice…saying, 'Write in a book what you see …' " (Rev. 1:10,11). This revelation process involved no left-brain functions (except the actual writing). Rather, I believe it flowed through the right side of the brain, coming from the heart. This process also resulted in a pure revelation, one that still stands today.

You can see that there are at least two different approaches you can use when receiving pure revelation: Luke's method and John's method. Both are valid. Both can result in purity. Both are to be honored. It is hard for us to honor the one who is different from us. The left-brain person is likely to characterize the right-brain person as flaky, impulsive and fly-by-night. The right-brain person is likely to describe the left-brain person as so analytical and academic that there is no possibility that the Holy Spirit could flow through him or her. Let us come to the place where we can honor both Luke's and John's approach to receiving revelation, knowing that the Holy Spirit can flow purely through both.

I do not equate the right side of the brain directly with the heart. Rather I would like to suggest that the capacities of the heart are to flow into both sides of our brains. We will discuss this in more detail in the next chapter.

Moving From Left to Right

People often ask, "How can I set aside my own reasoning and experience the inner intuitive flow?" Let us consider what Elisha did when he needed to hear a prophetic word from God. When he wanted to move from logic and reason (left-brain activity) to the word of the Lord spoken intuitively within (flowing through the right side of his brain), Elisha engaged in a right-brain activity: "Bring me a minstrel, so that I might hear the word of the Lord" (paraphrased from 2 Kings 3:15). The music drew him from the left side of his brain to the right side where he was perfectly positioned before the presence of the Lord, able to hear the spontaneous words that were spoken within.

Many people also find that the use of vision or enjoying the beauty of nature (both right-brain functions) position them properly before the intuitive voice of the Holy Spirit. In interesting university studies by Calvin Jeske, from Calgary, Canada, it has been shown that speaking in tongues stimulates right-brain electrical activity, as opposed to normal speech, which stimulates left-brain electrical activity. Therefore, I recommend that you use vision, music, nature, and speaking in tongues to help prepare yourself to more easily hear the intuitive voice of the Holy Spirit.

Summary

God yearns to be your Friend. He wants you to recognize His voice so that you can get to know Him personally. He longs for you to spend *yada* time with Him, having no agenda other than sharing love together. He wants you to offer Him your physical senses, the faculties of your soul, and the senses of your spirit so that you can *know* Him fully and deeply. He wants you to move out of your box and into His flow, out of your mind and into your heart, out of rationalism into true spiritual Christianity.

Personal Response

Write a love letter to Jesus. Tell Him how much you appreciate Him and how special He is to you.

Then let it become a two-way love letter. Let Jesus speak back to you. After you have written a paragraph or two to Him, fix your eyes upon Jesus, and tune to flowing thoughts. Let Him talk to you through a flow of thoughts which will simply appear in your mind as you fix your eyes upon Him. He wants to tell you of His love for you. As these thoughts begin to appear, simply write them down. While you write, they will continue to flow. You will discover you are having a two-way conversation with God, and recording it on paper. It will be very exciting!

Confirm this is God speaking to you by reading what you have written to your spouse or one of your spiritual advisors and asking if they sense it is from God. Don't forget to thank Him for seeking you out to be His friend!

Endnote

1. Documentation on the precise definitions of *ginosko* and *yada* may be found on pages 395-398 of *The Dictionary of New Testament Theology, Vol. 2* by Colin Brown.

CHAPTER 2

GOD'S VOICE SOUNDS LIKE...

Notes

In the title of this book we made you a promise. We declared that we were going to teach you how to hear the voice of God within your own heart. Through focused prayer and research, the Lord taught me four simple keys that unlocked the ability for me to discern the voice of God within me. Whenever I need or want to hear from God, I can, as long as I use all four of these keys. I have traveled all over the world teaching what I have learned, and the four keys have worked in every culture and every circumstance and every age group. God's people are able to recognize His voice, just as He promised.

Very simply stated, the four keys to hearing God's voice are:

Key # 1 — Recognize God's voice as spontaneous thoughts which light upon your mind.

Key # 2 — Quiet yourself so you can hear God's voice.

Key # 3 — Look for vision as you pray.

Key # 4 — Write down the flow of thoughts and pictures that come to you.

Simplifying even further are four words which summarize these keys:

> Stillness
> Vision
> Spontaneity
> Journaling

We will be exploring each of these keys in detail in the coming chapters, beginning with:

Key # 1 — Recognize God's voice as spontaneous thoughts which light upon your mind.

Our Father longs to share Himself with us in every way possible. Jesus wants to be our Way, our Truth, and our Life (John 14:6). He shows us the way to walk through His *Logos*, the Word: "Thy word is...a light to my path" (Ps. 119:105). He guides us through the counsel of our spiritual overseers (Prov. 11:14). Even circumstances are used to direct our way (e.g., Jonah). Jesus becomes our truth by illuminating Scripture to us, by leading us into truth, and by guiding us, through giving us peace or pressure in our spirits. We may receive guidance through dreams and visions (Acts 16:9), or the prophetic word.

Defining *Logos* and *Rhema*

One way Jesus becomes our life is by speaking His words directly into our hearts. In this chapter we want to examine this experience. Jesus says in John 6:63, "The words that I have spoken to you are spirit and are life." Probably each of us has experienced the breath of life as God's words have come clearly to our hearts, giving direction for the way before us, encouraging us, or strengthening us.

There are two Greek words in the New Testament that are translated "word:" *logos* and *rhema*. A "word" can be *logos* and *rhema* as you highlight either the content of the message or the way the message was received. If you use the word *logos*, you indicate that you are emphasizing the content of the message. Use of the word *rhema* demonstrates an emphasis on the way in which the message was received, specifically, through a spoken word.

A Biblical Example

Jesus refers to the same "word" or message twice in the seventeenth chapter of John, verses six and eight. In verse six the content is being emphasized, and therefore *logos* is used in the Greek. In verse eight, the fact that it was a spoken word is the focus, and therefore the word *rhema* is used.

Both *Logos* and *Rhema*

The Scriptures can be logos if I approach them simply for content. When I receive them as revelation from God, they can be called *rhema*. When God speaks a Scripture to me, it comes as a *rhema*. If God bids me note the content of the Scripture, I am then treating it as a *logos*. The Scriptures originally came as *rhema* to the writers (2 Pet. 1:21). Since they had content, they were also *logos*. The Scriptures are quickened to us by the Spirit and thus become a *rhema* to us in the same way that they were to the original writers. As we ponder the *rhema*, it becomes a *logos*, since we shift from emphasizing its manner of coming to its content.

We Need Both *Logos* and *Rhema*

The content of the Bible (*Logos*) is necessary because it gives us an absolute standard against which to measure all "truth." It is our safeguard to keep us from error, and our instruction manual for life.

Rhema is also necessary because it emphasizes the way the Bible was initially given — through individuals actively interacting with God — and the centrality of divine communication with man to the Christian message. It emphasizes the fact that God spoke and continues to speak to His children. We need to see that the men and women throughout the Bible model a way of living which involves ongoing contact with the God who created them. If the Bible tells us anything from Genesis to Revelation, it tells us that God desires to actively communicate with His children, and that we should expect to hear His voice and see His vision as we walk through life.

Before I found God, I lived out of myself. Now that I have found Him, I live out of His spoken word and vision within my heart. We do nothing on our own

1. LOGOS

The mind reading and understanding the Bible.

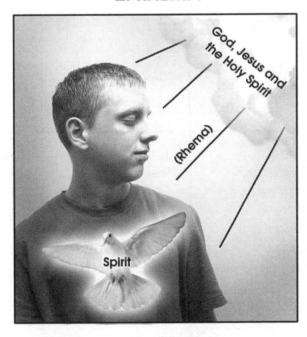

2. RHEMA

As I direct my heart and mind to seek the Lord, His Spirit speaks into my heart, directly impressing His thoughts and ideas upon it.

Figure 2.1

Notes

initiative, only that which we hear and see the Father doing (John 5:19,20,30). We see Jesus as a perfect example, modeling a way of living which we are to imitate.

Therefore, we need both the *logos* and the *rhema* in our lives. The following diagram may help.

Additional Distinctions Between *Logos* and *Rhema*

	Logos	*Rhema*	Distinctions between *Logos* and *Rhema*
Used in New Testament	331 Times	70 Times	
Dictionary of New Testament Theology Volume 3, Colin Brown	Literal Definition—"Collect, count, say, intellectual, rational, reasonable, spiritual."	"That which is stated intentionally; a word, an utterance, a matter, event, case."	"Whereas *logos* can often designate the Christian proclamation as a whole in the New Testament, *rhema* usually relates to individual words and utterances: man has to render account for every unjust word (Matt. 12:36); the heavenly ones speak unutterable words (2 Cor. 12:4)."
Vine's Expository Dictionary of New Testament Words, Vine	Literal Definition—"The expression of thought. Not the mere name of an object (a) as embodying a conception or ideal; (b) a saying or a statement."	"Denotes that which is spoken; what is uttered in speech...."	"The significance of *rhema* (as distinct from *logos*) is exemplified in the injunction to take the sword of the Spirit, which is the Word (*rhema*) of God. (Eph. 6:17); here the reference is not to the whole Bible as such, but to the individual Scripture which the Spirit brings to our remembrance for use in time of need, a prerequisite being the regular storing of the mind with Scripture."

Figure 2.2

Understanding the Power of *Rhema*: "The Spoken Word"

	Kind of *Rhema*	Biblical Examples
Most life-giving	I speak that which God is currently speaking with Him (i.e., my *rhema* comes forth from His *rhema*).	"...the words (*rhema*) that I say...I do not speak on My own initiative, but the Father abiding in Me does His works." (John 14:10) "...the words (*rhema*) which Thou gavest Me I have given to them...." (John 17:8) (See also Luke 1:38, 5:5; John 5:19,20, 30; 8:26,28,38; 3:34; 6:63; Acts 10:13; 2 Corinthians 12:4; Ephesians 6:17; Hebrews 11:3; 12:19.)
Somewhat life-giving	I speak the written Word of God.	"...stand and speak to the people in the temple, the whole message (*rhema*) of this Life." (Acts 5:20)
Neutral	I speak out of myself.	"...by the mouth of two or three witnesses every fact (*rhema*) may be confirmed." (Matt. 18:16)
Somewhat destructive	I speak the generalized word of satan, which I have heard in the past.	"...every evil word (*rhema*) that men shall speak, they shall render account for it in the day of judgment." (Matt. 12:36)
Most destructive	I speak that which satan is currently speaking with him.	"...we have heard him speak blasphemous words (*rhema*) against...God." (Acts 6:11) "The tongue is a fire...set on fire by hell." (James 3:6)

Figure 2.3

Our Goal: To produce the maximum amount of life by speaking that which the Father is currently speaking within us, through our fellowship with the Spirit (John 14:10,16).

Notes

I struggled unsuccessfully for years to see a distinction between *logos* and *rhema*. I observed that *logos* was often used for "spoken words," which I had been taught should be *rhema*. Finally, one day I noticed that the opposite was not also true, that *rhema* was never used in the context of "written words." I went through all 70 uses of *rhema* in the New Testament and observed that not once did *rhema* refer to the written word. So there was uniqueness about *rhema*!

As I learned much later in studying a master's thesis by Dr. Font Shultz, *logos* includes all aspects of communication, from the formulation of the ideas to be spoken, to the consideration of the language style, through the actual verbalization and reception by the hearer. *Rhema*, on the other hand, stands specifically for the "uttering" or "actual expressing." You may want to examine each occurrence of *rhema* in the New Testament yourself and note your observations concerning its distinctiveness. The references are listed in Appendix C.

How *Rhema* Is Sensed

Probably no question bothers Western Christians more than: "How do I discern God's voice within my heart?" We are now going to try to answer that.

I sought in vain for years to hear God's voice within my heart, but the only thing I found was many different thoughts. I could not hear any voice. This is precisely where many Christians stand frustrated. How can I possibly say "God said" when I am not able to discern His inner voice clearly? How can I move in word of wisdom, word of knowledge, prophecy, or interpretation of tongues if I cannot recognize God's voice? How can I get to *know* Someone who I cannot see, hear, or touch? Then the Lord finally began bringing the right teachers, revelation and understanding into my life and allowed me to "see" what I had been missing.

Rhema, or the voice of God, is Spirit-to-spirit communication — where the Holy Spirit, in union with your spirit, speaks directly to you.

Thoughts from my mind are **analytical**.
Thoughts from my heart are **spontaneous**.

So we can say that Key # 1 for hearing God's voice is recognizing that "God's voice is sensed as spontaneous thoughts which light upon your mind."

Biblical Support for the Concept That Spontaneous Thoughts Are the Voice of the Spirit World

1. All thoughts are not our thoughts.

*"For the weapons of our warfare are not carnal but mighty in God for pulling down strongholds, casting down arguments and every high thing that exalts itself against the knowledge of God, bringing **every thought into captivity** to the obedience of Christ...."* (2 Cor. 10:4,5 NKJV, emphasis added)

Why would we have to bring our thoughts into captivity? Is it not because some of them originate in satan or an evil spirit? If so, where may we assume that other of our thoughts come from? The Holy Spirit, naturally. We must come to terms with the truth that many of the thoughts in our minds are **not our thoughts**. What an incredible idea! I always believed that the thoughts in my mind were **my thoughts**. But in actuality, the Bible makes it clear that many of them are not. They are coming from the spirit world. You see, I am one whom another fills. I am a vessel, a branch grafted into a vine. I do not stand alone but someone else flows through me. I keep forgetting that and think that this is **me living**, when God has made it very clear that I do not live, but Christ lives in me (Gal. 2:20).

Therefore I accept the fact that spontaneous thoughts, ones I did not think up, do not come from my mind. They come either from my heart, the Holy Spirit within my heart, or an evil spirit trying to impress his ideas upon me.

Now let us look at some more biblical support for the concept that spontaneous thoughts are the voice of the spirit world.

2. *Naba* — "bubbling up"

Naba, the Hebrew word meaning "to prophesy," literally means to "bubble up." Therefore when the prophet would tune to the prophetic flow, he would tune to that which was bubbling up within him. In other words, he would tune to the spontaneous flow which he recognized as the voice of God within him.

Consider the distinctions between true prophecy and false prophecy in the following chart.

	True Prophecy	**False Prophecy**
Root Hebrew Word	*Naba*	*Ziyd*
Literal Definition	Bubble up	Boil up
Expanded Meaning	His prophecy bubbles up. His prophecy gushes up.	He boils up his prophecy. He cooks up his prophecy.
Inner Poise	Fix eyes on Jesus and tune to spontaneous flow.	Fix eyes on self's desires and devise a word or vision.

Figure 2.4

3. *Paga* — the chance encounter

The Hebrew word for intercession is *paga*, which literally means "to strike or light upon by chance" or "an accidental intersecting." Genesis 28:11 is an example of the use of *paga* as an accidental intersecting. As Jacob was traveling, he "lighted upon" (*paga*) a certain place and spent the night there.

Putting this literal definition of *paga* together with the idea of intercession, we come to a beautiful biblical example of Spirit-to-spirit communication that is familiar to almost every Christian. Can you remember a time when you suddenly had the impression that you should pray for someone? You had not been thinking about them; the thought just "came out of nowhere." That was *paga*. You were experiencing *rhema*, God's voice as a "chance idea" that intersects our minds, not flowing from the normal, meditative process, but simply appearing in our hearts. It seems to us it is just a chance idea because we didn't think it up. It is an idea from God lighting upon our hearts and being registered in our minds as a spontaneous idea. From God's perspective, it is divinely sent, and not chance at all.

4. The river of the Holy Spirit within the believer's heart

"On the last day, that great day of the feast, Jesus stood and cried out, saying, 'If anyone thirsts, let him come to Me and drink. He who believes in Me, as the Scripture has said, out of his heart will flow rivers of living water.' But this He spoke concerning the Spirit, whom those believing in Him would receive; for the Holy Spirit was not yet given, because Jesus was not yet glorified." (John 7:37-39, NKJV)

Now Jesus **is** glorified, and the Holy Spirit **has been** given. Jesus said it would be like a river within us. Therefore, when we tune to the bubbling flow within us, we are tuning to the Holy Spirit within us. **This is more than simply theology. This is an actual experience. There *is* a river within us**, and we **can** tune to it. This bubbling effortless flow *is* the Holy Spirit. It is so simple that even a child can do it. And that helps prove it is real, because Jesus said we needed to become like children to enter the Kingdom. If we make Christianity too difficult for a child, we most likely have it wrong. So when I tune to flow, I am tuning to the Holy Spirit within me.

5. We are a temple of the Holy Spirit.

"Or do you not know that your body is the temple of the Holy Spirit [who is] in you, whom you have from God, and you are not your own?" (1 Cor. 6:19 NKJV)

The Holy Spirit lives within us. We are not alone on the inside. And where the Holy Spirit is, there will be evidence of His Presence.

6. The Christian's spirit is fused to the Holy Spirit.

"But he who is joined to the Lord is one spirit [with him]." (1 Cor. 6:17 NKJV)

"The spirit of man is the candle of the Lord...." (Prov. 20:27a)

We are pure gold at the core of our being because we are joined to Almighty God by a miracle which He performed. When we touch our hearts, we also touch Him.

7. We are a branch grafted into a vine.

"I am the vine, you [are] the branches. He who abides in Me, and I in Him, bears much fruit; for without Me you can do nothing." (John 15:5 NKJV)

There is a flow of sap through living branches on a daily basis. The branch does not "crank it up." It just happens naturally. In the same way, there is a flow of spontaneity through each of us all the time. We don't crank God up; we just choose to honor the flow that is already there.

Say out loud as a confession: "I choose to honor the flow within me because it is the river of God in me by the working of the Holy Spirit."

Other Support for the Concept That Spontaneous Thoughts Are the Voice of the Spirit World

1. The experience of creative flashes

I am sure we have all struggled with a difficult situation and then experienced in an instantaneous flash a creative solution to the problem. Where did that flash come from? Was it my own greatness finally revealing itself? Or was it the creativity of the Creator Who lives within me? I believe that it was a *rhema* from Almighty God springing forth within my heart. I no longer take any credit for these creative insights but give it to God, the One Who lives within.

2. The experience of destructive flashes

Where do destructive and evil thoughts erupt from, when I am not thinking them up but they flash across my mind with a life of their own? I may be in prayer, and some perverted thought abruptly comes into my mind. I am fully convinced that they come from the destroyer, who is bombarding me with his evil thoughts. Therefore I do not accept guilt for evil thoughts that suddenly appear in my mind. I give proper blame to whom blame is due — satan.

3. Testimonies of "life after death" encounters

In books on "life after death" encounters, we find a confirming witness of what Spirit-to-spirit communication is. They tell of seeing Jesus or an angel speak.

Although they do not hear anything audibly, they instantly know within what has been said. They receive in their spirits the spontaneous, effortless flow of ideas that is Spirit-to-spirit communication (or *rhema*).

4. The example from nature

God often models spiritual truth in the physical world, which is why the whole earth reflects His glory. It is interesting to note that the Jordan River, which flows through the land of Israel, bubbles up from the depths of the earth and simply begins as a full-fledged river. As the Holy Spirit bubbles up from our innermost being and simply flows, the Jordan River emerges from the bowels of the earth and flows as a river throughout the land.

Qualities That Characterize God's Thoughts Interjected Into Your Heart

- They will be **spontaneous**, not **cognitive** or **analytical**, which means we move from living out of the use of our reason to living intuitively or spontaneously (i.e., living more like children — Matt. 18:3). This, of course, is countercultural to the Western worldview, so we are choosing to step out of our comfort zone and live from a biblical worldview. Jesus lived out of an inner flow of thoughts and pictures from His Father, doing nothing of His own initiative (John 5:19,20,30). We can do the same.

- God's thoughts are expressed through our personalities and style of speech. We notice that the Gospel of John reflects John's personality and the Gospel of Mark reveals Mark's individuality and manner. So the divine flow within us does not bypass or eradicate our personalities or style of speech. God is united with us (1 Cor. 6:17), flowing out through us. This is the wonder of Christianity — that God has joined Himself to man, and is expressing Himself through him. God's glory and splendor is being highlighted as it flows through your unique personality. So when you see your personality and vocabulary coming out in your journaling, do not reject it as being of self, but say, "The wonder of Christianity — Almighty God joined to me!"

- These thoughts come easily as God speaking in the first person.

- They are often light and gentle, and easily cut off by **any** exertion of self (our own thoughts, will, etc.), so we are careful to choose to honor the river over and above our own self effort.

- They will have an unusual content to them, in that they will be wiser, more healing, more loving and more motive-oriented than your thoughts.

- They will cause a special reaction within you, such as a sense of excitement, conviction, faith, life, awe, or peace, assuming you have taken a step of faith and believe that what you are hearing is from the God Who flows within.

- When embraced, they carry with them a fullness of strength to perform them, as well as a joy in doing so.

- Your spiritual senses are trained as time goes on, and you will more easily and frequently experience God speaking in this way. So don't quit if it is a bit awkward the first couple of times. It becomes easier quickly.

- Remember: God **is speaking** to you all the time, and you are receiving His interjected thoughts. Until you begin distinguishing them from your own, you are simply grouping them all together and assuming they are yours. In learning to distinguish His voice, you are learning how to separate the spontaneous thoughts that are coming from Him from the analytical thoughts that are coming from your own mind.

Testing Whether Flowing Thoughts Are From God

There are many ways of testing whether the spontaneous flow is your heart, the Holy Spirit Who is joined to your heart, or an evil spirit who is issuing an attack against you. An entire chapter will explore these later. However, let me offer a couple of easy tests right now that I currently use.

If you posture your heart properly, the flow within *will certainly be* the Holy Spirit!

John 7:37-39 tells us that we can sense a flow within us which is the Holy Spirit. It also lays out the prerequisites for positioning our hearts properly to ensure that this flow is coming from God and not self or a demon. The posture is clearly stated:

Biblical Statement (John 7:37-39)	Key Confession
If any one is thirsty	Lord, I am **thirsty** for Your voice
Let him come to Me	Lord, I **fix my heart upon You**
And drink	I **tune to flow**, drinking in Your words
He who believes in Me	I **believe** the flow within me is You!

Figure 2.5

Notes

The promised result is that we connect with the Holy Spirit! "From his innermost being **will flow** rivers of living water, but this He spoke of the Spirit."

Notice the Lord does not say that the Holy Spirit will flow:

- If you are fasting.

- If you have prayed much.

- If you have interceded greatly.

- If you have not sinned in a given period of time.

- If you are a longtime believer.

- If you have read your Bible regularly, or at length.

- If you are a deacon or an elder in the church.

- If you are an ordained minister.

- If you are in a religious atmosphere, for instance, in a church meeting.

- If you have done works for the Lord.

When I want to hear what God is saying to me, I position my heart properly before my King by saying, "God, I am one of Your 'anyone's.' Lord, I am thirsty for Your voice, vision and anointing. I fix my heart upon You. [I do this by using vision and seeing Him present with me — which the Bible clearly says is truth. You could also pray in tongues or listen to anointed music.] I tune away from my own reasoning, and I tune to Your voice, to flowing thoughts and pictures within me. I drink in Your words. Father, I believe the flow within me is the river of God, because You have declared it to be so. I banish all doubt. I believe that what the Bible teaches is true. Thank You, God, for the river of Your Holy Spirit within."

(As a side note: All the gifts of the Holy Spirit [1 Cor. 12:7-11] are received through exactly the same heart posture and in the same manner. When I need words of wisdom or knowledge, I tune to flowing ideas; for a prophecy, I tune to flowing words; for healing power or a miracle, to divine energy/light which flows out through me; for discerning of spirits, to flowing pictures, ideas or emotions; for faith, to a deep flowing emotion/confidence; for tongues, to flowing syllables; and for the interpretation of tongues, to flowing thoughts, emotions and pictures.)

As I journaled about releasing God's healing anointing to one who was very sick, the Lord said: "Mark, this day show love. That is the heart of My anointing — My love streaming forth, unhindered, and unearned. That is what is at the core of My being and that is what is to be at the core of your being, especially this day. It is not a day to judge. It is a day to love, to release My anointing through your love for My son and My daughter and to build them up in the Holy Spirit. My anointing is released through My love. So love unconditionally and you will see My anointing flow. It is about releasing My love. My anointing will never be separated from My love, saith the Lord of Hosts. So let love always be in the center of your heart and in the center of your actions."

Testing flowing thoughts against the Bible

Of course, you always test the spontaneous flow against the Bible, and you submit your journaling to your spiritual advisor(s) to see if they can confirm that it is from God. These two steps are critical and to be taken continuously.

Testing flowing thoughts by knowing where your eyes are fixed

It is a true principle that "the intuitive flow comes out of the vision I hold before my eyes." Therefore I ask myself if I had my eyes fixed on Jesus while I was tuned to spontaneity. If so, I find that, for me, the spontaneous flow is from God 95 percent or more of the time. We must acknowledge that we will always be vulnerable to mistakes. And that is okay. We can celebrate our mistakes, laugh at them, and learn from them (Eph. 5:20).

Generally when a person makes a mistake in his discernment of God's voice through journaling, I have learned to ask this one question: "Where were your eyes fixed when you wrote that section in your journal?" The correct answer, of course, is, "Upon Jesus." However, in nearly every case of error, the person will admit that they had dropped Jesus out of the picture, and they were staring at something else and then tuned to flow.

In some cases, they have been staring at the tension in a relationship, perhaps even with a spouse, and then had the flow say to them that this person was going to die. One person was focusing in his mind's eye on pharisees in the church, and then tuned to flow. His journaling became very vicious and destructive. You can always test your own journaling by going back over it and asking, "Where were my eyes fixed when I wrote this section?" If they were not on Jesus, then that section is suspect.

Sorting Out Three Categories of Thoughts in Our Minds

1. <u>Spontaneous Positive Thoughts</u> that line up with the names/character of the Holy Spirit, including Edifier, Comforter, Teacher, Creator, and Healer, Giver of Life, we will assume come from the Holy Spirit.

2. <u>Spontaneous Negative Thoughts</u> we assume come from demons, and thus will line up with the names/character of satan, which include Accuser, Adversary, Liar, Destroyer, Condemner, Thief and Murderer.

3. <u>Analytical Thoughts</u> come from self, from our own reasoning process, and are sensed as cognitive, connected thoughts. They are limited by our own knowledge, wisdom, understanding, and abilities. For example, you may "think" one plus one equals two. In this case, the thought would be correct ("true") if you were only talking about decimal or base 10 math. However, in binary math (the language of computers and engineering), it would not be true. (In base two, one plus one equals 10.) So "reasoned truth" is only little glimpses of partial truths.

It had never crossed my mind to develop a biblical understanding of the three sources of thoughts within my head. I had just assumed they were all my thoughts since it was my head! This simple step has helped me greatly in my life and my Christian walk for now that I have identified the different types of thoughts, I have made the choice to only accept those from Category One. Category Two thoughts are rejected as soon as I am aware of them. Category Three Analytical Thoughts are replaced with "Spirit-led reasoning," which we will discuss later in this chapter. You may refer to Appendix D for a deeper philosophical and theological look at the three sources of thoughts.

Personal Application

Write down a question in your journal that you would like to ask the Lord. It can be any question that you choose, as long as it is not one of the most traumatic questions of your life. Those issues cause you to become tense; they tend to inhibit you from maintaining the biblical poise of stillness that is commanded as we approach God (Ps. 46:10), especially when you are just learning the skills of journaling. Here are some ideas of questions I recommend you begin with:

> Lord, do You love me?
> Lord, what do You want to say to me?
> Lord, what do You want to say to me about the truths in this chapter?

Take a moment, choose a question, and write it down.

After you have written the question, ask Jesus to open the eyes and ears of your heart so that you can receive what He wants to share with you. Then picture Jesus in a comfortable setting. He may be sitting next to you, or walking along the Sea of Galilee with you. Become a child. Take His hand. Look into His face. See His joy and expectancy and excitement over sharing this time with you. (If you can't see His face at this time, don't worry about it. His face will become clearer the more you use vision.) This is what He longs for more than anything else. See His long robes. See the sandals on His feet. Relax and put a smile on your face. Enjoy being alone with Him. Then as you gaze upon Him, ask Him the question that you have written down.

Tune to spontaneity, fix your gaze upon Him and write what begins to flow within you. Don't test it now. Just write in simple childlike faith. You can test it later. If it is not too private, share it with a spiritual advisor for confirmation. It is important especially during your first weeks of journaling that you share much of what you receive with your advisor so you are established in faith that you are on the right track and truly hearing His voice. During this learning time, ask simpler and more general questions, rather than questions about decision-making or predictions of what is going to happen or extremely sensitive issues. One good introductory line for your journaling is to say, "Good morning, Lord, I love You! I give You this day. What would You like to say to me?"

Enjoy an example of the journaling of one of my students:

"Lord, what would You like to say to me?"

"You are too hard on yourself. I don't expect you to be perfect. I called you out so that I could live in you and so that we could both experience what the combination of the two of us looks like when we are expressing our personalities through this one body. When we are separate I am like chocolate and you are like peanut butter. Blend us together and the result is a tasty treat. Except that there is only one like us in the whole world. Together we are a RARE tasty treat!"

Biblical Meditation: Turning *Logos* Into *Rhema*

One way you experience *rhema* is when the Holy Spirit causes Scripture verses to leap off the page and hit you between the eyes. We have all had this happen, and it is exciting! The written Word becomes illumined in our hearts as a specific spoken word for us at this present moment of our lives. So how and why does this occur? Could it happen every time I read the Bible? If so, what would I have to do for this wonderful experience of divine revelation to take place continuously? Here is the answer!

I cannot turn *Logos* into *rhema*. That only happens by the movement of the Holy Spirit. However, I can poise myself attentively before the Word and the Spirit, giving myself prime opportunity to hear what the communicating God wants to speak to me. In this way, I can receive revelation consistently as I turn to His Word.

God longs to speak to us through the *Logos*. He wants to give us a spirit of revelation, to open the eyes of our hearts (Eph. 1:17,18), to cause our hearts to burn within us (Luke 24:13-32). He desires for the Logos to be transformed from simple words to personal heart revelation and conviction as we pray over the Scriptures, allowing the Spirit to make it live in our hearts.

How can *Logos* become faith-giving *rhema*? How can I precipitate its happening? By choosing "Biblical Mediation" over "Western Study." Biblical meditation involves opening all five senses of my spirit to be filled with *rhema*. That places me in prime position to receive and provides God with the maximum opportunity to grant revelation within my heart. Below is a simple chart which compares study and meditation.

Since study is so central in Western education, it is startling to discover that the word "study" is only found **three times** in the King James Bible, and in none of

STUDY
(Greek/Western)

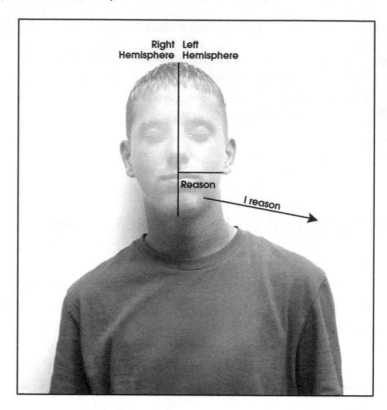

"Application of the mental faculties to the acquisition of knowledge"
(*Webster*)

STUDY (**My use of one part of one hemisphere of my brain**)

1. Is nowhere endorsed in Scripture (2 Tim. 2:15 is a mis-translation in the KJV Bible).
2. Is self in action (Humanism — a false god).
3. Is self using reason (Rationalism — a false god).
4. Results in wisdom from below— earthly, natural, demonic (James 3:15). For example, reason caused Peter to be at odds with the purposes of God (John 18:10,11).

STUDY **violates the following biblical principles:**

1. Gal. 2:20 — I resurrect self, which no longer lives.
2. Rom. 12:1 — I am using my faculties rather than presenting them to God to use.
3. Is. 1:18 — I'm reasoning, rather than reasoning together with God.
4. Gen. 3:5 — I've fallen prey to the temptation of the Garden of Eden that "I can know good and evil."

Figure 2.6

these references is study as we understand it endorsed or recommended. The verses are as follows:

- *"And further, by these, my son, be admonished: of making many books there is no end; and much study is a weariness of the flesh."* (Eccles. 12:12)

MEDITATION
(Hebrew/*Lamad*)

"To murmur; to converse with oneself, and hence aloud; speak; talk; babbling; communication; mutter; roar; mourn; a murmuring sound; i.e., a musical notation; to study; to ponder; revolve in the mind; imagine; pray; prayer; reflection; devotion" (*Strong's Exhaustive Concordance*)

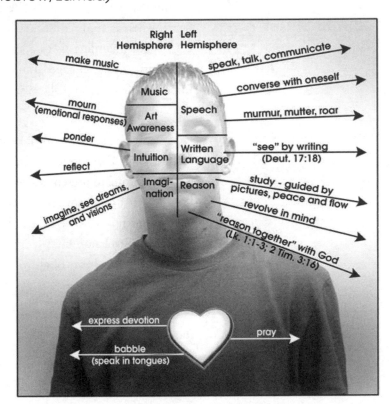

MEDITATION (**God's use of every part of both hemispheres of my brain as He fills and flows out through my heart by His Spirit**)

1. Is endorsed 18 times in the KJV Bible.
2. Is God in action within the individual.
3. Is God granting revelation through the heart and mind which has been yielded to Him.
4. Results in wisdom from above — pure, peaceable, gentle (James 3:17).

MEDITATION **applies the following biblical principles:**

1. Gal. 2:20 — I let Christ live through me.
2. Rom. 12:1 — I am yielding my outer faculties to the indwelling Spirit (to "flow" — John 7:38).
3. Isa. 11:2 — When reasoning together with God, I receive a **spirit** of wisdom and understanding and knowledge.
4. John 5:19,20,30 — I'm living as Jesus did, out of divine initiative, doing what I see and hear my Father doing.

Figure 2.7

- *"And that ye study (literal Greek is to "be diligent") to be quiet, and to do your own business, and to work with your own hands, as we commanded you."* (1 Thess. 4:11)

- *"Study (literal Greek is to "be diligent") to shew thyself approved unto God, a workman that needeth not to be ashamed, rightly dividing the word of truth."* (2 Tim. 2:15)

The New American Standard Bible translates 1 Thessalonians 4:11 and 2 Timothy 2:15 correctly as "be diligent." Diligence, of course, is an attitude of the heart, whereas study is a function of the left hemisphere of the mind. So 2 Timothy 2:15 is commanding us to come to the Bible with a properly postured heart, rather than with a fully engaged mind. This is a huge difference, and it will have a great impact on what you walk away with when you have completed your "Bible study" time.

So we see that nowhere does the Bible command us to study it, or to study anything, for that matter. "Study" is me using my mental faculties myself. What God wants is for me to present my entire self (this includes my brain) to Him and the Holy Spirit so that God can use and flow through me. I am to do nothing on my own initiative. Einstein said, "I want to know God's thoughts; the rest are details." He understood that revelation knowledge which comes through a biblical process called "meditation" is at the heart of all wisdom, knowledge and understanding.

The Scriptures use the word "meditation" as an alternative experience to "study." In the King James Version of the Bible, there are 20 uses of the words "meditate" and "meditation."

We find that we <u>can</u> meditate (Ps. 5:1), and that meditation takes place in our hearts (Ps. 19:14; 49:3; Isa. 33:18). We can meditate in the fields in the evening (Gen. 24:63) and in our beds during the night times (Ps. 63:6). We are encouraged to meditate on God's law all day long (Ps. 119:97). We are to meditate upon the Lord (Ps. 104:34) and upon His Word (Josh. 1:8; Ps. 1:2; 1 Tim. 4:15), upon His ways (Ps. 119:15), His statutes (Ps. 119:23; 119:48) and His precepts (Ps. 119:78). We are to meditate on all His works (Ps. 143:5). When we do this, we have more understanding than all our teachers (Ps. 119:99).

It is clear that God wants us meditating, rather than studying. You can see from the chart on "Study vs. Meditation" that while study is me using one faculty in one hemisphere of my brain, meditation is me inviting the Holy Spirit to use every ability in both hemispheres of my brain. This is obviously a far superior process and will grant a far superior end result. Study gives me *reasoned* knowledge, whereas meditation gives me *revelation* knowledge. Study is man in action. Meditation is God in action. Study gives me what Paul called "knowledge," whereas meditation gives me what Paul called "true knowledge," or what we might term revelation knowledge, or knowledge birthed in the Spirit of God.

You will note that the definition of "meditation" includes "study." If I combine study with all the rest of the experiences that are part of the meditation process, then study is an acceptable activity. For example, I am often led by the Holy Spirit to look up the Greek or Hebrew root meaning of a word in a verse. The Lord will tell me what I am to be looking for, and make it leap off the page when I see it.

So the entire studying process, when it is part of meditation, is guided by the flow of the Holy Spirit and wrapped with pictures or imagination. I am allowing flowing thoughts and flowing pictures to guide my reasoning process. I call this "Spirit-led reasoning" or "anointed reasoning." I believe the best biblical phrase for this is "meditation."

Biblical Meditation
Resulting in illumination, revelation knowledge, anointed reasoning

Do Not Do This: **Left-brain** **Study/Rational Humanism**	But Do This: **Whole-brain/Heart** **Meditation/Divine Revelation**
1. Have unconfessed sin	1. Be washed by Jesus' blood
2. Have a pre-conceived attitude	2. Have a teachable attitude
3. Be independent: "I can..."	3. Pray: "Lord, show me"
4. Read quickly	4. Slow down, ponder, muse
5. Rely on reason & analysis only	5. Combine anointed reason, flowing pictures, music & speech
6. Read without specific purpose	6. Read with focused purpose
7. Take credit for insights	7. Glorify God for insights

The Seven Steps of Biblical Meditation Explained:

1. **Lord, cleanse me by Your blood:** Since receiving divine revelation is at the heart of biblical meditation, you must prepare yourself to receive from the Holy Spirit by repenting and being cleansed by the blood of the Lamb. You must be obedient to

previous revelations from God (Matt. 7:6), and confess any sin in your life, so you are not cut off from ongoing revelation (Isa. 59:1,2; 1 John 1:9).

2. Lord, grant me a teachable attitude: Revelation is given to those who maintain an attitude of humility, and it is withheld from the proud and the arrogant. So keep an open, humble attitude before God, allowing Him the freedom to shed greater light on any ideas you currently hold and to alter them as He sees fit (James 4:6; 2 Pet. 1:19).

3. Lord, I will not use my faculties myself: You can do nothing of your own initiative but only what you hear and see by the Spirit (John 5:19,20,30). You do not have a mind to use, but a mind to present to God so He can use it and fill it with anointed reason and divine vision (Prov. 3:5-7; Rom. 12:1,2). If you use your mind yourself, it is a dead work (Heb. 6:1,2).

4. Lord, I pray that the eyes of my heart might be enlightened: Slow down as you read, mulling the text over and over in your heart and mind, praying constantly for God to give you a spirit of wisdom and revelation in the knowledge of Him (Eph. 1:17,18; Ps. 119:18).

5. Lord, I present the abilities to reason and to imagine to You to fill and flow through by Your Spirit: Meditation involves presenting your faculties to God for Him to fill and use. These include your left-brain reasoning capacities as well as your right-brain visual capacities. Look for the river of God (i.e., "Spirit flow") to guide and fill both hemispheres, granting you anointed reasoning and dream and vision (John 7:37-39). Music can assist you, as can muttering, speaking, and writing as you go through the discovery process (2 Kings 3:15).

6. Lord, show me the solution to the problem I am facing: Focused attention brings additional energies of concentration of heart and mind, which help release revelation. For example, think about the difference between a ray of sunlight hitting a piece of paper, and sunlight going through a magnifying glass to hit a piece of paper. The focused energy creates a ray so concentrated that the paper bursts into flames. When you have a hunger to master a new understanding and discipline, that hungry and searching heart will cause you to see things you would not normally see (Matt. 5:6).

7. Thank You, Lord, for what You have shown me: Realizing that the revelation came from the indwelling Holy Spirit, give all the glory to God for what has been revealed (Eph. 3:21).

God commands us to reason together with Him (Isa. 1:18). This involves the flow of His Spirit within us, guiding our thoughts. Vision is a key element in this process, as seen in Isaiah 1:18. God goes straight to pictures after He says, "Let us reason." He continues, "Though your sins be as scarlet, I will make them white as snow." That is reasoning with pictures. That is biblical reasoning. It is very different than the Western way of thinking which centers in logic. Luke 1:1-3 gives another good example of "Spirit-led reasoning."

I believe verses become *rhema* as a result of biblical meditation. I believe they remain simply black and white print when we use Western study. I have therefore purposed in my heart to only use biblical meditation when I come to the Bible. I will not use Western study as I approach the Bible, or any other book for that matter, since I am not interested in simply my own knowledge or understanding but earnestly desire the Spirit's revelation on everything I learn.

You, also, may want to pray, saying, "I choose biblical meditation over Western study from this point on in my life. Father, by Your grace I will use biblical meditation when I come to the Bible and to every other book or area I explore, because I want divine revelation, not man's reasoning. Holy Spirit, please remind me whenever I slip back into mere study. Thank You."

Since it is a heart/spirit activity, following are the faculties (senses) of my heart which I present to the Holy Spirit to be used in biblical meditation.

- **Ears of my heart** — I direct my whole attention to God's Word as I begin to read. I incline my ear to His words and have an attentive attitude so that I hear what He is saying to me from the passage. Since His voice comes to me as flowing thoughts, I tune to these as I read the Scriptures.

- **Eyes of my heart** — I sanctify my imagination, deliberately offering up to Father the eyes of my heart to be filled with pictures and visions of the eternal reality that I am reading about in the Bible. I picture the biblical scenes as I am reading and I tune to flow, inviting the Holy Spirit to make them come alive and to minister anything to me He wants to reveal to me. As flow bubbles up and the scenes come alive and begin moving, the pictures in my mind transition from godly imagination to divine visions.

- **Mind of my heart** — Throughout the day and night, I ponder the words and visions I have received, seeking greater revelation and how they are to be integrated into my life.

- **Will of my heart** — I set my will to fully understand and obey all that God has spoken to me. I confess verses and truths and principles out loud, personalizing them by putting my name in the Bible promises I am meditating upon.

- **Emotions of my heart** — My deep underlying emotions are stirred as I gaze at the picture I am holding on the screen of my heart. These emotions move me to action. In addition, I have a sense of peace and assurance in my heart when the Holy Spirit is saying "yes" or unrest when He is saying "no." My heart lets out a victory cry when it gains new insights through the Holy Spirit, and when He convicts me of sin, it is broken and contrite before Him.

As I prayerfully fill all five senses of my spirit with the *Logos*, I provide a **maximum opportunity** for God to move within my heart and grant revelation. The

Notes

summary diagram on the following page confirms this truth. Fill in the Scripture verses on the lines provided in the diagram.

"Pondering" by Maurice Fuller (one of Mark Virkler's long-time friends and spiritual advisors)

"There are times when a believer will think things through with his own human intelligence, without the Spirit of God. This is the way the word 'ponder' in Psalm 73:16 is used. It is the Hebrew word *chashav* (pronounced *kashav*). In the Piel stem of the verb, the stem that is used in this passage, it means 'the result of a thought process that (usually) brings one to a wrong conclusion.' The Psalmist at first reasoned without revelation and got it all wrong. Then, in the presence of God, he received revelation that enabled him to see all things clearly.

"It is used in Psalm 77:5,6. Here the Psalmist reasoned in his 'heart' and his 'spirit' but he still got it wrong. The significance of 'heart' and 'spirit' here is that even when thoughts come from the very deepest part of us, from the very core of our being, if they are uninformed by the Spirit, they can still be completely wrong. *Chashav* does not always indicate a thought process devoid of the Spirit, though. In Psalm 119:59, when the Psalmist 'considered' (*chashav*) his ways he saw them clearly and realized he should turn his steps to God's testimonies.

"The central idea of *chashav* is to compare an unknown thing with known things so as to clarify and define it. It is a very deep and thorough process yet, without the Holy Spirit, it can be dead wrong. The word also occurs in Proverbs 16:9 and 24:8, Daniel 11:24, Hosea 7:15 and a few more. In some of these passages it has the idea of carefully laid plans which, if they do not include God's guidance through the Spirit, are futile.

"I would say that, yes, Spirit-led reasoning is a gift and when it is well developed, as it is in left-brainers, it is especially useful. Right-brainers need to learn how to utilize this capacity just as we left-brainers had to learn how to hear from God. If they don't they will think every thought that comes into their head is from God, no matter how wonky, not realizing how our own defective theology can distort divine revelation.

"Flaky prophets suffer from underdeveloped analytical abilities. The balanced person is the one who is able to compare new revelation with his storehouse of knowledge gained from former revelation, from life experience, from the Scriptures, and from what other godly people have shared with him. Maybe there needs to be a special course on Spirit-led reasoning for super-intuitive people!"

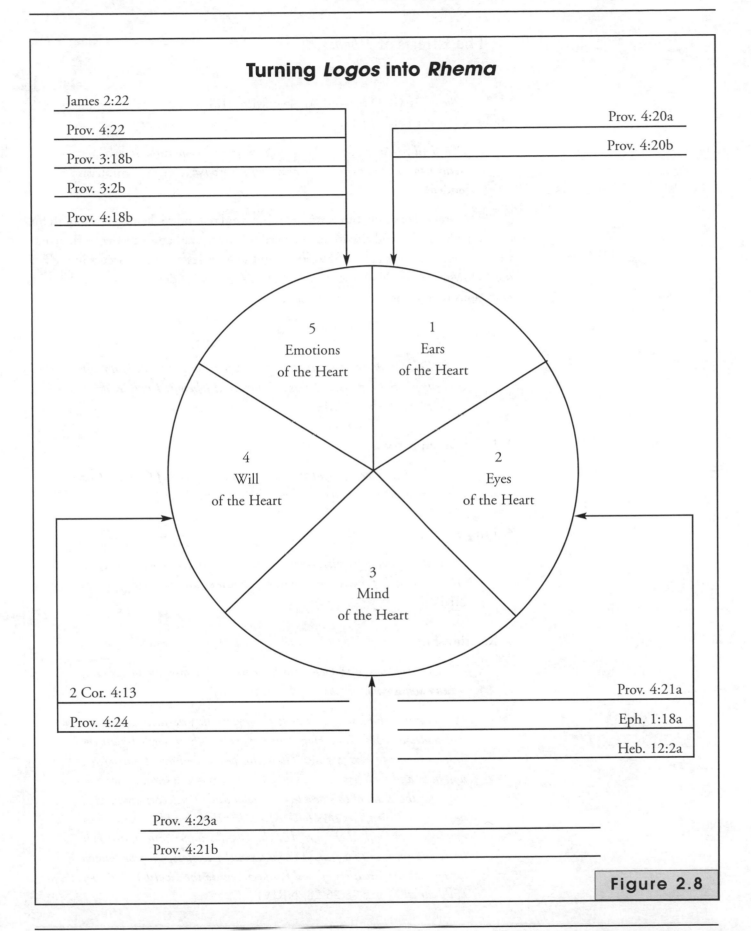

Turning *Logos* into *Rhema*

James 2:22

Prov. 4:22

Prov. 3:18b

Prov. 3:2b

Prov. 4:18b

Prov. 4:20a

Prov. 4:20b

5
Emotions
of the Heart

1
Ears
of the Heart

4
Will
of the Heart

2
Eyes
of the Heart

3
Mind
of the Heart

2 Cor. 4:13

Prov. 4:24

Prov. 4:21a

Eph. 1:18a

Heb. 12:2a

Prov. 4:23a

Prov. 4:21b

Figure 2.8

The Effects of *Rhema*

Rhema is **GOD'S** word, spoken with **HIS** mouth, which produces **HIS** results. Consider Isaiah 55:11:

> *"So shall My word be which goes forth from **My mouth**; it shall not return to Me empty, without accomplishing what I desire"* (emphasis added).

Logos is the whole Bible. *Rhema* is the word of God spoken by His mouth for the immediate time and situation. We need to understand and experience rhema as well as *Logos*. *Rhema* is used over 70 times in the New Testament. It occurs in each of the following verses. Note the powerful effects and write down your thoughts and reflections on each of these uses of *rhema*.

1. Productivity

> *"But Simon answered and said to Him, 'Master, we have toiled all night and caught nothing; nevertheless at Your word [**rhema**] I will let down the net.'"* (Luke 5:5, NKJV)

2. Effective ministry

> *"For He whom God has sent speaks the words [**rhema**] of God, for God does not give the Spirit by measure."* (John 3:34, NKJV)

3. Life

> *"It is the Spirit who gives life; the flesh profits nothing. The words [**rhema**] that I speak to you are spirit, and they are life."* (John 6:63, NKJV)

4. Relationship

> *"He who is of God hears God's words [**rhema**]; therefore you do not hear, because you are not of God."* (John 8:47, NKJV)

> *"So when they did not agree among themselves, they departed after Paul had said one word: 'The Holy Spirit spoke rightly through Isaiah the prophet to our fathers, saying, "Go to this people and say, 'Hearing you will hear, and shall not understand and seeing you will see, and not perceive; for the heart of this people has grown dull. Their ears are hard of hearing, and their eyes they have closed, lest they should see with their eyes and hear with their ears, lest they should understand with their heart and turn, so that I should heal them.'" Therefore, let it be known to you that the salvation of God has been sent to the Gentiles, and they will hear it!'"* (Acts 28:25-28, NKJV)

5. Authoritative teaching

"Do you not believe that I am in the Father, and the Father in Me? The words [rhema] that I speak to you I do not speak on My own authority; but the Father who dwells in Me does the works." (John 14:10, NKJV)

6. Fullness of desire

"If you abide in Me, and My words [rhema] abide in you, you will ask what you desire, and it shall be done for you." (John 15:7, NKJV)

7. Faith

"So faith comes from hearing [akoe] and hearing by the word [rhema] of Christ" (Rom. 10:17). *Akoe* means "to have audience with, to come to the ears" (**Abingdon's Strong's Exhaustive Concordance**). Thus, the verse expanded and personalized would read:

So faith comes by having audience with God through the fellowship of the Holy Spirit, and hearing His voice in my heart.

The Alternative to God's Spoken Voice: God's Laws

It seems that we as humans often prefer a list of rules to a relationship. I suppose we find a security in rules which is somewhat lost in a growing relationship; and since we are creatures of habit, we prefer not to change.

When God wanted to have a relationship with the Israelites and speak to them directly from the mountain, they chose instead to be governed by a set of laws. Please read Deuteronomy 5:22-31 below from the New American Standard Bible Updated.

"These words the LORD spoke to all your assembly at the mountain from the midst of the fire, of the cloud and of the thick gloom, with a great voice, and He added no more. He wrote them on two tablets of stone and gave them to me. And when you heard the voice from the midst of the darkness, while the mountain was burning with fire, you came near to me, all the heads of your tribes and your elders. You said, 'Behold, the LORD our God has shown us His glory and His greatness, and we have heard His voice from the midst of the fire; we have seen today that God speaks with man, yet he lives. Now then why should we die? For this great fire will consume us; if we hear the voice of the LORD our God any longer, then we will die. For who is there of all flesh who has heard the voice of the living God speaking from the midst of the fire, as we have, and lived? Go near and hear all that the LORD our God

says; then speak to us all that the LORD our God speaks to you, and we will hear and do it.' The LORD heard the voice of your words when you spoke to me, and the LORD said to me, 'I have heard the voice of the words of this people which they have spoken to you. They have done well in all that they have spoken. Oh that they had such a heart in them, that they would fear Me and keep all My commandments always, that it may be well with them and with their sons forever! Go, say to them, "Return to your tents." But as for you, stand here by Me, that I may speak to you all the commandments and the statutes and the judgments which you shall teach them, that they may observe them in the land which I give them to possess.'"

In the verses above, God is offering the Israelites a relationship. He offers them His voice. He offers to restore the fellowship Adam and Eve had in the Garden of Eden. They turn down His precious gift because with His voice comes fire, where they will be required to put to death their own fleshly desires so they can be alive in the Spirit. The Israelites don't want that much heat in their lives, so they tell Moses he can go and have a relationship with God, and he can report back to them what God says, and they will keep the laws he gives them.

So the Israelites turn down God's offer of a relationship, saying, "No, I prefer law, please." I believe God's heart is broken here, just as any parent's would be if their child told them he did not want a relationship with them.

God was not going to stop speaking. He told the Israelites they could go back to their tents if they wanted, but if Moses wanted to have a relationship, he could stay close. So Moses got a relationship and the Israelites received laws, commandments, statutes and judgments. Law was added to law until the burden became heavy.

Yes, there is some good in trying to live under law (v. 28), because it is a tutor that brings us to Christ (Gal. 3:24) as we realize we can never keep the law (v. 29).

The author of Hebrews comments on this situation in Hebrews 12:18-29. Please read it now.

In verse 19, the word *rhema* is used. They did not want to hear the sound of His voice. In verses 22 and 23, we, too, have come to the Holy Mountain, Mount Zion. In verse 25, He gives us a warning:

"See to it that you do not refuse Him who is speaking."

Why? Because, if we do, we will forsake the relationship with God that is to characterize Christianity, and we will return to life under the law, even as those in the Old Testament did. Our minister will hear from God and, like Moses, will give us the laws under which we are to live. How sad that we might not avail ourselves of the living Holy Spirit within our hearts and live in communion with Him, choosing instead to live only out of the New Testament laws and thus become legalists or pharisees.

Anyone who has tried to do this has found, with me, how burdensome it becomes. The load becomes heavy instead of being light as Jesus promised. As we grow as Christians, we discover more laws to obey until eventually the list becomes more than we can handle. The choice often becomes either to stop growing or to abandon Christianity altogether. The Pharisees of Jesus' day had 613 laws they were imposing on Israel. Jesus rebuked them for the heavy load they were laying on the people.

Therefore, we, like the Israelites, are faced with a decision: either we hear God speak and live in relationship with Him, or we must live under the New Testament laws we discover. I believe it is **imperative** that we learn to discern God's voice and live in it so that our **relationship** is not **reduced** to a **religion**.

Speak this aloud as your confession: "Lord, I choose relationship rather than rules. Please draw me into a full and complete relationship with You, Almighty God."

Personal Application — Bible Meditation Exercise

Meditate on the following passages: John 7:37-39; Revelation 22:1,2; Psalm 1:2,3; John 15:4-8. Picture each scene and then ask God for a spirit of wisdom and of revelation in the knowledge of Him. Pray, "Lord, please enlighten the eyes of my heart" (Eph. 1:17,18). Now tune to flowing thoughts and flowing pictures as you wait in His presence.

Ask Him, "Lord, please show me where the river within me comes from, what it feels like within me. What is this flow designed to produce? What will be the effects of what is produced? How important is it to live out of this river? What happens if I neglect the river and live out of self's initiative? And Lord, is there anything else You want to show me in this biblical meditation?"

Record what God reveals to you in your journal. (You can keep your journal on your computer if you desire. I do, and since I can type with my eyes closed watching vision and tuned to flow, it is all much easier than writing things out by hand.) Once you have written out the illumined truths you receive from your meditation on the Scripture passages, fix your eyes on Jesus, and journal about what He has shown you. Ask, "Lord, what do You want to say to me personally about what You have shown me from these passages? How would You have me change?" Picture Jesus in a comfortable setting, tune to flow, and write down the spontaneous thoughts (i.e., His voice) that come back to you. Submit this to your spiritual advisors for confirmation. Then run with it.

Do this NOW, before proceeding on to the next chapter. It is only what you DO that changes your life, not what you read and think would be nice to do!

An Overview of the Four Keys to Hearing God's Voice

Remember: "Hearing God's voice is as simple as quieting yourself down, fixing your eyes on Jesus, tuning to spontaneity, and writing!" You can ensure that what you have written came from God by sharing it with your three spiritual advisors to confirm that their hearts bear witness that it is from God.

Memorize those two sentences so you can share them easily, and help your friends greatly.

Speak these aloud, as your declarations:

- I choose to honor the river of God within me. I choose to tune to it (Him) and to honor spontaneous thoughts and spontaneous pictures that light upon my mind, as I believe they are coming from Almighty God.

- I choose to posture my heart properly before God so I can receive divine flow continuously. I choose His anointing upon and through me. I choose divine initiative over my initiative.

CHAPTER 3

HOW I CAN BECOME STILL

Let's begin with a review of the four fundamental keys to hearing God's voice:

Key # 1 — Recognize God's voice as spontaneous thoughts which light upon your mind.

Key # 2 — Quiet yourself so you can hear God's voice.

Key # 3 — Look for vision as you pray.

Key # 4 — Write down the flow of thoughts and pictures that come to you.

In this chapter we will explore in depth:

Key # 2 — Quiet yourself so you can hear God's voice.

In order for us to hear the still, small voice of God within us as spontaneous thoughts, we ourselves must become quiet. God says, "Be still and know that I am God" (Ps. 46:10, NKJV). Other renderings of the verse exhort us to "cease striving, let go, relax and know that I am God." David commanded his soul to wait in silence for God only (Ps. 62:1,5, NASB), and to rest and wait longingly for God (Ps. 37:7).

Often we miss the importance of quieting ourselves when we approach God. Our lives are such a rush; we just run up to God, blurt out our prayers, and rush away again. I am convinced we will never enter the realm of the Spirit that way.

If we are going to commune with God, first we must become still. Habakkuk went to his guard post to pray (Hab. 2:1). In the early morning when it was still dark, Jesus departed to a lonely place to pray (Mark 1:35). And after a day's ministry, Jesus went to a mountain to be alone with His God.

In order for our inner man to commune with God, we must **first** remove external distractions. We must find a place where we can be alone and undisturbed, so that we can center down into our hearts without being distracted by our external circumstances. Ask your family to help you by intercepting phone calls, young children, or other interruptions that would distract you from your *yada* time. Set aside a specific time and place for your personal conversations with your God. As you go there regularly, you will find His Spirit waiting there for you. If you don't already have such a time and place identified, do so now before reading any further.

Second, we must learn to quiet our inner being — all those voices and thoughts within us that are calling for our attention. Until they are quieted, we most likely will not hear His voice.

Several means can be used to quiet the voices within you. First, you can write them down to be taken care of later. Second, you can quiet your inner members by focusing them on Jesus. Open your eyes and see in the Spirit the vision that Almighty God wants you to behold. This will bring your inner attention to the Father and the Son.

Sense the "cry of your heart" and repeat it over and over. The cry of your heart is whatever your heart is trying to express at any given moment. I often notice it as a song I spontaneously sing in the early morning. Whenever we need to sense our hearts, we can listen for the spontaneous song bubbling within and go with the flow of it.

For example, one day when my life was crumbling around me and God seemed so distant that I could not see Him or sense Him in any way, I found that the spontaneous song that bubbled up from my heart was only two words: "Lord, arise." As I sang those words over and over, I eventually began to sense the Lord rising within me, and His vision and presence being restored in my life. We should sing the song on our heart until it realizes its goal.

You may find tension in your body as you seek stillness. That, too, should be released so you are fully open to receive from God without being distracted or hindered by bodily discomfort. Be in a comfortable, relaxed position when you pray (1 Chron. 17:16). Consciously relax the parts of your body that are tense. Have you noticed how calm your breathing is when you first awaken? On the other hand, when I first began public speaking, I would be terrified and my breathing would be short and fast. I found I could calm my body by breathing more deeply and slowly. Check your breathing and use it to help you relax.

Biblically speaking, there is a very close connection between breath and spirit. Both breath and spirit come from one word in the Greek, as well as the Hebrew. When our breath is gone from our bodies, our spirit is gone. I do not believe it is an accident that these words are so closely connected in the Bible. I have found I can breathe in the pure Spirit of Christ as I breathe out the contaminated spirit of self.

"Be still and know." Stillness is not a goal in itself. I want to become still in mind and body so my heart can know and sense God moving within. His promptings are gentle, and until my own inner and outer raging is quieted, I will not sense His inner moving.

In becoming still, I am not trying to **do anything**. I simply want to be **in touch** with the Divine Lover. I am centered on **this moment** of time and experiencing Him in it.

Becoming still cannot be hurried or forced. Rather, it must be allowed to happen. At a point in your stillness, God takes over and you sense His active flow within you. His spontaneous images begin flowing with a life of their own. His voice begins speaking, giving you wisdom and strength. You find that you are "in the Spirit" (Rev. 1:10).

Becoming still is an art to be learned, especially for those of the Western culture who are always on the go. However, our communion with the Lord must begin here. When you pray, take the first few minutes to become centered, and proceed **only after** you have become still. Out of your stillness, you will sense God. Then you will be able to commune. You will find that the more you practice becoming still, the easier it becomes and the more quickly it happens. Many also find that being in a group that is seeking to become quiet together helps them quiet down. An atmosphere of quiet engenders quiet.

How Elisha and David Stilled Themselves

It is interesting for me to study the great prophets of the Bible to see what they did when they wanted to touch the divine flow. Think of Elisha, for instance. In 2 Kings 3:15, we find that when Elisha wanted to receive a prophetic word from God, he said: "'But now bring me a minstrel.' And it came about, when the minstrel played, that the hand of the Lord came upon him. And he said, 'Thus says the Lord....' "

Elisha used music to help him tune to the voice of God within and away from outer reasoning. It is interesting to note that reason is a left-brain function, while both intuition and music are right-brain.

May I suggest that when you want to move from reasoning, which flows through the left side of the brain, to intuition, which flows through the right side of the brain, you can do as Elisha did and use music (which also stimulates the right side of the brain)? This will cause a shift internally from the left hemisphere to the right hemisphere. It is so simple and so thoroughly biblical. Of course, David also did this when he wrote his psalms, musical records of his encounters with God.

I have found it effective for me to sing a quiet love song to the King of kings and picture the words that I am singing. (Vision also flows through the right side of the brain.) This poises me instantly before the intuitive flow that springs up from my heart, and I begin to record the precious words that come from my Lord.

Doing any right-brain activity moves you from the left side of the brain to the right. Therefore, normally I will do **several** right-brain activities **together** to ensure a smooth and complete transition from the left side of my brain to the right side. I will fix my eyes on Jesus, sing softly in the Spirit, relax by putting a big smile on my face, and, perhaps picturing myself as an eight-year-old, look at the beauty of God's creation as I stand with Jesus near the Sea of Galilee. Then I write down a question I want to ask Him. In that posture, I tune to spontaneity and record the flow of thoughts which come. It is God's voice, and I confirm it is God's voice by submitting it to my three spiritual advisors.

The chart below will review some effective ways of quieting yourself.

REMOVING INNER NOISE
(Voices, Thoughts, Pressures)

Problem	Solution
1. Thoughts of things to do.	1. Write them down so you don't forget them.
2. Thoughts of sin-consciousness.	2. Confess your sin and clothe yourself with the robe of righteousness.
3. Mind flitting about.	3. Focus on a vision of Jesus with you or do any right-brain activity.
4. Need to get in touch with your heart.	4. Begin singing and listening to the spontaneous song bubbling up from your heart.
5. Need for additional time to commune when your mind is poised and still.	5. Realize that times when you are doing automatic activities (e.g., driving, bathing, exercising, routine jobs, etc.) are ideal times for hearing from God.

Identifying the State of Being Still

The five key ingredients of the contemplative or meditative state are physical calm, focused attention, letting be, receptivity, and spontaneous flow. The opposites of these characteristics are physical tension, distraction, over-control, activity and analytical thought. These could be placed on a continuum as follows:

Physical Tension   Physical Calm

0	1	2	3	4

Distraction   Focused Attention

0	1	2	3	4

Over-control			Letting Be		*Notes*
0	1	2	3	4	
Activity			Receptivity		
0	1	2	3	4	
Analytical Thought			Spontaneous Flow		
0	1	2	3	4	

Meditation is commanded throughout the Scriptures, and so is each of these elements that make up the meditative pose. Consider the following with me.

The Biblical Exhortation Concerning Physical Calm

"There remains therefore a Sabbath rest for the people of God. For the one who has entered His rest has himself also rested from his works, as God did from His. Let us therefore be diligent to enter that rest, lest anyone fall through following the same example of disobedience." (Heb. 4:9-11)

"And to whom did He swear that they should not enter His rest, but to those who were disobedient? And so we see that they were not able to enter because of unbelief." (Heb. 3:18,19)

The Biblical Exhortation Concerning Focused Attention

"...let us...lay aside every encumbrance, and...sin which so easily entangles us, and let us run...fixing our eyes on Jesus, the author and perfecter of faith...." (Heb. 12:1,2)

"Truly, truly, I say to you, the Son can do nothing of Himself, unless it is something He sees the Father doing; for whatever the Father does, these things the Son also does in like manner." (John 5:19)

The Biblical Exhortation Concerning Letting Be

"Cease striving [marginal reference: let go, relax] and know that I am God." (Ps. 46:10)

"Be anxious for nothing, but in everything by prayer and supplication with thanksgiving let your requests be made known to God. And the peace of God which surpasses all comprehension, shall guard your hearts and your minds in Christ Jesus." (Phil. 4:6,7)

The Biblical Exhortation Concerning Receptivity

"Abide in Me, and I in you. As the branch cannot bear fruit of itself, unless it abides in the vine, so neither can you, unless you abide in Me.

Notes

I am the vine, you are the branches; he who abides in Me, and I in him, he bears much fruit; for apart from Me you can do nothing." (John 15:4,5)

The Biblical Exhortation Concerning Spontaneous Flow

"He who believes in Me, as the Scripture said, 'From his innermost being shall flow rivers of living water.' But this He spoke of the Spirit, whom those who believed in Him were to receive...." (John 7:38,39)

On the following lists, check those characteristics that represent your meditative state and your lifestyle, since meditating or abiding is to be a way of living. This will assist you in cultivating the art of stillness before Almighty God.

Physical Calm

_____   My heart beats calmly and evenly.

_____   My breathing feels calm, easy, even and complete.

_____   My muscles don't feel tight or clenched.

_____   I don't feel restless or fidgety.

_____   I don't feel tense or self-conscious when I say or do something.

_____   I don't feel uncomfortable, hot and perspiring.

_____   I don't feel the need to go to the bathroom when I don't have to.

_____   I feel coordinated.

_____   My mouth isn't dry.

_____   I feel awake and refreshed.

_____   I don't have a headache.

_____   I don't have a backache.

_____   I don't feel unfit or heavy.

_____   My shoulders, neck or back is not tense.

_____   The condition of my skin is healthy.

_____   My eyes are not watery or teary.

_____   My stomach feels calm.

_____   My appetite is okay.

Focused Attention

_____   My thoughts are not scattered.

_____   I have little trouble remembering what I am doing.

_____   I feel very conscious of things.

_____   When disturbed, I find it easy to get back on track.

_____   My mind feels clear.

_____   I feel centered.

_____   I am not indecisive.

_____   My goals and priorities are clear.

_____   I keep things simple, doing one thing at a time.

_____   My mind is steady and focused.

_____   I concentrate on what I am doing.

_____   I seem to be quite perceptive.

_____   My mind is not confused.

_____   I don't let interruptions disturb me.

_____   I keep my mind on what I want to do.

_____   Even if things get hectic, I feel I can work in a calm and orderly manner.

_____   I feel quite alert.

_____   I devote my full attention to what I decide to do.

_____   I feel absorbed.

_____   My attention doesn't wander.

_____   Things seem lucid and clear.

_____   It is fairly easy to keep my mind on my task.

_____   I don't feel divided between different courses of action.

_____   I seem quite aware of things.

_____   I don't wander from what I set out to do.

_____   I finish one job before starting something else.

_____   I live in the present, fully experiencing every moment.

_____   My mind is like a mirror, clearly reflecting the physical and spiritual worlds without distortion.

Letting Be

_____   My wants and desires do not drive me.

_____   I am not hard on myself even though I have some imperfections.

_____   I don't feel as though I have to urgently push or rush myself.

Notes

Notes

_____ I can accept things that cannot be done or understood.

_____ It feels okay to say "live and let live" about some of my problems.

_____ I can put things that really matter in perspective.

_____ I don't get worked up over things that can't be changed.

_____ I feel I can let go and be myself.

_____ I feel flexible.

_____ Some of my wishes seem less important when seen side by side with things that really matter.

_____ When I have worked enough, I can easily let go and relax.

_____ I feel patient.

_____ It feels okay not to worry needlessly about yesterday's or tomorrow's problems.

_____ It feels okay to let some things be.

_____ I feel as though I could accept my problems philosophically.

_____ I don't feel as though everything has to be done at once.

_____ I feel things aren't so bad even when they don't go the way I want.

_____ I don't get caught up demanding things I cannot have or that don't really matter.

_____ I don't feel particularly self-conscious or as though I have to be overly concerned with doing the right thing or making a good impression.

_____ I don't feel as though I have to have everyone's acceptance and approval.

_____ I feel part of a larger purpose or scheme of things.

Receptivity

_____ I am aware of God flowing through me.

_____ I live in an active dependence upon the Holy Spirit.

_____ I acknowledge the Holy Spirit's presence.

_____ I do not tackle projects with a dependence upon my own abilities.

_____ I offer one word or sentence prayers when in need.

_____ I am instantly aware when pride or self dependence encroaches upon me.

_____ I picture myself as one filled with Another.

_____ I recognize that my strength comes from God.

_____ I recognize that my wisdom comes from God.

_____ I recognize that God is my Source.

_____ I picture myself as one through whom Another flows.

_____ I am aware that I can do nothing on my own.

_____ I am aware that my righteousness is that which is imputed through Christ.

_____ I see myself as clothed with Christ's righteousness.

_____ I picture myself as a container filled with Another.

_____ When I succeed, I am immediately aware that it is Christ's victory.

_____ When I fail, I am aware that I have not drawn on the One Who lives within.

_____ I do things without undue strain or effort.

Spontaneous Flow

_____ I live tuned to spontaneity.

_____ I recognize that the Holy Spirit's flow is like a river within me.

_____ I feel willing and comfortable living in flow.

_____ I feel uncomfortable living in "boxes."

_____ I feel that pure analysis is not as profitable as allowing spontaneity to flow together with analysis.

_____ I am comfortable going with inner promptings.

_____ I feel spontaneous and free.

_____ I feel as though I go with the flow of things.

_____ I can sense when I am in flow.

_____ I purposely relax when working so I can enter the flow experience.

_____ I am aware of creative expression flowing within me.

_____ I seek out quiet, relaxing settings so my creativity can be maximized.

_____ I seek out and enjoy relaxed, spontaneous sessions with others.

_____ I quiet myself, focus myself and relax so the flow can begin.

_____ When in flow, I seek to continue with what I am working on until it is completed.

_____ I do not begin working until I sense the flow experience.

_____ I tackle projects when I sense them flowing within me.

Notes

_____   As I practice living in the flow experience, I sense it operating more readily and easily within me.

_____   I understand that all that lasts comes out of the flow experience.

Brainwave Activity Levels

Some of the research being done in sleep laboratories is interesting as it relates to quieting ourselves and becoming still. It has been discovered that when we are wide awake and alert, *beta* level waves go through our minds. However, when we relax or enter sleep, these waves slow down and become *alpha* level waves. This is a measurable physiological effect of stilling ourselves as God commanded.

I share this because it helps me, a logical left-brain Westerner, to realize that quieting myself before God is not just a nebulous experience. I actually enter a different state of being (i.e., heart awareness), and the physical manifestations of this state can be measured through tools like biofeedback. Such tools could possibly help you learn how to quickly enter this state of rest, which the Bible calls *stillness*. They did me.

A pastor friend and I together purchased a $49 biofeedback system that measured galvanic skin response called the "The GSR2 Biofeedback Device," and a more complete system, the "GSR/Temp 2X Biofeedback System" (both available at www.mindgrowth.com). I used them for a few weeks while I was learning to quiet myself in the Lord's presence. I found it very helpful since it measured the state of relaxation within me. I could quickly discover which things relaxed me and which things didn't. For instance, I discovered that singing rowdy praise songs did not relax me. Neither did singing quiet praise songs, if I was lunging emotionally at God, telling Him how much I loved Him. However, if I quietly spoke the words, "I love You" as I sang gentle worship songs, I found that I entered the stage of relaxed stillness that the Lord had commanded.

Another fun tool for helping you learn to live in rest can be purchased for only a few dollars. A "Stress Rate Card" will change colors when you hold your thumb on it for 10 seconds, turning black when stressed, red when tense, green when calm and blue when relaxed. It is an excellent tool to help you learn to relax.

The chart on the following page gives an overview of brainwave activity levels.

Similarity to Eastern Religions?

Some have wondered about the similarity of what I have described above to Eastern religions. You may be surprised that my response is, "Well, I would hope what I am doing is similar to the counterfeit!" I expect satan's imitation to be similar to the real. Satan is not an originator. He is a copycat, and he only counterfeits those things

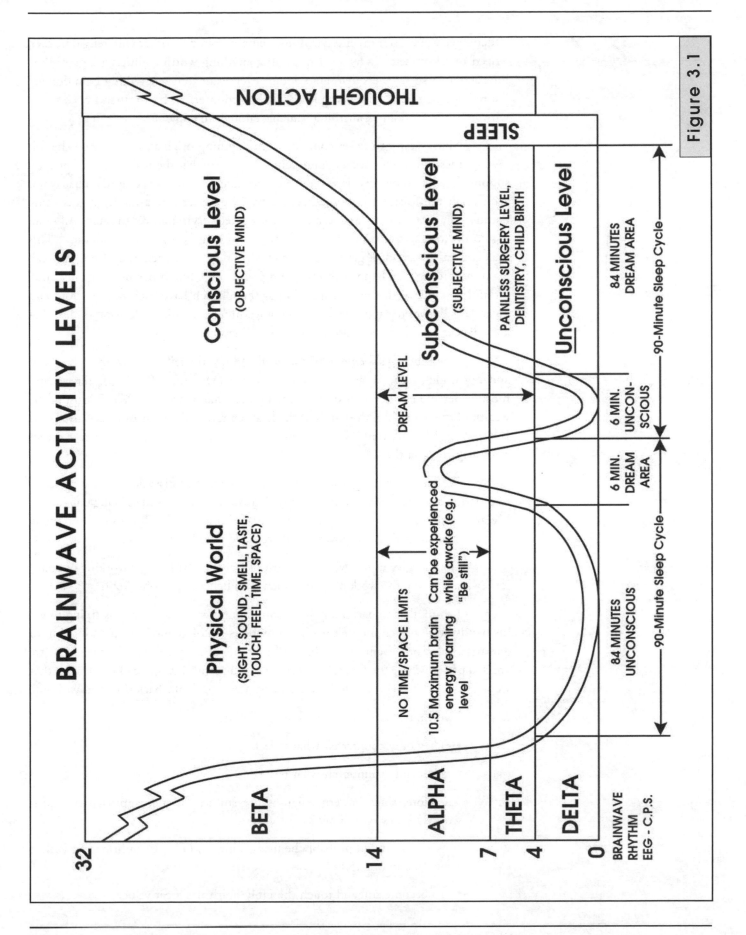

which have value. So if my lifestyle is not being imitated by other false religions, then I need to ask myself, "Why am I not doing anything worth counterfeiting? Are my life's activities so valueless that satan doesn't even want to fake anything I am doing?" I sure hope that what I am doing looks like the counterfeit. If not, then I need to get with it, and start doing something valuable enough to copy.

Since satan can never come up with anything original, I ask myself the following question when I see a counterfeit: "I wonder what the real thing is that I am supposed to be doing, that is so valuable that satan is counterfeiting it?" That is not a question the fearful ask. Some people say, "We better stay away from this thing because satan can use it," and as a result they give everything over to satan. All satan has to do to take something valuable away from some people is to imitate it. This makes them so afraid of getting close to it that they even back away from the real. Satan accordingly ends up with everything, and the Church has nothing. Just look around you and see if this isn't true. We as the Church have backed away from and given largely over to satan the following: government, politics, television, radio, theater, dance, pageantry, education, business, money, and computers.

The Bible says we are to be the head and not the tail, we are only to be above and not underneath, we are to lend and not borrow (Deut. 28:12,13). Yet we find most leadership positions filled by heathen rather than Christians. Why? Most of the wealth of the world is in the hands of the heathen rather than Christians. Why? Is the Bible wrong? I think not! We are wrong in that **we live under a spirit of fear rather than a spirit of faith.**

We have been taught to be so afraid of satan and his wiles that we cower in trepidation and back away from anything that could be perceived as being dangerous. We are supposed to be people full of faith and abundant life. But instead too many are full of neurotic fear and poverty and are ruled over by the heathen.

God, forgive us for living in a spirit of fear (i.e., faith in the working of satan) rather than "doing the work of God, which is to believe…" (John 6:29).

I think that to back away from something just because satan is trying to get his hands on it and counterfeit it is a horrendous sin of giving in to the kingdom of darkness. I, for one, want to take back all that satan has stolen, and I believe that we are in a period where the Church is doing just that. And this is one of those areas that we will redeem. I invite you to become a conqueror and take back this land with me.

Two things stand out about counterfeiters:

- They only counterfeit what is real.

- They only counterfeit what has value.

Therefore, since Eastern religions use stillness as they approach the spirit world, I know two things:

- We, too, should probably be using stillness. (This is confirmed in Psalms 46:10 and 62:1,5.)

- To become still and touch the Holy Spirit has great value.

Since the Eastern mystic does not go through Jesus Christ, he becomes ensnared by the evil one as he enters the spirit world. However, some of the **paths into** the spirit world are neutral. They may be used by either cultists or Christians. On the other hand, some paths are not neutral. A non-Christian may use drugs to enter the spirit world. This is an illegal entry for the Christian and strictly forbidden in the Bible. The word for witchcraft in the Bible is *pharmecea* which is, of course, connected with drugs.

Since the Christian goes through Jesus Christ, Jesus guides him safely through the snares of the trapper and into the throne room of God — as He did John in the book of Revelation.

Two Approaches to Overcoming Self: Attacking Self vs. Refocusing

Throughout the last 2000 years, the Church has presented two different ways of dying to self so we could become more Christ-like:

"Stripping away" — In this approach, you attack the desires and lusts of the flesh and try to kill or remove them from you. A lot of self whipping tends to take place, at least verbally and sometimes even physically. Things like lying on a bed of nails have been advocated, along with many other fairly painful rituals. I see this as self attacking self. No one wins because the self that is attacking has the same strength as the self that is being attacked!

"Coming to the light" — In this approach, you overcome your sinfulness and darkness by coming into Christ's light. You fix your eyes upon Jesus, and are transformed "while you look" into His wonderful presence (Heb. 12:1,2; 2 Cor. 3:18; 4:17,18). When you lift your hands during a worship service and find yourself in the presence of the King, you discover that all your negative attitudes and weaknesses melt away and you find faith, hope, love, peace, and joy flowing effortlessly within you.

I have personally chosen this approach to overcoming self. I feel it is what the New Testament teaches, and it is what works most effectively in my own life. So, for example, when I want to overcome rational thinking, I never attack my thoughts and tell them to stop (which I found doesn't work), but instead I refocus from self to Jesus. I picture myself together with Jesus in a comfortable setting, and I write down a question I want to ask Him. I put a smile on my face, tune to spontaneity and write down the flow of thoughts which come while my eyes are fixed on Jesus.

Removing All Idols in Your Heart Instantly by Fixing Your Eyes on Jesus!

This teaching on praying with an idol in your heart will provide tremendous insight for you in the area of purifying your journaling. The key is to be aware of where you are fixing your eyes when you are praying. Consider the following.

"...any man in the house of Israel who sets up his idols in his heart, puts right before his face the stumbling block of his iniquity, and then comes to the prophet, I the Lord will be brought to give him an answer in the matter in view of the multitude of his idols." (Ezek. 14:4)

This brings into focus a startling truth concerning an inappropriate method of prayer, which I am afraid has been practiced by many: They have fixed their eyes on the thing they are praying about more than on Jesus. The principle is: "When anything is larger than Jesus in the eyes of your heart, that thing has become an idol."

When I come to the Lord in prayer, I am to be a living sacrifice. I must lay down my will and be totally sold out to God's will concerning the issue about which I am praying. If that is not my mindset, I should pray for God to form that attitude within me before I begin praying about the issue at hand. If I pray about the issue while I have a definite direction about it in my own heart, that "definite direction" of my own will interfere with the signals coming from the throne of God and cause me to believe that God is confirming the direction I felt, whether He actually is or not.

In other words, if I pray about something and the item is more prominent in my eyes or my consciousness than my vision of the Lord, the answer that comes back will be through the item and will be deceptive rather than a pure answer from the heart of the Lord. On the other hand, if my vision of the Lord is more prominent in my consciousness than my vision of the issue I am praying about, then the answer will be a pure answer from the Lord's heart and not contaminated by my own desires.

The Principle of Pure Focus is this: "The intuitive flow comes out of the vision I am holding before my eyes." That is why I am commanded to fix my eyes on Jesus, the Author and Finisher of my faith. That will make the vision pure.

An example of a seer having his vision clouded and receiving damaging direction can be found in the story of Balaam in Numbers chapter 22. Balak had sent messengers to Balaam asking him to come and curse the Israelites. When Balaam sought God about it, God was very clear: "Do not go with them; you shall not curse the people; for they are blessed" (Num. 22:12).

Balak again sent messengers, more distinguished than before, with the offer that Balak would honor Balaam greatly and do whatever he asked if he would only come and curse the Israelites. Apparently gold and riches were on Balaam's mind because he said, "Though Balak were to give me his house full of silver and gold, I could not do anything ..." (Num. 22:18). However, he invited them to stay, saying, "I will check with the Lord again."

Since he so desperately wanted to receive the honor, gold and riches (and was probably picturing a house full of silver and gold), he went to the Lord again in prayer, this time with an impure heart. As could be expected, the Lord gave him an answer consistent with the idol in his heart. He said, "Sure! Go ahead!" However, God was angry with Balaam and He sent an angel with a sword to block his path (Num. 22:22).

There are other examples of Israel praying with an idol in their hearts and receiving the answers to their prayers that eventually brought hurt in their lives. Israel begged God for a king, and even though He didn't want to give it to them, He gave in to their whining. Israel lusted for meat in the wilderness, and God gave it to them, but along with it He sent a wasting disease (Ps. 106:14,15).

In conclusion, when we pray with an idol in our hearts, we may get an affirmative answer from the Lord, but it will bring us to destruction. Therefore, when we pray, we must be certain that our vision is purified, and that we see Jesus as One Who is MUCH LARGER than the object or issue for which we are praying. Only then will our answer be pure and life-giving.

The diagram below demonstrates these two approaches in prayer.

Praying with an Idol in Your Heart
Ezekiel 14:4
Praying with an idol

"The Thing" is held more prominently in your consciousness and vision than is Jesus.

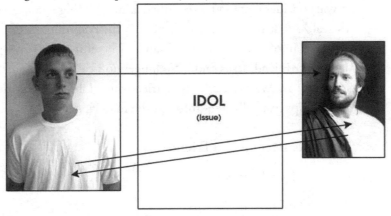

IDOL
(Issue)

The answer comes back through the idol: "Yes."

Praying without an idol

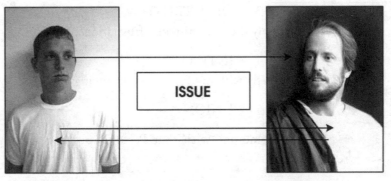

ISSUE

Jesus is held more prominently in your heart and mind than is "The Thing" for which you are praying.
The answer comes back from Jesus: "Caution—No."

THE PRINCIPLE: The intuitive flow comes out of the vision being held before one's eyes.

AN EXAMPLE: Balaam — Numbers 22:15-35

Figure 3.2

Personal Prayer Application: If you realize you have prayed in the past with an idol in your heart, stop now and repent, asking the Lord's forgiveness. State your intention to fix your eyes upon Jesus as you come to Him in prayer from this point on. Receive His cleansing, and put on the robe of righteousness. Ask the Holy Spirit to remind you anytime you are praying with an idol in your heart, and declare that by His grace you will honor that inner prompting and immediately fix your eyes back on Jesus. Ask God to take any mistaken decisions you have made in the past and to work His purposes out even through your mistakes. He is well able to do that. He brought Jesus Christ through David's biggest mistake, adultery with Bathsheba, the murder of her husband and the deaths of many other men on the front lines of battle.

What Is Prayer, Anyway?

Prayer is two lovers sharing love together. If you look back to the Garden of Eden and see how God walked and talked with Adam and Eve in the cool of the day, if you consider that God is described as manifesting incomprehensible love, you begin to realize that our sharing with Him is the communion of two lovers. You can find many examples of this in the Psalms. Therefore, when we pray, we are coming to Jesus, our Friend. Jesus said, "No longer do I call you servants, I now call you friends" (Jn. 15:15). We are building a friendship. I have found that the development of friendships generally goes through the following steps.

Prayer Is Becoming a Friend

(Not doing something, but being with Someone)

1. STAGE 1 — CASUAL
    I speak of the world outside me (sports, weather).

2. STAGE 2 — BEGINNING TRUST
    I speak of what I think and feel.

3. STAGE 3 — DEEP TRUST
    I share my dreams, mistakes, frustrations.

4. STAGE 4 — INTIMACY
    I sit quietly with my Friend, experiencing a Presence beyond words.

5. STAGE 5 — UNION

I become one with that Person, speaking, feeling and acting with His reactions.

We do not intrinsically become Jesus. But when we have gazed upon Him (Heb. 12:2) with loving affection for so long, we become a reflection of His glory (2 Cor. 3:18), taking on His character (Gal. 5:22,23) and His power (1 Cor. 12:7-11). A union has taken place in our spirits (1 Cor. 6:17), and "I have been crucified with Christ; and it is no longer I who live but Christ lives in me...." (Gal. 2:20) See also Romans chapter 6.

A Poem About the Present Tense God

A key to living with God is to live in the present tense. As I was learning this art, I discovered this beautiful poem which may be a blessing to you also.

I was regretting the past
And fearing the future.
Suddenly my Lord was speaking:

"My name is I Am." He paused.
I waited. He continued,
"When you live in the past,
With its mistakes and regrets,
It is hard. I am not there.
My name is not I Was.

"When you live in the future,
With its problems and fears,
It is hard. I am not there.
My name is not I Will Be.

"When you live in this moment,
It is not hard. I am here.
My name is I Am."

Helen Mallicoat

Prayer: "Lord, may we become still so that we may sense Your Spirit."

The Four Keys

Once again I want to remind you of the four words that summarize the four keys to hearing God's voice:

Stillness
Vision
Spontaneity
Journaling

So far, we have explored spontaneity and stillness. In the next chapter, we will delve into the exciting subject of vision — seeing with the eyes of our hearts.

Personal Journaling Application

Write the following questions in your journaling notebook or in a journaling file on your computer:

1. "Lord, what means have I used to effectively still myself?"

2. "What methods would You like me to cultivate?"

Now relax. Picture yourself with Jesus in a comfortable gospel setting — maybe walking along the Sea of Galilee or strolling through the fields of Judea. Turn to Him. See His love and compassion, and joy and excitement at being able to spend this time with you. Smile! Become a child and take His hand. Let the scene just happen as He wants it to. Ask Him the question on your heart. Tune to spontaneity and write down the answer He gives you. Do not test it while you are receiving it. Stay in simple childlike faith. You will have plenty of time to test it after the flow is finished.

CHAPTER 4

HOW I AM TO USE
THE EYES OF MY HEART

 We are now ready to explore key number three for hearing God's voice:

Key # 1 — Recognize God's voice as spontaneous thoughts which light upon your mind.

Key # 2 — Quiet yourself so you can hear God's voice.

 Key # 3 — Look for vision as you pray.

Key # 4 — Write down the flow of thoughts and pictures that come to you.

*"I will pour forth of My Spirit…and your young men shall **see visions**, and your old men shall **dream dreams**."* (Acts 2:17, emphasis added)

Daniel **looked** toward Jerusalem as he prayed (Dan. 6:10).

Habakkuk kept **watch** to see what God would speak (Hab. 2:1-3).

John looked inwardly for a **vision** and heard a voice say, "Come up here, and I will show you what must take place after these things," and immediately he **saw a vision** (Rev. 4:1,2).

Jesus spoke the things He had seen in the presence of His Father (John 8:38).

Our ability to see in the spirit is a primary sense by which we perceive the spiritual dimension. Since Christianity is a heart-to-heart or Spirit-to-spirit relationship, we would expect this faculty to be central in our relationship with God. Unfortunately, it is not used as much as it should be because we have been trained to live out of our head rather than our heart. We tend to live more in the world of logical concepts and rational thinking than in the world of heart impressions, dreams and visions. If we are going to allow our hearts to be released, we must learn to live in the world of the dream and the vision (John 5:19,20; 8:38).

God wants to communicate through the eyes of our heart, giving us dreams, visions and godly imagination, but first we must recognize this sense within us and the importance it can have as we present it to be used by Him. For ten years as a Christian, it never occurred to me to use the eyes of my heart or look for vision. As a result, I never received any visions. Now that I've learned to look, I find vision readily appears to me.

Obviously, the "eyes of our hearts" (Eph. 1:17,18) is a sense of our hearts. It is one of the ways man's heart communicates — possibly one of the primary ways. I have found that the key that unlocks the door to the inner world is the use of vision. Many spiritual leaders agree with this. Dr. David Cho, pastor of the world's largest church with over 750,000 members declares, "The language of the Holy Spirit is the dream and vision" (*Fourth Dimension*). Watchman Nee, pastor and writer, states that, "The picture is the Holy Spirit memory" (*Anointed Preaching*). These statements are astounding in the value they place on seeing in the Spirit.

I have come to the conclusion that the ability to think in terms of images is extremely important in the Christian's life. I believe that maturity involves knowing how to present both our logical faculties and our visionary faculties to the Holy Spirit to be used by Him. The results are Spirit-led reasoning and godly imagination, visions and dreams.

If we look at Scripture, we see that dreams and visions have been prevalent throughout the history of God's dealings with men. See Appendix F for a complete list of all Scriptural references to dream and vision. If you have any doubt about the validity of dream and vision, or about the place of seeing with the eyes of your heart as an integral part of your Christian life, I strongly encourage you to look up each of these verses and find out exactly what the Bible has to say. Our opinions and beliefs are only as strong as the Scriptural foundation upon which they are built.

Appendix G offers a brief look at the place dream and vision have held throughout Church history. Please refer to it now.

Words Describing Dream and Vision

In the Greek New Testament, there are many different words and phrases used to describe encountering God through dream and vision, and experiencing revelation. They are as follows:

Onar — a common word for "dream." Precisely, it is a vision seen in sleep, as opposed to waking. It is used in Matthew 1:20; 2:12,13,19,22 and 27:19.

Enupniom — a vision seen in sleep. It stresses the givenness, almost surprise quality, of what is received in sleep. It is used in Acts 2:17 and Jude 8.

Horama — translated "vision." It can refer to visions of the night or sleeping experiences, as well as to waking visions. It is used in Matthew 17:9; Acts 7:31; 9:10,12; 10:3,17,19; 11:5; 12:9; 16:9,10 and 18:9.

Opasis — can signify the eye as the organ of sight, an appearance of any kind, even a spectacle; but there are also two instances where it means a supernatural vision: Acts 2:17 and Revelation 9:17. The distinction between the perception of the physical and the nonphysical is lacking in the Greek. Both "seeings" are genuine perception.

Optasia — translated "vision." It has the sense of self-disclosure, of "letting oneself be seen." It is used in the following four passages: Luke 1:22; 24:23; Acts 26:19 and 2 Corinthians 12:1.

Ekstasis — the word from which the English word "ecstasy" is derived. It literally means "standing aside from oneself, being displaced or over against oneself," and ordinarily there is a sense of amazement, confusion and even of extreme terror. It may refer to either sleeping or waking experiences. Psychologically, both the dreams of sleep and the imagery that occurs on the border of wakefulness, hypnagogic or hypnopompic imagery, fit the condition that *ekstasis* describes. Although translated "trance," it is misleading to use the word "trance" as a direct translation. It is used in Mark 5:42; 16:8; Luke 5:26; Acts 3:10; 10:10; 11:5 and 22:17.

Ginomai en pneumati — translated "to become in Spirit" (Rev. 1:10). This signifies a state in which one could see visions and be informed or spoken to directly by the Spirit. Related phrases are found in Matthew 4:1; Mark 1:12; Luke 1:41 and 4:1.

Ephistemi, paristemi — simply referring to the fact that some reality stands by in the night or in the day. It is used in Luke 1:11; Acts 10:30; 16:9; 23:11 and 27:23.

Angelos or angel — meaning an actual physical envoy, a messenger, or a divine being sent by God, and *daimon, daimonion, diabolos* or demon, devil and satan, referring to nonphysical entities or powers from satan. Both angels and demons can be encountered in dreams and visionary experiences as shown in the following references: Acts 10:3; Jude 8; and many instances in the book of Revelation.

Blepo and *eido* — meaning "to see," "to perceive." These words are used to mean "see" in the normal outer sense, yet are also used to refer to seeing in the spiritual sense as evidenced in the following passages: Revelation 1:2,11; Mark 9:9 and Luke 9:36. Obviously, because of the dual use of these words to describe both inner and outer sight, the early Church considered visionary experiences to be just as easy to perceive and observe, to be given as often, and to be equally valid as the perceptions one has of the outer physical world.

Blepo simply means physical seeing but *eido* has the additional meaning of seeing all that is there, the essential nature of a thing, perception.

Apokalupsis — translated "revelation," literally means disclosure, divine uncovering or revelation. It is used in Romans 16:25; 1 Corinthians 14:6,26; 2 Corinthians 12:1,7 and Galatians 2:2.

Notes

When considering the great variety of words New Testament Christians had to choose from to describe their visionary experiences, it is evident that they were able to very precisely define the exact type of visionary encounter they were having. Probably our poverty of vocabulary in finding one or two suitable words to clearly define our visionary experiences demonstrates the scarcity of direct spiritual encounter we all experience in the Western culture. May we restore to our vocabulary a host of suitable words to clearly define the variety of inner spiritual experiences we are having!

Defining Kinds of Vision

The following summary may help us draw together all of the expressions above and gain a clearer understanding of the kinds of experiences we can expect as believers.

1. Spontaneous Vision on the Screen Within Your Mind

We may receive a spontaneous inner picture in the same fashion as we receive spontaneous *rhema*. God may give a vision of the face of a friend or relative, and we just know we are to pray for them. The picture is light and gentle, and is seen within. It may be sharp or hazy, precise or unclear. As I poll Christian groups, I find that almost everyone has had this type of vision.

2. Spontaneous Vision While in Prayer

These are identical to the previous level except that we receive them while seeking God in prayer. We have no part in setting them up. They just "appear," or pop into our minds. We may even find ourselves trying to change them in some way (although really we don't want to change them, because we want His visions, not ours). However, this in turn helps us to realize that it was His vision initially that lighted upon our minds (Dan. 7:1,13,14). About 70 percent of the Christians I poll have experienced this type of vision.

3. Seeing a Vision Outside of Yourself

On this level, a person actually sees a vision outside himself, with his spiritual eyes. For example, Elisha prayed and said, "'O Lord, I pray, open his eyes that he may see.' And the Lord opened the servant's eyes, and he saw; and behold, the mountain was full of horses and chariots of fire all around Elisha" (2 Kings 6:17). Only about 15 percent of the Christians I poll have experienced this type of vision.

4. Vision While in a Trance

A vision can be seen while in a trance. Peter had this experience in Acts 10:10-23. Trance-like visions are not very common in Scripture or in the contemporary Church. About 5 percent of the Christian groups I poll have had trance-like visions.

Ekstasis, being taken outside of oneself, is reserved for those with strong preconceived notions, which close them off from God's voice. Peter, who believed firmly that Gentiles could not be saved without first becoming Jews, had to be taken (with some sense of force) outside of his stubborn self and be shown the vision of the unclean animals and then be commanded to "rise, kill, and eat". Those whose spirit is open to God's voice seldom experience *ekstasis*, or trances. Trance is the common experience of New Age channellers, such as Edgar Cayce, who are used by evil spirits.

5. The Visionary Encounter of Dreams

Paul received a vision in the night as he slept (Acts 16:9,10). Dreams are common in Scripture (about 50), and they are also common today. About 85 percent of Christians have had a dream that they recognize as coming from God.

Visions on each of these five levels are equally valid and spiritual, and all are to be thoroughly tested, weighed and considered.

Full-Color or Black and White Pictures?

The groups I poll are about evenly divided between those who see visions in full color and those who see in black and white. Some people seem to have much better internal antennas and clearer reception than others. My visions are nebulous, and black and white. Some people's are sharp, clear and full color; they roll off almost like a video tape.

I am more left-brain. My experience indicates that left-brain people (analytical, logical) generally do not see as clearly as those God has gifted with more right-brain leanings (intuitive and visionary). That is fine. When I need to know more clearly, I simply team up with a seer, one who can see more clearly than I can. Jesus taught cooperation; He sent the disciples out in twos. In the book of Acts at least one of the teams was composed of a prophet and a teacher. It is likely that the teacher was more left-brain and the prophet more right-brain. We are not in competition with each other. We use our giftedness to serve one another. I think it is wise for you to minister with a person who is the opposite of yourself, and honor the different-ness of each other's gifting. Much more complete ministry is offered this way, and more people will be truly helped.

My First Steps in Beginning to See Vision

The Bible says we have not because we ask not. For years I never saw, because I never looked, nor did I ask to see. As I teach people to look, I witness their experience of becoming seers. This sounds simple and it is for many, particularly those who are intuitive, spontaneous, and visionary by nature, those who have not cut off their natural spontaneous openness to vision because of the pressure of a culture that idolizes logical, analytical and cognitive functions.

However, for those like me who were born with the natural tendency toward the analytical and cognitive and who have had these leanings reinforced by the rationalism of their culture, becoming a "seer" may not be so easy. Often the intuitive and visionary functions have literally atrophied or died through lack of use. Therefore, it is not as simple as just "looking" and "seeing." When a muscle has atrophied, it must first be exercised and strengthened before the body can call it into use again. In the same way, our weakened, dormant capacity for visualization must be exercised and strengthened before the Holy Spirit can fill it and call it into use.

The first step is to believe in the value of living in the world of dreams and visions. We must see it as the language of the heart, a primary means that God wants to use to communicate with us.

As pastors have often preached, our hearts are like a radio — we must tune them so we can hear God's voice. We must also tune them to see God's vision. Unfortunately, my heart's radio was not only out of tune, it was broken and in need of complete renovation by the Master. I began the process of restoration by repenting of having scorned my visionary capacity. I asked God's forgiveness for not honoring and using what He had created and bestowed upon me as a gift. I also repented of my participation in making an idol of logic and analytical thinking, a form of thinking that had bewitched me as well as my culture. I covenanted to seek and honor His ability to flow through vision as much as I sought and honored His ability to flow through analytical thought. If you need to pray the same prayer of repentance, do so now.

I next asked God to breathe upon my visionary capacity and restore it, to bring it back to life and teach me how to allow Him to flow through it.

Then I was ready to take my first few wobbly steps. As I sat in my study seeking God's face, I was drawn to a scene from the fourth chapter of John in which Jesus sat by the well and talked with a Samaritan woman. Sensing that God wanted to sit and talk with me, I pictured the scene with a slight adaptation. Instead of the woman, I was the one sitting there next to Jesus. I prayed and asked the Holy Spirit to take over this godly imagination, and I tuned to flow. The scene came alive through the Holy Spirit. Jesus moved and gestured, as someone does when he is talking. With His movement, there came into my heart spontaneous or flowing thoughts, His words and directives for my life.

This was the first time I had ever sought for vision in this way, and I was thrilled to see that Scripture could so readily come alive and be moved upon by the power of the Holy Spirit. I had, in essence, poised myself for the divine flow by choosing a Gospel story, meditating upon it, and asking God to fill it. I found as I repeated this experiment in later days that God continued to move through these Gospel scenes, causing them to come alive with His own life and become supernatural visions direct from the throne of grace.

You, too, will find that the more you present this channel to the Lord, the more it will be used. It will grow and grow until you reach the place to which God directed Dr. Cho, which was that "he must always be 'pregnant' with dreams and visions." Our Lord Jesus set the example, for He did nothing Himself unless it was something He saw the Father doing (John 5:19,20).

The Bible says as we come to God, we must come in faith. We must also come to the world of dream and vision in faith. "Without faith, it is impossible to please God" (Heb. 11:6). If we enter the world of dream and vision with doubt, we will find it taking us nowhere.

As we grow up, instead of rejecting the inner world as many of us were taught to do, we must learn to distinguish it from the outer world, yet live in it comfortably.

When we look at life, we see that we are more deeply affected by pictures than by simple cognitive communication. For example, we prefer television over radio, a speaker who tells vivid stories over a didactic lecturer, a testimonial over a book of theology. Analytical thought does not have the same power as thinking in images. Pictures give us a way of thinking that brings us closer to actual experiences of the spiritual world than any concept or merely verbal idea. Dr. Cho found that the ability to become creative came into his life only when he learned to "incubate" the visions and dreams God gave to him.

I desire earnestly to live as Jesus did, out of the Father's initiative, doing only what I see my Father doing (John 5:l9,20; 8:38). However, before I can live that way, I need to learn how to become a seer. In a rationalistic culture where "seeing" is generally looked upon with scorn, it takes a monumental effort to become at ease with seeing vision as Jesus did.

Lookers Become Seers

The spirit world is there, whether I am seeing it or not. By becoming a seer, I am simply beginning to see what is. I am learning to bring alive an atrophied sense (i.e., my visionary ability) and present it to God to be filled. Once my visionary sense has been restored to life and is presented before Almighty God, I have the opportunity to live as did Jesus of Nazareth, out of the continuous flow of divine vision.

My experience, as well as the experience of many others, has convinced me that once we have grown accustomed to looking expectantly into the spirit world for a vision from the Lord, it readily appears. The simple act of looking in faith opens us up to begin seeing what is there.

Notes

The expression "I was looking" is found about 13 times in Daniel alone (NASB).

"You...*were looking* [in the dream] and behold...." (Dan. 2:31, emphasis added)

"I saw a dream...and the visions *in my mind*...." (Dan. 4:5, emphasis added)

"Now these were the visions *in my mind* as I lay on my bed: *I was looking*, and behold...." (Dan. 4:10, emphasis added)

"*I was looking* in the visions in my mind; *I was looking* as I lay on my bed, and behold an angelic watcher, a holy one, descended from heaven." (Dan. 4:13, emphasis added)

"...Daniel saw a dream and visions *in his mind* as he lay on his bed; then he wrote the dream down and related the following summary of it. Daniel said, '*I was looking* in my vision by night, and behold....'" (Dan. 7:1,2 emphasis added)

"*I kept looking* until...After this *I kept looking*, and behold...After this *I kept looking* in the night visions, and behold...." (Dan. 7:4,6,7, emphasis added)

"*I kept looking* until thrones were set up, and the Ancient of Days took His seat...." (Dan 7:9, emphasis added)

"Then *I kept looking* because of the sound of the boastful words which the horn was speaking: *I kept looking* until...." (Dan. 7:11, emphasis added).

"*I kept looking* in the night visions, and behold, with the clouds of heaven One like a Son of Man was coming...." (Dan. 7:13, emphasis added)

"*I kept looking*, and...." (Dan. 7:21, emphasis added)

"A vision appeared to me...and *I looked* in the vision, and it came about while *I was looking* that...and I looked in the vision...Then I lifted my gaze and *looked*, and behold...While I was observing...then I heard a holy one speaking...When I, Daniel, had seen the vision...." (Dan. 8:1-5,13,15, emphasis added)

"And I heard the voice of a man between the banks of Ulai, and he called out and said, 'Gabriel, give this man an understanding of the vision.' So he came near to where I was standing, and when he came I was frightened and fell on my face; but he said to me...." (Dan. 8:16,17).

The prophets of Israel could simply say, "I looked," and as they quieted themselves before God "they saw" (Dan. 7:2,6,9,13).

Notes

When we first begin to look for vision, it seems awkward and almost forced, anything but natural. For this reason, its very unfamiliarity makes some people suspicious of it. As we do it more and more, however, it becomes a natural posture that we do almost without conscious thought. Those who have walked in vision since early childhood find discussing it comparable to discussing the dynamics of breathing.

Since I have reclaimed the use of my visionary ability, I too can simply quiet myself in the Lord's presence, look, and see the visions of Almighty God. I am a "seer" simply because I have become a "looker."

Ways to Strengthen the Eyes of Your Heart

Summarizing the lessons I learned, if you want to become a "seer," here are five things you can do to open yourself up to a divine flow of dreams and visions:

Principles of Visionaries

1. Our goal is to be like Jesus Who was a constant visionary (John 5:19,20; 8:38), "The Son can do nothing of Himself, unless it is something He *sees the Father doing....*"
   - ❑ I accept this as my goal in life.
   - ❑ I am currently living this way.
   - ❑ I will seek to learn to live this way.

2. We are looking for vision (Hab. 2:1,2). "I will keep watch to see what He will speak to me...Then the Lord answered me and said, 'Record the vision.'" "Watch and pray...." (Matt. 26:41) "Fixing our eyes on Jesus...." (Heb. 12:2)
   - ❑ I generally look for vision when I pray.
   - ❑ I don't look for vision when I pray.
   - ❑ I will look for vision when I pray.

3. We are looking **in the vision** until the vision has stopped flowing (Dan. 4:10, 13; 7:2,9,13 NASB). "I was looking...." "I was looking in my vision by night...." "I kept looking until thrones were set up and the Ancient of Days took His seat." "I kept looking in the night visions...."
   - ❑ When a vision begins, I continue to watch it.
   - ❑ When a vision begins, I quickly turn away from it.

Notes

❑ I have rarely received vision because I haven't looked for vision when I pray.

❑ I will begin looking steadfastly at the visions that begin to flow within me.

4. We must realize that we can have encounters with Jesus, God, and angels in vision **in our minds, and that these are actual spiritual encounters** (I Kings 3:5-15; Dan. 4:4,5,10,13,14; 7:1, 13-16; Matt. 1:20: 2:12,13,19,22).

❑ I have met Jesus in a vision in my mind.

❑ I have not met Jesus in a vision in my mind.

5. A natural way to present the eyes of our hearts before God is to visually enter a Bible story in prayerful contemplation and allow God to move in it as He wills, or to fix our eyes upon Jesus, the author and perfecter of our faith, asking Him to meet us and shower us with His grace (Heb. 12:1,2; Rev. 4:1,2).

❑ I have met Jesus visually in the midst of Gospel stories.

❑ I have not met Jesus visually in the midst of Gospel stories.

But — But — But!

Before we go any further, let's consider some common questions you might have.

First, "Don't I limit God by forcing Him to move in a Gospel story that I present before Him to fill?" The answer is "Absolutely yes!" Of course, God has some flexibility as He speaks through the Bible story. He can move it in one direction or another. However, if the Gospel story is totally removed from what God wants to show me, I may find that nothing happens. The vision does not come alive. It remains dead. God is not able to move in it. I have had this happen, and in response I have simply relaxed and said, "God, what would You like to say to me today?" With that, God implants the vision through which He can and does move.

The question follows, "Well then, why don't I just look for His vision in the beginning, rather than starting from a Bible story?" As I have said before, this works fine for the naturally intuitive and visiosnary person. However, the person with an atrophied visionary capacity will often need a learning tool to get him started. Once he is accustomed to vision, he will be able to discard the learning tool and simply "look" and "see."

Someone else may ask, "Am I saying that my 'godly imagination' is a divine vision?" Of course not! My image is my image. God's supernatural vision is His vision. We never mix up the two. We never say that my *priming of the pump* is God's vision. It is simply my *priming the pump*. However, when I invite the Holy Spirit to take over the scene in my mind and the inner flow is experienced and the vision moves with a life of its own, flowing from the throne of grace, it is obviously no longer my own. At this point it has become God's. My godly imagination (1 Chron. 29:18) is mine, and God's vision is God's.

Another may question, "Where in the Bible does it teach that we are to set the scene ourselves in order for God to begin flowing in vision?" Part of my response is, "Where does it say in the Bible that we are not to set a scene and ask God to fill it?" Since there is no clear verse for either position, we resort to pulling together several verses, which we then interpret in light of our chosen position. An alternative to this approach is to allow our brothers and sisters the Christian liberty to work out their own understanding in this area, since there is no absolutely clear biblical teaching on the issue.

To most of the world, who have not been steeped in rationalism and analytical thinking, openness to the realm of the Spirit is a natural part of human awareness. Only to us in the Western world does it seem strange to the point of at first being scary. When we begin to do it, it soon becomes a part of our normal awareness, and we become whole persons again, just like the rest of the world!

Seeing in the Spirit, Not Worshiping an Image

Perhaps the verses that most nearly can be interpreted as speaking against setting a scene are those that prohibit setting up a graven image.

God commanded the Israelites not to "make a graven image or any likeness of what is in heaven above or on the earth beneath or in the water under the earth. You shall not worship them or serve them; for I, the Lord your God, am a jealous God" (Exod. 20:4,5). Therefore, we must carefully distinguish between seeing in the spirit and idolatry.

There is obviously no problem in receiving a vision from God as one prays and waits before Him. This has occurred throughout the Bible, one example being in Revelation 4:2. Here John receives a heavenly vision of Christ, given by God, and as it unfolds, John becomes actively involved, dialoguing with heavenly and angelic beings and participating in the vision (Rev. 10:8-11).

However, when I set the first scene and look for a vision of Christ, do I find myself in violation of Exodus 20:4, because I am making a likeness of a god that I am then bowing down to and worshiping? No, definitely not.

A graven image is "an object of worship, carved usually from wood or stone" (*Webster's Ninth New Collegiate Dictionary*). Obviously, the scene we set in our minds is not carved wood or stone, or worshiped, but simply serves as a stepping stone to the living flow of divine images.

God incarnated Himself in Jesus of Nazareth, "the image of the invisible God" (Col. 1:15). This God/Man then lived out a full life in our midst, showing us pictorially, over and over, the "radiant glory of God" (Heb. 1:3), revealing to us, image upon image, the kindness, gentleness, mercy and power of God. God is not only invisible, He is also visible in Jesus of Nazareth — the greatest of all images given to man — through the Gospels as they record for us the powerful, life-changing stories of His life.

Now we have an image that is not a man-initiated representation of the likeness of God, but a God-given picture, perfectly portraying Himself to us in the multiplied stories He has recorded for us. We can turn to the Gospels, open to the story of His choice, and see the invisible God in visible action. Often, the story itself will give us the precise answer to our need.

For example, in asking the Lord one day how I should counsel in the situation of an illegitimate pregnancy, the Lord immediately reminded me of the story of Jesus saying to the woman caught in adultery, "Go and sin no more." He did not condemn, reject or hate her; He received, protected and loved her, sending her on with His instruction. Thus was brought before my heart the story, complete with sound and vision — the story I could enter into and feel — the story and image of God's choice.

I did not bow down and worship that image of Jesus forgiving the adulterous woman. Rather, that picture instantly helped me to focus on the eternal, invisible God Who revealed His love and mercy.

Carrying this one final step, I have found that when I want to commune with God in general, share love together, or share our lives together, I can focus my inner being on the invisible, intangible God and tune to Him by focusing on His Son, Jesus Christ, in one of the casual, relaxed scenes from the Gospels. He becomes alive as His indwelling Holy Spirit quickens Him within me, and we commune together and experience any vision that He chooses to bring forth. We may walk together along the Sea of Galilee, sit on a mountainside, or experience any other scene He chooses to quicken to my heart. It is clearly commanded in Scripture that I "fix [my] eyes on Jesus, the author and perfecter of faith" (Heb. 12:2).

John "looked to see" (Rev. 4:1) what the Lord wanted to show Him, the Holy Spirit took over, and a heavenly vision unfolded before him. We, too, can look to see what God wants to unfold. I have looked at Jesus sitting on the edge of a well (John 4) and asked Him to speak to me the things He desires; and He has, through a gentle flow of spontaneous thoughts. When I first began to use vision I would see Jesus from the shoulders down, and just sense His loving countenance. I did not see His face. After working with vision for a few weeks, I began to see Him more clearly. I saw His eyes full of laughter and a great big smile on His face. Others have told me that when they began to use vision, they, too, did not see Jesus' face. So be patient if that is your experience, also.

In no sense do I feel we are making a "graven image" or a "likeness." Rather, we are tuning in to God's image, Jesus Christ. Nor are we worshiping an image, because the image is readily alive with the moving of the Holy Spirit as He leads us into an encounter with and the worship of the ever-living, invisible Almighty God.

Differences Between Idolatry and Setting an Image in One's Mind		
	Idolatry	**Image**
Authorized By	Man (Exod. 32:1)	God (Exod. 25:8-22; Col. 1:15; Heb.12:2)
The Goal	Worship the idol (Exod. 32:8)	Never worship the image; use image as stepping stone into divine flow. (Rev. 4:1)
The Action	Idol remains dead (Isa. 44:19)	Divine flow is prompted (Rev. 4:2)
The Prayer	Pray to idol (Isa. 44:17)	Never pray to image; as divine flow is activated communication with God is established. (Rev. 4–22)
The Purpose	To worship "the thing" (Isa. 44:15)	To focus your heart before God (2 Cor. 3:18; 4:18)
The Attitude	Stiffnecked; proud of heart (Exod. 32:9)	Seeking God humbly (Prov. 2:1-5)
The Control Issue	Manipulating God; magic (I Kings 22:20-23)	Watching God in action; Christianity (Rev. 4–22)

Figure 4.1

Protestantism's 500-Year-Old Bitter Root Judgment and Inner Vow

I believe that when Protestantism protested and left the Roman Catholic Church, it reacted against Catholicism's use of imagery. I believe Protestants have held an ungodly belief that "All use of images constitutes a graven image." Their corresponding inner vow was that they would "Reject all uses of imagery in their Christian lives." The result is that most Protestant books on systematic theology do not even include a section on dream, vision, imagination, or any other application of the eyes of one's heart. This is startling considering that the biblical stories and actions which came as a result of dreams and visions form a section of Scripture equal in size to the entire New Testament! Their ungodly belief has given them the right to ignore one-third of the Bible.

Another fruit is that Protestants do not lead in drama, theater, or the arts. Protestants have great conservative political think tanks (i.e., a left-brain function), but few great Christian performing or visual arts (i.e., a right-brain function). We need to repent of this ungodly belief and inner vow for ourselves and our forefathers, and receive all that the Bible says is ours.

On the Positive Side

On the positive side of this question of man's capacity to think visually, I would like to make two points. 1) All of the children and two-thirds of the adults I have polled **usually** picture Bible scenes as they read them. As we are picturing these Bible stories and praying for a spirit of revelation (Eph. 1:17), God causes the story to come alive and speaks to us out of it. This is essentially the same process we are describing, of setting scenes in our minds and asking God to grant us revelation, then tuning to the flow of the Holy Spirit and watching the scene come alive as God speaks to us. 2) One-fourth of the adults I have polled normally picture the scenes of songs when they worship. As God inhabits our praises, the scenes come alive and move with a life generated from the throne of God. Both of these illustrate the very process I am describing.

Man's ability to think visually is currently being used unknowingly by many Christians, particularly those who are intuitive and visionary by nature. In reality, visual thinking is not a new thing. We are just defining and clarifying what has been happening naturally for some. As a result of this clear definition and statement, all believers can now be taught to become more sensitive to the divine flow within us.

A Temporary Learning Tool

It must be remembered that setting a scene is a temporary learning tool needed only by some. The naturally intuitive person may not need this device. He will simply look to see, and the vision will be there. The analytically-oriented person may put aside this learning tool shortly, as he, too, learns how to open himself naturally and normally to vision.

If we lived in a more biblical culture, perhaps we would not have so many obstacles to overcome before we could live easily and naturally in the divine flow of vision. If our dreams and their spiritual meaning were a typical part of our conversation at breakfast with our families, as they were for Joseph and other Hebrews, we would find a natural skill built into our lives concerning visionary things. However, who in America takes his dreams seriously, discussing them regularly in a family gathering? Practically no one. If we did, we would be considered crazy. Is it any wonder that skill and openness to visions are almost totally lacking in our culture?

As a Church, we need to repent for allowing the rationalism of our time to distort our own perspective of a balanced lifestyle. Some people fear that there may be seeds of Eastern thought in some of the teaching of the Church today. Did we ever stop to realize that Jesus was not a Westerner? God did not give us logic to idolize and put on a pedestal. He did not give us vision for us to squelch it with our scorn. No, it was others who encouraged these attitudes. If you need to repent, please do so now.

Church, let us come back to the balance of Jesus of Nazareth, who did nothing on His own initiative, but only that which **He saw and heard** the Father doing (John 5:19,20,30; 8:26,28,38). I have shared my struggles and experiences that have brought me closer to an ability to live this way. I challenge you to find the way that will **work for you.** The veil is torn, access is available, fellowship with the Holy Spirit is possible. Will you enter in? Will you seek the way? Will you go within the veil and experience God in direct encounter, or will you be satisfied to experience Him secondhand through the Book He has written?

Making Jesus Our Perfect Example

God is calling for those who will make Jesus their perfect Example, who will aspire to live and walk as He did, who will do nothing on their own initiative, but will live out of a constant flow of rhema and vision within them. Will you search until you find the way to that lifestyle and experience? Will you continue on until you discover Him?

"You search the Scriptures, because you think that in them you have eternal life; and it is these that bear witness of Me; and you are unwilling to come to Me, that you may have life." (John 5:39,40)

Prayer: Lord, we come to You in repentance for allowing our culture to dictate to us, telling us that we are to scorn a part of our inner capacity that You have created and placed within us. We seek Your forgiveness and ask that You restore to our hearts a proper use of dream and vision. Restore our ability to hear and to see. Draw each of us into all that You have for us.

Summary So Far Concerning Dream and Vision

1. God does speak to us through dream and vision, as attested by hundreds of verses.

2. Since Jesus is our perfect Example, we are to learn to live the way He did, that is, constantly open to the divine flow of vision.

3. The Bible tells us that God provides a ready and free flow of dreams and visions since we have received the outpouring of the Holy Spirit. Therefore, the normal Christian life is to experience vision readily (Acts 2:17).

4. Samuel established schools of the prophets to train men to become seers (the original term for prophets). There is no indication that this process would not be continued.

5. It is also interesting that one of the prophets' constant statements was, "I looked." The Bible clearly tells us that we have not because we ask not. Therefore, if we want vision, we most certainly will begin looking and asking for it, something that many of us have never been taught to do. The best way to train a person to become a seer is to train him to become a "looker." Probably the major reason people are not seers today is because no one is instructing them to become lookers. We must once again learn to *look to see.*

6. We are plainly commanded to fix our eyes upon Jesus (Heb. 12:1,2). The Greek for fixing our eyes is *aphorao* which literally means "to view with undivided attention by looking away from every other object; to regard fixedly and earnestly, to see distinctly" (*The Analytical Greek Lexicon,* Zondervan). According to the above definition, part of fixing our eyes upon Jesus is "to see Him distinctly." This is precisely what I am encouraging the Church to do as they pray, worship and walk through life.

Notice that *aphorao* is made up of *apo,* "away" and *horao,* "a visionary seeing." So, we are commanded to look away from other objects and to see Jesus in vision. Visions of Jesus, far from being unusual and infrequent, should be an essential part of our daily Christian experience.

7. May I suggest as an interpretation of Revelation 4:1,2 that John is preparing himself to visually receive the bubbling flow of the Holy Spirit's vision here? In chapter four, verse one, John said, "I looked," and then he went through a door in the heavens. *Immediately following* his decision to answer the urging to go through this door, verse two records, "*At once I came under the [Holy] Spirit's power, and lo…*" (AMP).

It is interesting that the Greek behind this specifically states at the beginning of verse two, *rather than the beginning of verse one*, that John came under the Holy Spirit's power. May I suggest that since John felt a desire to meet God in the spirit realm, he visualized an open door in the heavens and, upon walking through it, "came under the [Holy] Spirit's power," finding an active flow of divine vision issuing forth.

Admittedly this is a somewhat personal interpretation and you should feel free to set it aside if you are not comfortable with it. The interested student may want to search for other places in Scripture where this process is indicated or taught. It is fascinating to me that John was priming the pump for this vision by picturing a scene in his mind which was the **last scene** of the **previous vision** he had received from the Lord (Rev. 3:20). We can do the same thing! Try it!

8. God uses images extensively in His communion with us, as evidenced by the following:

- God knows our needs. He knows that we are very aware of our own history and frequent failure. He has provided in the Bible a story, recording His dealings with mankind. As we prayerfully ponder these Bible stories, we discover them merging with "our story" as God speaks to us from them. Although parts of the Bible contain systematic theology, God has made the Bible mainly narrative.

- When God designed the Holy of Holies, the place where man would stand directly before the presence of God, God used an image to represent Himself to Moses and the other high priests. If God were opposed to the use of images to symbolize Himself to man, He could have had Moses stand alone in an empty room and speak to Him face to face and mouth to mouth without the use of images. However, God chose to use a symbol — the Ark of the Covenant and the mercy seat with cherubim on top.

- Individuals, laws, feasts, rituals, sacrifices and events were used throughout the Old Testament as types or pictures that help us grasp and appreciate the complexity and beauty of New Testament realities.

Notes

- Rather than just telling us how glorious and splendid and full of love He is, God sent His Son Jesus Christ to be the "radiance of His glory and the **exact representation** of His nature (Heb. 1:3, emphasis added)." Colossians 1:15 tells us that Jesus is "the image of the invisible God." Jesus said to Philip, "He who has seen Me has seen the Father" (John 14:9). When God most clearly and powerfully revealed Himself to us, He did not do so with words and rational concepts but with the life of a person, His Son Jesus Christ, Who was a living image of all God is. The truths of the invisible God have been revealed to us through Jesus' life story. When the theology is beyond our understanding, we can look at the life of Jesus and if we walk in Christ, we walk in God.

- Matthew 13:34 says, "**All** these things Jesus spoke to the multitudes **in parables**, and He was **not** talking to them **without a parable**" (emphasis added). Jesus turned everything in life into a parable. He converted issues into symbols of heavenly values and realities. All of life was a meaningful story to Him. Jesus lived, thought and spoke in the world of the vision (or parable), and that is an important key to the release of God's power through Him. Jesus turned the matter of getting a drink of water into a discussion of living water (John 4). He saw in a field white for harvest the spiritual reality that the people of the earth need to be spiritually harvested into the storehouse of heaven. The commonplace pictures before Jesus were constantly used as stepping stones into images of spiritual realities.

9. I believe it is proper to enter into an image or picture to meet God in a direct spiritual encounter because the structure of the entire Bible is such as to lead us into this experience. As we have noted earlier, the Bible is primarily a book of powerful, life-changing stories, rather than a book of analytical theology. We are commanded to come unto the Lord as little children. When a child reads a story, he pictures the scene and action as he reads or listens. Most adults do so as well.

According to Ephesians 1:17,18, God wants to open the eyes of our hearts, granting us a spirit of wisdom and of revelation as we read His Word. The process of Bible meditation, as God has designed it, involves entering into a Bible story, allowing God to speak to us out of the midst of the vision (created by the Word) which is before our eyes, and living out that response.

10. When the vision within our hearts comes alive, we may encounter and interact with heavenly beings *in the vision.*

- In Daniel 4:13,14, King Nebuchadnezzar encountered an angel in a vision **in his mind**. "I was looking in the **visions in my mind** as I lay on my bed, and behold, an angelic watcher, a holy one, descended from heaven. He shouted out and spoke as follows…" (emphasis added).

- Daniel encountered the Ancient of Days and one like a Son of Man in a vision he had in his mind. "In the first year of Belshazzar king of Babylon Daniel saw a dream and **visions in his mind** as he lay on his bed; then he wrote the dream down and related the following summary of it…. I kept looking in the night visions, and behold, with the clouds of heaven one like a Son of Man was coming, and He came up to the Ancient of Days and was presented before Him…. As for me, Daniel, my spirit was distressed within me, and the **visions in my mind** kept alarming me" (Dan. 7:1,13,15, emphasis added).

We see, therefore, that it is very biblical to encounter God, Christ and angels **in the visions of our minds** as these visions come alive with the flow of the Holy Spirit within us.

11. Our ability to see in the spirit was designed to be presented to God and filled by God. We know **everything** God created was good, and that "everything" obviously has to include our visionary capacity. As all that God has created is presented before Him to fill, God's kingdom is realized and His purposes established. When we present the eyes of our hearts to Him, His vision fills our spirits. Our responsibility is to present all our abilities quietly before Him, allowing Him to move upon and through them. That includes our minds, our hearts, our hands, our mouths and our visionary capacity, along with everything else that we are.

God will not force Himself upon anyone who is not opening himself before Him. We generally will not speak in tongues until we offer Him our mouths. We probably will not receive words of wisdom and knowledge until we offer Him our minds. We normally will not receive visions until we offer Him the eyes of our hearts.

Therefore, in cultivating our visionary capacity, we are presenting the eyes of our hearts before God, asking Him to fill them.

Allowing God to Restore Your Visionary Capacity

Some people find that seeing vision is almost impossible. They are not even able to call a picture of their loved ones onto the screen of their minds. There may be several reasons for this. It is best to seek the Lord for revelation concerning what the block or hindrance is, and then ask for His revelation of the steps to take to heal the problem. The following are some common problems that I have run into, along with some solutions that have proven helpful.

Problem # 1 — Disdaining the Visual and Idolizing the Rational

Some people have unwittingly been swept into the Westerner's idolization of logic and his disdain (or disregard) of the visionary. Westerners generally do not believe in the value and power of the visionary capacity within them. They do not hold it in esteem and honor, as one of the gifts that God has placed within man. This was my problem.

To heal this problem, you must: 1) Repent for not fully honoring and using a gift and ability that God has placed within; 2) Repent for idolizing logic and cognition; 3) State your commitment to present both your visionary and analytical capacities to the Holy Spirit to fill and to use; 4) Ask God to breathe upon and restore your visual capacity; and 5) Begin practicing and exercising it by learning to live in pictures as readily as you live in thoughts. Then you are ready to begin presenting the eyes of your heart to God to fill, **by looking** for His vision as you walk through life.

Problem # 2 — Fear of Entering into Cultism

Some are unable to use their visual capacities effectively because they have been taught that it is cultish.

To heal this problem, you must: 1) Realize that the ability to think and see using pictures was given to you by God, not by satan; 2) Realize that even though satan seeks to fill your visual abilities, so does God; 3) Realize that satan can attack the thought processes as easily as he can attack the visionary processes; therefore, both must be presented continuously before the Lord for Him to fill and to flow through; 4) Acknowledge that God does not want you to turn away from use of the visual capacity, but rather He wants you to present it continuously to Him to fill; 5) Renounce fear of receiving a satanic counterfeit, while confessing faith in God's ability to fill the visual capacity; 6) Confess fear as sin and receive God's gift of faith.

Problem # 3 — Cutting Off the Visual Capacity in Order to Avoid the Sin of Lust

Some people have chosen to deal with the problem of lust by simply making a decision to cut off all use of the visual capacity. These people probably cannot visualize anything, including their living room couch.

To heal this problem, you must: 1) Realize that there are effective means of dealing with lust, other than cutting off one of the capacities that God has placed within. It is infinitely more effective to fix our eyes upon Jesus with our visionary capacity when we are tempted by lustful images than it is to refuse to use our visionary capacity at all. Moreover, when we constantly fill our vision with Jesus, we will find that destructive images simply cannot and do not intrude. It is the idle and empty mind that falls prey to sin; 2) Learn to appropriate some of these other alternatives to effectively deal with the sin of lust; 3) Repent for cutting off the visual capacity; 4) Ask God to restore it and recreate it; 5) Begin using it again; and 6) Ask God to fill it with His divine vision.

Problem # 4 — Shutting Down the Visual Capacity in Order to Avoid Some Unpleasant Visual Scene

Some people have shut off their sensitivity to the visual capacity because they are trying to avoid seeing a scene of pain in their lives. This may be an experience of molestation or a recurring nightmare or some other terrifying scene. They have decided that the most effective way of handling these frightening scenes is to cut off their visual capacities. These people probably cannot visualize anything, not even their family pet.

To heal this problem, you must: 1) Recognize and discover the precipitating reason for cutting off your visual sense; 2) Offer the scene to God, asking Him to walk into it and heal it with His loving, all-powerful presence. Seek the help of someone skilled in the ministry of inner healing if necessary to help you receive the complete healing God has for you; 3) Ask God to restore the use of your visual capacity; 4) Begin again to use pictures and visions as you walk through life; and 5) Present the eyes of your heart to God for Him to fill and flow through.

Suggestions for Becoming Open to Seeing in the Spirit

Part of the solution for each of the preceding problems was presenting the eyes of your heart to the Lord and beginning to use pictures in your daily life. Here are some suggestions that may help you begin to be open to God, allowing Him to fill the eyes of your heart with His dream and vision. When you want to strengthen your arm muscles, you do push-ups. These are "eye-ups" that will help you strengthen the eyes of your heart.

1. You must "be still" outwardly and inwardly so the Holy Spirit can issue forth with a flow of living images. Review the chapter on stillness. You will sense a bubbling flow within you as the vision comes alive with a "life of its own" (i.e., the Holy Spirit's life).

2. Enter a biblical story by picturing the scene. This is probably the most common method Christians use. Simply allow yourself to see what you are reading. And you can do more than just imagine the scenes yourself. Ask God what He wants to show you from what you are seeing, and then tune to flow. A flow of inner images can take over that is directed by God.

3. Open the eyes of your heart during your quiet times, allowing God to show you things. I have found that **focusing intently** upon Jesus while asking the Holy Spirit to take over the vision will cause the scene to come alive.

4. In intercession for others, see the person for whom you are praying, and then see Christ meeting that person. Relax and ask the Holy Spirit to show you what Jesus wants to do in the situation. Allow the vision to move under the direction of the Holy Spirit. Watch what He does, then pray that into existence.

5. Listen to your dreams, which are a natural expression of the inner world. Ask God to speak to you during the night (Ps. 127:2). When you awaken, **immediately** record your dreams and then ask God for an interpretation. He will give it. We have a book and cassette series available entitled ***Hear God Through Your Dreams***

which will teach you how to receive God's counsel to you during your dreams at night.

6. Praying in the Spirit opens up communication with the Holy Spirit and allows Him to flow, especially if you are presenting the eyes of your heart to God to fill.

7. Quiet prayer, simply affirming your love for Jesus and His toward you, opens you up to reflections and insights that are a form of vision in action.

8. When you come before the Lord in praise and worship, open the eyes of your heart to see what you are singing and allow the Holy Spirit to carry the vision where He wants.

One Inner Screen

In the verses from Daniel quoted earlier, you may have noticed where the vision was that he was looking at: "in [his] mind." That is where you will normally see visions also — in your mind. The kind of vision which you see "outside of your-self" is very unusual, both in Scripture and in today's experience.

The following diagram may help you see and understand that the eyes of your heart can be filled by self or satan or God. But it will almost always be the same "screen" that each uses.

One Inner Screen — Three Projectors

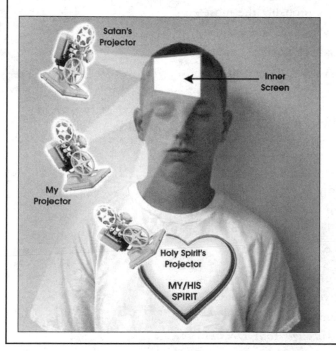

1. I am to instantly cut off all pictures put before my mind's eye by satan.

2. I am to present the eyes of my heart to the Lord to fill. In this way I prepare myself to receive.

3. The Spirit projects on my inner screen the flow of vision which He desires (Rev. 4:2).

Figure 4.2

Improper Uses of Man's Visual Ability

When I use my own projector to create a slide show or movies out of my own heart and mind, I get in trouble. The Bible warns of several misuses to which I might put the eyes of my heart.

1. One can follow the imagination of his own heart.
"But have walked after the imagination of their own heart, and after Baalim, which their fathers taught them." (Jer. 9:14)

In this case, man is using his capacities and God-given giftedness himself, rather than yielding it to God to use and fill.

One disappointing contemporary focus is the eschatology of the antichrist terrorizing the Church during a period called "the Great Tribulation." This new doctrine was first introduced to the Church in 1830 by J.N. Darby, the founder of the Plymouth Brethren and was not a teaching during the first 1800 years of Church history. It is tragic that many of the same people who are against the use of the eyes of one's heart in their approach to God are at the same time very comfortable using the eyes of their heart to picture the terror of this dismal theology which exaggerates the power of satan and diminishes the triumph of Christ discipling this world through His Church. Lord, forgive us!

2. Evil men will use their imaginations the same way they use every ability they have — for evil.
"But they hearkened not, nor inclined their ear, but walked in the counsels and in the imagination of their evil heart, and went backward, and not forward." (Jer. 7:24)

3. Man can imagine evil against one another.
"How long will ye imagine mischief against a man? Ye shall be slain all of you...." (Ps. 62:3)

Anyone can use his imagination to imagine evil, mischievous and vain things.

4. Carving a graven image and worshiping it is strictly forbidden.
"The workman melteth a graven image, and the goldsmith spreadeth it over with gold, and casteth silver chains." (Isa. 40:19)

"Thou shalt not make unto thee any graven image, or any likeness of any thing that is in heaven above, or that is in the earth beneath, or that is in the water under the earth." (Exod. 20:4)

"And the residue thereof he maketh a god, even his graven image: he falleth down unto it, and worshippeth it, and prayeth unto it, and saith, 'Deliver me; for thou art my god.'" (Isa. 44:17)

"Graven" image in the Hebrew literally means "to carve, whether wood or stone."

Fashioning an image of our own choosing and then bowing down and worshiping it is strictly forbidden.

5. Using our visual capacity in lust is strictly forbidden.
"I say to you, that every one who looks on a woman to lust for her has committed adultery with her already in his heart." (Matt. 5:28)

Summary: Why Is Using the Eyes of Our Hearts Important?

1. God has commanded us to imagine His Word ("meditate" — Josh. 1:8; 1 Chron. 29:18).

2. Divine creativity comes through image (Exod. 25:9-22; 35:35).

3. When God reasons, He uses imagery (Isa. 1:18).

4. When Jesus taught, He used imagery (Matt. 13:34).

5. As Jesus lived, He ministered out of vision (John 5:19,20).

6. God has declared that one of the primary ways He communicates with us is through dream and vision (Num. 12:6; Acts 2:17).

7. God counsels us through our dreams at night (Ps. 16:7).

8. Sight is better than blindness (Jesus healed the blind — Mark 10:46-52).

9. The Lord's Supper utilizes imagery ("This is My blood, this is My body, do this in remembrance of Me" — John 6:53,54; 1 Cor. 11:23-25).

10. Personal transformation occurs while we look into the spiritual realm (2 Cor. 3:18; 4:18).

11. Pictures are powerful and produce heart faith (Gen. 15:1,5,6).

12. The Bible is full of pictures, dreams, visions, metaphors, similes, parables, and images (Genesis through Revelation).

13. Our prayers are to be full of imagery (Ps. 23).

14. Our worship is to be full of imagery (Ps. 36:5,6).

My Journaling About Using Vision

"The speaking of your spirit is to be the speaking of My Spirit, and it will be if you are centered and focused on me. As you look clearly and only to Me, the intuitive impressions you receive are from Me."

"Lord, when you say 'look to Me,' do you mean inner vision?"

"It is not absolutely necessary, although it is extremely helpful. Remember the pattern of My Son. He saw and heard. The looking with inner vision facilitates an easy, pure flow. However, the flow can come through inner dependence — simply 'relying on.' When looking to Me, you will find that intuition progresses beyond your subconscious knowledge to things that I reveal."

Suggested Books Applying Vision to Your Encounter With God

The Bible teaches us that God gives dreams (Acts 2:17) and that He counsels us at night through our dreams (Ps. 16:7). This is a wonderful and fascinating area which we cover in our book *Hear God Through Your Dreams*. You can freely download key principles for interpreting your dreams from the "Free Books" section of our website (www.cwgministries.org).

For a description of the practical way Dr. Cho lives, pregnant with dream and vision, read his book *The Fourth Dimension*.

For a good book describing the use of vision in the ministry of inner healing, read *You Can Be Emotionally Free* by Rita Bennett.

(An example of the use of vision in inner healing in the New Testament is the twenty-first chapter of John where Jesus heals the deep hurt in Peter's heart caused by his threefold denial of his Lord. In order to minister profound, lasting healing, Jesus used imagery to deepen the reality of the forgiveness and love He was offering Peter.

Both the hurt and the healing happened: 1) at dawn, 2) around a charcoal fire, and 3) involving a threefold confession. The Lord brought about an encounter that served to remind Peter of his denial. Here the Lord showed something of what "drama" in His hands can do by way of healing memory and equipping for service. Simultaneously, **what had been** and **what was going to be** were present in Peter's mind and heart — a moment of intense, deep imagining and cleansing. It may well be compared with the Lord's use of "drama" in the parables; for all who are responsive, "my story is being told there." The Lord is **at work** in this activity. It is central to His ministry.)

Personal Application — Journaling Exercise

In a separate journaling notebook or on your computer, write down the following three questions: "Lord, how important is it to use the eyes of my heart? How have I been using them? How would You have me use them?"

Notes

Picture yourself and Jesus in a comfortable Gospel story. See the scene around you. Then fix your eyes on Jesus. Smile! Enjoy His presence. Ask Him the questions written above. Tune to spontaneity and begin to write the flow of thoughts and pictures that come back to you. Do not test them while you are receiving them. Stay in faith. Know that you can test them later.

Prayer: "Thank You, Lord, for what You say to us. May the eyes of our hearts be constantly filled with Your vision."

CHAPTER 5

RECORDING MY CONVERSATIONS WITH GOD

 We have come to our fourth essential key to hearing God's voice:

Key # 1 — Recognize God's voice as spontaneous thoughts which light upon your mind.

Key # 2 — Quiet yourself so you can hear God's voice.

Key # 3 — Look for vision as you pray.

Key # 4 — Write down the flow of thoughts and pictures that come to you.

Two-Way Journaling: A Means of Discerning God's Voice

Two-way journaling is a biblical method that can help you grow in the discernment of the voice of God in your heart. It has been a most helpful tool for me, probably the key tool that has taught me to discern the Lord's voice. "Two-way journaling" or simply "journaling," as I use the term, is basically recording your prayers and what you sense to be God's answers. The psalms are an example of this process, as well as the books of the prophets and Revelation. Clearly, it is a common biblical experience.

To be precise, I try to say "two-way journaling" to ensure that people know I am talking about a dialogue with God where both you and God are talking and you are recording it all on paper. When I say "journaling" I still mean "two-way journaling." In two-way journaling, I want God to do most of the talking, since His words are life (Jn. 6:63), not mine. The Bible clearly tells us to limit our words when we are before His throne and to let Him do most of the talking. Make sure you do this!

"Guard your steps as you go to the house of God and draw near to listen rather than to offer the sacrifice of fools; for they do not know they are

Notes

doing evil. Do not be hasty in word or impulsive in thought to bring up a matter in the presence of God. For God is in heaven and you are on the earth; therefore let your words be few." (Eccles. 5:1,2, NASB)

Some people have asked me if it is not true that the journaling commands and examples we find in Scripture are different from the journaling we are doing, since in the Bible all the journaling became the inerrant Word of God. Not so! In 1 Chronicles 28:12-19, we have an example of journaling that did not become Scripture, exemplifying the exact procedure we are recommending. In verse 19, David says, "The Lord made me understand in writing by His hand upon me, all the details of this pattern." What he received was the blueprint for the temple, which is not recorded in Scripture in its entirety.

God is speaking to His children much of the time. However, we often do not differentiate His voice from our own thoughts, and therefore, we are timid about stepping out in faith. If we can learn to clearly discern His voice speaking within us, we will be much more confident in our walk in the Spirit. Journaling is a way of sorting out God's thoughts.

One of the greatest benefits of using a journal during your communion with the Lord is that it allows you to receive freely the spontaneous flow of ideas that comes to your mind, **in faith** believing that they are from Jesus, without short-circuiting them by subjecting them to rational and sensory doubt while you are receiving them. Journaling allows you to write in faith believing the flow of thoughts and pictures is from the Lord, knowing that you will be able to test them later.

I found that before I began keeping a journal, I would ask God a question, and as soon as an answer came into my mind, I would immediately wonder whether the idea was from God or from self. In doing so, I was short-circuiting the intuitive flow of the Holy Spirit by subjecting it to rational doubt. The flow of God is arrested by doubt. He that comes to God must come in faith (Heb. 11:6). I would receive one idea from God and doubt that it was from Him, and therefore receive no more. Now, by writing it down, I can receive whole pages in faith, knowing I will have ample time to test it later. Keeping a journal greatly facilitates the flow of *rhema* into your heart.

Also, maintaining a journal keeps your mind occupied and on track as you are receiving God's words. My mind wants to do something while I am receiving revelation from God. If I tell it to be quiet and do nothing, it has a fit and starts critiquing every word I write. So I tell my mind to help me by spelling the words correctly. Even though I am not a great speller, my mind is happy to be helping. Journaling puts my mind on my side as a facilitator of divine encounter, rather than an attacker of it.

Another advantage of writing revelation down is given in Habakkuk 2:2,3. Habakkuk was told that he should write down what he received, because there would be a period of time before it came about. Therefore, your journal becomes an accurate reminder of revelation God has given you that has not yet come to pass.

After keeping a journal for more than 25 years, I cannot fully express how it has deepened my relationship with Christ. It has been one of the most helpful tools I have discovered for growth in the Spirit.

The Difference Between Journaling and Automatic Writing

Obviously automatic writing is satan's counterpart to journaling. Those who have experienced automatic writing before becoming a Christian tell me that in automatic writing, a spirit comes and controls the person's **hand**, whereas in journaling there is a spontaneous flow of ideas birthed by God in their **hearts** and then recorded in their journals by a hand freely under the person's own control. Therefore in journaling, the entire being is involved, the heart, the mind and the mind's guiding of the hand in writing, whereas in automatic writing only a limp hand is involved. The rest of the individual is bypassed by the evil spirit that controls the hand.

The Difference Between Journaling and Adding to Scripture

One objection to journaling is that it seems to come perilously close to writing new Scripture and, thus, adding to the Word of God. Some take this objection and use it against hearing from God in any fashion apart from reading the Scriptures. This is an honest objection and we must not dismiss the matter lightly.

The Bible is complete in that it contains the revelation God desires to give us in order to grant us salvation and to restore us to a life of fellowship with Him. Nothing needs to be added to it! It is inerrant and inspired by the Holy Spirit and has been the best-selling Book in all of history, even after 2000 years!

This does not mean that God has stopped speaking to His children. On the contrary, the Bible says God does continue to speak to us even as He did from Genesis to Revelation (John 10:27). We still get to take walks with God in the garden in the cool of the day and dialogue with Him. This does not mean that all our personal dialogue now needs to become Scripture. No, it is just two lovers sharing love together. Our journaling does not become Scripture.

Practical Suggestions for Journaling

1. Since you are coming to meet with your Creator and Sustainer and commune with Him, your time of journaling should be when you are in your prime condition and not overcome by fatigue or the cares of the world. I find early morning best for me. Some find the middle of the night best for them. Find your best time with God and use it.

2. A simple spiral-bound notebook is sufficient. If typing comes easily for you, you may want to type rather than write. Some people use a cassette recorder and commune with God while driving in their cars. They simply speak the words they feel are coming from God. I have found journaling on my computer is the easiest for me. I can type much faster than I can write, and I can put it through spell checker when I am done. Then I can email any journal entries I would like to my spiritual advisors for their input, and generally have an answer back within 24 hours.

3. Grammar and spelling are not critical when journaling.

4. Keep your journal secluded and use codes when necessary. As you bare your soul to God and He counsels you, some of your material will be of a private nature and should be kept confidential.

5. Date all entries.

6. Include in your journal your communion with God, your dreams and their interpretations, visions and images the Lord gives you, and personal feelings and events that mattered to you (e.g., angers, fears, hurts, anxieties, disappointments, joys, thanksgivings).

7. When you begin journaling, you will find that the Holy Spirit gives you healing, love and affirmation as He speaks edification, exhortation and comfort to your heart (1 Cor. 14:3). He will lead you into a fuller love relationship with Jesus and provide the encouragement and self-acceptance the Divine Lover wants to give to you. Then, as time goes on, you may allow your journaling to expand into a flow of the gifts of the Holy Spirit (e.g., prophecy, word of wisdom, word of knowledge, discerning of spirits, etc.). If you try to use your journal to cultivate the gift before you have sharpened your journaling ability through use, you may find that your mistakes will set you back so severely that it will be hard to press on with use of a journal. After you are firmly established in journaling, you will find the gifts of the Holy Spirit beginning to flow naturally through it. Allow them to come in their time.

8. Have a good knowledge of the Bible so that God can draw upon that knowledge as you journal. Not only is *rhema* **tested against the *Logos*, but it is also built upon the *Logos*.** God told Joshua to meditate, confess and act upon the Law of God day and night so that God could give him success (Josh. 1:8). If I fill my heart and mind and life with God's principles, and then pause in dependence upon Him in a given situation, my spirit will bring forth, through a flow of spontaneous thoughts, a perfect construction of exactly the right biblical principles. Thus I am able to speak a more pure, life-giving word from God. *Rhema* is built upon the *Logos*, in that God, by His Spirit, is selecting, through illumination, the specific principles that apply and then is constructing them in precise order. My mind cannot pick out and construct with nearly the precision that His Spirit can. Thus, *rhema* is grounded in *Logos* and is illumined by *Logos*.

9. If you want to add more structure to your journaling, you may use the first few pages to list people and items God is burdening you to pray for regularly. You

may also want to list the seven areas of prayer on a summary page at the back of this manual. You would want to be sure to stay tuned to flow as you prayed through these lists.

Notes

10. When you begin to journal, **write down** the question you have, rather than just thinking it. This simple act will assist greatly in facilitating the Lord's response.

11. As you are learning the art of journaling, you may want to journal daily until it is established in your life. Then you should be free to be spontaneous about your journaling. I generally journal several times a week.

12. Skip a line in your journal when you move from God speaking to you speaking, and vice versa. This will help you keep the transitions clearer when you reread it.

13. Reread your last journal entry before you begin your next day's entry. It helps you check whether or not you have been obedient to the previously spoken *rhema* word.

14. I review my entire journal when the notebook is full and write a brief summary of the key themes God has spoken about to me. I put this summary in the front of my next journal.

15. I have found that every time I have asked the Lord for a date, the dates have always been wrong. Therefore I have stopped asking. When God speaks, He simply says "soon," which means anytime in the next 1,000 years! He says, "Trust Me." Therefore, I recommend that you don't ask for specific dates in your journal.

Safeguards for Journaling

1. Cultivate a humble, teachable spirit. Never allow the attitude, "God told me, and that's all there is to it." All revelation is to be tested. In learning any new skill, mistakes are inevitable. Accept them as part of the learning process and go on.

2. Have a good knowledge of the Bible so that you can test your *rhema* against the *Logos.*

3. God gives us revelation for the areas in which He has given us responsibility and authority. A homemaker will receive revelation for within the home and family. A husband will receive revelation for caring for his family and functioning in his business. A pastor will receive revelation for the church for which God has made him responsible. Along with a God-given ministry comes God-given revelation to wisely fulfill the ministry. Therefore, look for revelation in the areas in which God has given you accountability.

Stay away from the ego trip in which you begin seeking revelation for areas where God has not placed you. When Peter asked Jesus for information about John, Jesus essentially told him it was none of his business and he should worry about being obedient to what the Lord had spoken to him. As a result of Peter's curiosity about something outside his area of responsibility, confusion and false information spread through the Church (John 21:18-23). You do not want to be the cause of such error!

4. Be fully committed to sharing with two or three spiritual advisors on an ongoing basis. Walk together with others who are seeking spiritual intimacy with Almighty God. Realize that until your journaling is confirmed, it should be regarded as "what you **think** God is saying." Time is also a confirming factor, as "wisdom is vindicated by her fruit" (James 3:13-17; Luke 7:35).

5. Occasionally I might write something down and the flow stops or seems to become impure or unusual. In this case I assume that I have gotten my eyes off the Lord. I simply re-focus and ask God to speak again because I feel I've gotten off-track. The Lord is always gracious to repeat Himself and I can usually see where I missed Him.

6. Check to be sure your journaling experiences are leading to greater wholeness and ability to love and share God. If your experiences become destructive to you, you are contacting the wrong spirits and you should seek out your spiritual advisors immediately.

An Example of a Prophetic Word Through Journaling

After you have acquired skill in journaling by doing it regularly for six months to a year, you may find the gifts of the Holy Spirit beginning to flow through your heart and pen. One of these gifts is prophecy. I have found that I can ask the Lord for a prophetic word for our Sunday service, and He will give it to me before the service begins — possibly even several days before. I write it down and share with the pastor in charge of the service that I have a word from the Lord. He then calls on me to share it at an appropriate time. One such prophecy which I shared on December 5, 1987 follows.

"My children, fear not your weaknesses. Be not discouraged by them. Are they mightier than I? Are they greater than the living God? NO! They are not! No! They are simply to be consumed by MY Power. Even as you are consumed in MY Presence, so are your weaknesses consumed by MY Power. MY Power and MY Presence are one. Therefore when you are consumed in your weakness, you are not consumed in MY Presence. Conversely, when you are consumed in MY Presence, MY Power has consumed you, and your weaknesses are no more. So come, My children, unto Me, and you shall be healed."

Mistakes in Your Journaling: Celebrating the Learning Curve!

There will be times, especially when you are just beginning, that you will find errors in your journaling. How do you handle this? I didn't deal with it very well at first. Usually I would become angry, fearful, discouraged — tempted to throw my journal down and quit. I did that at least a half-dozen times during my first year. I was of the opinion that since it was supposed to be God's words, it had to be right; and if it wasn't right, then it wasn't God, and the whole exercise in journaling was a farce.

As I reflect on my initial responses, I realize how immature they were. Who does anything perfectly the first time? Who ever began riding a bike without falling more than once? Who ever learned to play tennis without missing the ball? The fact is, there is always a practice time before we perfect any skill. And even when we have become skillful, we still make mistakes from time to time. We must carry this same attitude and realization into our spiritual growth as well. If we do, the pressure of having to be perfect in our journaling is removed. We will allow ourselves the freedom to fail at times, without giving up the whole enterprise. We simply laugh and say, "Whoops, that was a mistake!" and go on. I encourage each of you to adopt this attitude.

Some of the Most Common Reasons for Mistakes in Journaling

1. **Improper focus.** Sometimes you may discover yourself inadvertently praying with an idol in your heart. That is, you are focusing more intently on the "thing" you are praying for than you are on Jesus Christ. Thus the answer comes back through the "thing" rather than purely from Jesus' heart.

    The solution — Fix your eyes on Jesus as you pray. Watch Him address the thing you are praying about.

2. **Improper interpretation.** Sometimes I think God has said a certain thing. I go out and act on it, but it doesn't come to pass as He said it would. I have often found that when I go back and read the actual words which are in my journal, they are different than I had thought them to be. I had immediately jumped to a conclusion, interpreting the words in a certain way. However, when I looked again at the precise words, I found that these actual words were fulfilled. It was my interpretation that was wrong.

    The solution — Be careful not to interpret what God says. Ask Him to interpret it. He will!

3. **Not acting as God instructs.** I have found that if I do not act on the words of God in the way and according to the timing which He gives me, the release of God's perfect will into the situation can be hindered.

The solution — Do what God says, when He says it, the way He says to do it. Our actions become acts of faith, prophetic actions and acts of obedience, and as such they open the door for God's miracle-working power to be released.

4. **Not a large enough conduit to release God's power.** God chooses to have His power flow through channels, allowing His will to be released. These channels most often are individual Christians. If God has spoken that His will is to do a supernatural feat through me, and my channel is clogged through improper spiritual care and exercise, my constricted channel can thwart God's miracle, and my journaling may appear to be wrong. However, my journal probably did reveal God's perfect will, but it was not accomplished because of the channel being too small to allow a sufficient amount of the Holy Spirit's energy to touch the point of need.

    The solution — Take good care of your spirit through continually praying, spending time with Jesus, meditating on the Word, picturing what God has promised as already fulfilled, confessing all sin and obeying the voice of God in your heart. You may also be interested in our book *How to Release God's Healing Power Through Prayer.*

5. **Not having the right word in my vocabulary to fit the feeling within my spirit.** As God grants impressions within our hearts, our spirits search for an adequate vocabulary to attach to these impressions so they become understandable. If I do not pause to get exactly the right word, or if I do not have the right word in my vocabulary, I can hastily assign a wrong word to the inner sensation and find I have messed up my journaling.

    The solution — Wait for the "right" word to be formed within your heart, the word that fully and completely conveys the feeling of your spirit.

6. **Blocking the divine flow by having my sights fixed on a limited number of options.** Sometimes when I ask a question I am looking for a "yes" or a "no" and have thus closed my heart to other creative possibilities. Often God has ingenious approaches to situations which I never hear because I am locked into a narrow framework. In this case I may find myself journaling the answer I most want to hear, since I have blocked the divine flow.

    The solution — Be careful to be open to limitless possibilities.

7. **My advisors may answer quickly without hearing from God.** Sometimes when you share your journaling with your spiritual friend, he may disagree with what you have written. In this case, make sure that he has not just answered "off the cuff," or just given you "his best opinion" concerning the issue. You are not asking for his best judgment; you are asking him to seek God's voice in his heart concerning the issue.

   The solution — Ask him to pray about it and tell you what God says to him.

8. **Some of God's commands in my journal are never meant to be fulfilled.** They are simply positioning moves. "Now it came about after these things, that God tested Abraham, and said to him, 'Abraham!' And he said, 'Here I am.' And He said, 'Take now your son, your only son, whom you love, Isaac, and go to the land of Moriah; and offer him there as a burnt offering on one of the mountains of which I will tell you" (Gen. 22:1,2). Later the angel of the Lord countered this command, saying to Abraham, "Do not stretch out your hand against the lad, and do nothing to him; for now I know that you fear God…" (Gen. 22:12).

   I wonder if God was concerned with Abraham making an idol out of Isaac, so He had to show Abraham that nothing, not even a miraculous offspring, could be allowed to come between Abraham and God. God "tested" Abraham (Gen. 22:1) and when He saw that Abraham was willing to offer Isaac as a sacrifice, He said, "…now I know that you fear God." "Fearing God" means coming completely out of all idolatry and worshipping God only.

   I believe this happens numerous times in our lives. God speaks a certain thing, moving us in a certain direction for a period of time, and then after getting us to a specific point or action, He totally reverses His command. I believe this is done in order to position our attitudes in holiness before Him, and to more effectively place us and others for future purposes which He has planned.

   Therefore, we must be open to this eventuality and hold on to all words loosely. It is Christ Himself, and Christ only, to Whom we hold tightly. All words, visions, and journaling are held loosely.

9. **God will not violate man's free will.** God desires that all men come unto repentance; however, some do not. Therefore, God's perfect will is not always realized in each person's life. When we are journaling, and a word is given that involves another person, we need to realize that that person can choose a direction contrary to God's perfect will and that our journaling, even though it may be reflecting God's perfect will, may not be fulfilled.

Notes

10. **Reject any journaling that speaks of the death of someone of whom you would like to be freed.** If you believe you are being told that your spouse is going to die and you are going to marry another, this should be dismissed. Every close relationship contains a certain amount of stress. There may be a conscious or unconscious desire to be freed from the relationship. This unconscious desire can emerge in your journal and appear to be the voice of God. If it is truly of God, it will happen. If not, it will simply be forgotten.

Do not incubate such a vision or speak it or act upon it. Instead, focus your journaling on ways of enhancing your relationship with that person and give increased attention to cultivating your relationship with the Lord.

Destructive journaling is almost always from the deceiver. This is one of the ways satan comes to us as an angel of light. He will use Scripture to prove his point; however his message betrays him. He is speaking of death. It should be actively resisted and rebuked in the name of Jesus. My spiritual advisor's wife had a feeling soon after their oldest daughter was born that she was not going to live very long. He sensed immediately that it was from satan and together they rebuked his lie in Jesus' name.

11. **Beware of your own strong desires as you journal.** If you feel strongly about a certain thing, it is very easy for your own desires to come through your journaling. Prominent examples would include: romance, sexuality, power, greed, lust, fame. These things can flow so easily and effortlessly into your journal that you are most certain it is Christ, yet it is only a reflection of your own desires. Therefore, crucify your own desires daily, and walk near the cross of self-sacrificing love. Make sure your journaling comes only from that vantage point. Share any questionable journaling in these areas with your spiritual advisors for their input.

These cover a few of the most common reasons we discover errors in our journaling. Accept your errors with grace and laughter and go on, knowing that **practice makes perfect** (Heb. 5:14).

Samples of Journaling

Often individuals have me read entries from their journals to help them in confirming that it truly is the voice of God speaking to them. Several of these individuals have allowed me the privilege of passing their journal entries along to you so you may be blessed by hearing the kinds of things which the Lord is speaking into their lives. Celebrate the goodness and greatness of God as you read.

The process is where it is at! (Mark)

*"You feel the immediate victory and slaughter of the evil one is the goal. I feel the process is the goal. You see, I can instantly slaughter the evil one. Yet I have not. I am letting him perform his greatest efforts against My body and then I shall utilize **both his and My efforts together** to demonstrate My victory. Thus I shall rule over all — both the forces of good and the forces of evil. And My triumph shall be unquestionable.*

"Therefore fear not the process nor the intertwined defeats. I shall in My time thoroughly and totally defeat the enemy and shall be Lord over all.

"Has not the process always been integral to My plans? Consider Joseph's many years of slavery before being exalted to Pharaoh's right hand. Consider Moses' 40 years on the backside of a desert before being exalted by My right hand. Is not the process integral to the victory? Consider My Son's death and torment before being exalted to My right hand.

"Fear not the process. Fear not for the victory, for it shall surely come SAITH THE LORD.

"CELEBRATE the process. CELEBRATE the struggle. CELEBRATE the defeats, for all shall be swallowed up in My victory and I shall be Lord over all. I shall rule over the light as well as the darkness. My glory shall shine forth as never before and all mankind shall see it."

A Pastor's First Three Journal Entries (Della)

"You still have many things you fret about. Fix your eyes on Me, not just for journaling. I do care for you and I meet your needs one day at a time. You feel that you are unprotected and need to take action for the future, but you have always been under My wings, daughter. I have always been there protecting you. These are just facades and they are coming down for you. Let them fall down.

"Go to the edge of the cliff and just jump. I will catch you. You will learn to enjoy life as you asked and you will see Me. Keep your eyes fixed. You are making progress. Let go, and let Me. I do have somewhere that I am taking you and it is a journey. Let the heaviness and pressures go. It is OK to be lighthearted and carefree, especially because I care for you and about you. You have many that love you. Keep your eyes on Me."

"Lord, what would You like to say to me today?"

"Come and sit in My lap today. This weekend I have been doing many things in your life and in the lives around you. Remember to take quiet time and rest in Me. Mondays are really your Shabbat. You need to find your peace and center in Me. You are learning that I can do more than you possibly could think about. I have surprised you this weekend to show you I am working in these relationships.

"Lay your head on My chest. Let Me hold you tight. It is OK to let go of everything and relax in Me. When I massage your temples, your stress will leave because that is

where it is held. Quit thinking so much and sense your spirit. Stay focused in vision and expecting vision. I will come to you in vision and you will see Me clearly. You will see clearly. Letting go is a process. This is the day to let go and download."

"Thanks, Jesus."

"Dear Jesus, why do I want to eat all the time?"

"*There have been great disappointments inside of you. With the disappointments come great emptiness and that is what you have been trying to fill. It is true that food isn't that filling. It's just a habit that is associated with pleasure. You have been making great strides in bringing your disappointments to Me and acknowledging them. It will get better in this area. You are pressing into Me and finding out about My nature. I am not troubled or concerned with circumstances as you are. I have a much larger plan and a larger view.*

"*As you continue to trust in Me and envision Me, you are seeing Me in a new light. I don't want you cloaked in heaviness, nor with the cares of this world. It is true that you have come such a long way this past year. This year will be lighter and freer for you. You will experience more joy and deeper intimacy with Me. It will be worth all your prayers and perseverance. The river is coming and your heart is being healed. My daughter, I have gifts for you. Get ready to open them. Receive them, believe in them and use them. They will help others get set free. Rest your chest on My heart today. Lean into Me.*"

"Thanks, Jesus."

Using What God Puts in Your Hand (Paul from England)

"I saw the Lord next to the sea; I joined Him and began to skim stones on the water. I got three skips. The Lord did the same and it skipped to the horizon. He grinned. I did it again and this time did better - five skips. Again the Lord did it and it went to the horizon. As I bent to get another stone He stopped me and gave me a stone. It didn't look like a good skimming stone, but I took it. I threw it and it skimmed TO THE HORIZON. The Lord looked at me with a smile and said, '*Paul, what I put in your hand goes further than the things you pick up.*' WOW...it has caused me to ask the question when things are offered me and invitations come, is this what the Lord is putting in my hand or is it something I am picking up!"

The Battle With Doubt (Mike)

"Father, I realized again, over the weekend, talking with my friend Wayne that I have such a hard time really believing You and Your words to me. I want to and I try but find myself doubting so much. I believe, but help thou my unbelief. Why do I have such a hard time believing? How do I simply believe and trust You?"

"*As you repeatedly listen, hear and take to heart what I am saying, you will begin to believe with your whole heart. There is a chipping away at the walls and patterns of unbelief that have been a part of you for so long. Also, as I show you specific areas of doubt and unbelief, you must bring them to Me, lay them down and repent of that which you have held on to; to the lies and misconceptions of Me and also of who you think yourself to be. I am not in many ways who you think I am and you are not in many ways who you think you are.*

"As I mentioned earlier, your ungodly beliefs lead you to failure over and over again. Unbelief is sin. It is one of the most damnable sins that a Christian indulges in. It is one of the root causes why My children go into all sorts of sins and failure. You see yourself as such a failure, such a hopeless case and therefore you already have given up and thrown in the towel to defeat and failure. You convince yourself even before the fight that you will not win, which results in certain failure and defeat. When one goes into battle already believing that they will lose, then there is no hope or strength to conquer. Defeat is inevitable.

"But I do not see you that way! I am not convinced or persuaded of those lies and misconceptions. You are My son. Bought with My precious blood. More than a conqueror! An overcomer! A delight to the Father. You are overturning many years and generations of ungodly belief and ungodly structures that have been set up against the knowledge of God. I will help you to identify and then to pull down ungodly patterns of unbelief in your life. I will bring you to a place of utter rest in Me and to a place of great intimacy which will result in great exploits that will reach the nations. FIX your eyes on Me! I am able to do this. I am the Great I Am.

"You are no different than My disciples were. They were also steeped in great unbelief as they walked with Me and saw all that I did and yet they were still engulfed in unbelief and ungodly patterns of thought. But I brought them to a place of great faith and relationship with Me. I am faithful. Great is My faithfulness to you. You are Mine. You are Mine just as much as the apostles were Mine. They were not more My children or more favored than you. You are just as much a child of Mine as they were. Continue to acknowledge and repent of your sin of unbelief and turn your attention and focus to Me, to My words for you and you will continue to experience a transformation in your life that will revolutionize your world that will in turn, revolutionize all those that you are called to affect.

"Trust Me like a little child would trust his father. Remember Josiah at a young age when you repeatedly told him to trust you when he was ready to jump into your arms in the water? He was so afraid to jump, but you persuaded him to trust, to jump, because you knew you would not fail him. And you did not. He jumped, then again and then again until his fear of the water was overcome. Trust was built and established. Now, trust Me and jump. I will catch you. You can do it. Jump! I cannot fail you. I will not fail you. I will catch you. You are forever safe in My arms. You will not drown. I will not fail you. Trust will be built and established."

Death of a Vision (Karen)

"Father, what do You want to say to me today? What would You have me do?"

"Karen, look to Me. I know you are uncomfortable and wondering how this is all going to come out. Yes, you are in the death to the vision stage wherein you think life is falling apart on you, and you realize there is nothing you can do about it. You see doors closing on you and none opening at the moment. You feel boxed in with no place to go. This shall soon pass.

"I am Your place and I want you to simply trust Me. The ministry I am calling you to is to be accomplished by My power so all will know it is from Me. When I am lifted up, I will draw all men unto ME. I will provide for you as I have promised. I know your needs. I know all about the bills. I know your desire to give more into My kingdom. You are important to Me, so important that I am taking special care to teach you these lessons. Relax, and enjoy Me and the life I have set before you. I am always with you and I am giving you time to come apart with Me in this wilderness. Rejoice in My love and that all is well even though to you it doesn't seem that way. I am refining you so you can be the clean, pure vessel of gold that you desire to be for Me and so I can work mightily through you. You have nothing to fear."

"Thank You, Father. Take me. Work out Your precious will. By the power of the Holy Spirit, I take my hands off my life, my finances, my health, the ministry You are calling me to, work, everything."

Interpersonal Relationships (Benji, a 10-year-old boy)

"Why does Dad always get so mad all the time?"

"Benji, I'm bringing you through many tests right now. And I'm teaching you and him many things. You are now going into spiritual adulthood, and you must learn many things. Your dad and mom will get stricter on you for a short time, and during this time I will teach you many things. Some of your friends will dislike you because you are getting wiser and more spiritual. I love you and your parents love you, and I will be interceding for you at the right hand of the Father during this time."

"Lord, will You help me have a better attitude towards my elders and my schoolwork?"

"Yes! All you have to do is ask for My help!!"

"Please help me have a better attitude."

"OK. But first I want you to yield yourself to Me and allow Me to take control."

"OK. I want You to take all control over me and I yield myself to You."

"Benji, you will have a better attitude all the time. You are very very special to Me. Thank you for yielding to Me!"

"I love You very much!"

"I love you, too, Benji."

Brokenness (Jean from England)

"Lord, please speak to me about this Discipleship Training School as I walk through these delightful grounds. Lord, I feel Your presence, Your closeness in the beauty of this place."

"What do you see lying on the ground?"

"Lord, I see many fallen chestnuts. Some are completely exposed, their hard, prickly shells have long since broken open and they are bright and shiny."

"What else do you see?"

"Lord, some have only a crack in their shells, others are partly exposed and some are still unripe and are on the trees."

"My child, this is a picture of the different stages of My children within this school. Some have allowed Me to break open their hard shells that they had placed around themselves for protection. They are open and exposed, and My Holy Spirit will continue to do a deep work in their lives. Others are partly open and, as the power of My Holy Spirit is released, their bondages will break asunder. Others are in different stages of openness, and some are not ready at this present time. Remember the chrysalis? It is not My purpose to wrench away hard shells before the maturing process is completed. If you help the butterfly to break the shell it will be damaged and it will die. My timing is always perfect. So allow Me to initiate and My people to respond at their own pace."

God's Voice Even as We Jog! (Lynda)

"I was going out to jog (after about a three-month break) and was trying to determine how much to run. Against my feeling of compulsion, I listened to what was coming from within. I was able to run this amount, realizing that if I had followed my compulsion, I would have failed to succeed in the goal. As I thought on this (nearing the end of my jog) I felt God saying to me *'Lynda, I want you to succeed.'* This was a revelation to me.

"The next day in my journal I said to God, 'Lord, I have so many questions, what is real faith? What is success? Why is it so hard for me to believe You really have my best in mind? Speak to me, Father.'

"Yes, My child, I do want you to succeed. It has always been My plan that you would have success. But as your mind is telling you right now, the success I have for you, and for all My children, is not the success as the world knows, or measures. Your success is measured by your oneness with Me. That is how I made you to be. You become truly you, truly human, when your oneness with Me is complete.

"The Father and the Son are one. Jesus did nothing out of His own initiative. He only did what He had already seen the Father do. That is why I want you to come to Me...to rest in Me, to spend time with Me, so you will truly know Me and thus be able to follow in My ways.

"As you have been gathering faith in My love for you, your ability to express that genuinely for others has increased. As you have shed tears over My mercy and grace and the price I paid for you, you have shed tears for others, and with compassion reached out in My name.

"My Son did not have success in the ways of this world. He largely spent His time with 12 men and of those, primarily three. He had contact with a lot of people, healed many (but could have healed more) but He poured His life into that motley crew...fishermen, ordinary people. The more of an agenda these men had, the harder it was to truly see Me and be one with Me.

"It's not that I don't want you to have visions and dreams and aspirations, but I want them to be seated in your oneness with Me...for I want you to succeed, to accomplish what I made you for...not because that is where or how you earn your value and love. Your value is a given. It just is. You are My daughter, My precious child. My love for you is complete. You have nothing to prove or accomplish or do to make My love any greater for you. Neither will you ever lose or be separated from My love.

"You are beginning to discern some of your own deception of your strengths and weaknesses and even wisdom. Your deception comes from a yet unhealed heart. You are only beginning to grasp My view of you...it will take you time to put to death your view of you, and own how I see you. This is part of the renewal of your mind.

"When you place faith and confidence in your old structures and behaviors and ways of thinking...you will fail. The old way is built on law, on striving, on succeeding by will power. The new way, My way, is based on rest, on humility, on becoming childlike, on dependency. These ways continue to be foreign to you but you are walking in them more and more. It is My desire to see you succeed, to see you one with Me, to let the river of life flow freely from you.

"Don't look at this as somehow losing yourself. In fact, it is really becoming more of who you really are. What you are putting to death is the mask, the facade, the fortress that holds you in, imprisoning who you really are. Work with Me. Like Joshua, listen to Me. Sometimes you will think My instructions foolish, or of making no sense...but the walls come down. Be strong and courageous...in following My ways. For I will be with you. Do not be afraid or discouraged, for I will be with you. I AM WITH YOU NOW. Be still, rest and know that I AM GOD."

"Don't Wait So Long to Come to Me" (Lynda)

"My child why do you wait so long to come to Me? I have seen your pain, I have heard your cries, and yet you do not come to Me. How long will it be until you learn to seek Me first as your source of comfort and confirmation?

"I see your loneliness, I feel your rejection, I see the fear you have of being rejected again by others...BUT I AM...not like others. Until you learn that I will never leave, until you learn I will never forsake you, you will also have fear with Me. You must learn to trust Me. That means stepping out, trying Me, testing Me when your feelings are telling

you otherwise. When My Son responded to the Tempter, 'You should not put God to the test,' this is not the type of testing He (Jesus) was referring to. What I am asking of you is to push your faith, build it.

"I am with you always. I am in you. Stop thinking of Me being separate from you...it is too easy for you to then think rejection. But if you remember we are one as the Father and Son are one, then you will know your acceptance, your approval, your right-eousness is secure in Me. I cannot reject Myself. Rest in Me. Trust Me. Believe in Me. Let Me hold you when you need to cry. Know My heart beats with yours.

"And when you fall, remember I was wounded for your transgressions, I was bruised for your iniquities, the chastisement of the whole world was placed upon Me. Repent and go on. Your prolonged sorrow for the things I have already paid for is not help-ful. Your guilt for your actions that are less than perfect, is futile. Remember 'metaxi.'* You are not yet in heaven. I don't expect perfection from you. It is your heart that mat-ters to Me. I love you, My child...come away and love with Me."

"Love yourself. I will show you how to love you. That will also help you in lov-ing others, but right now I want you to joy in My joy over you, delight in My delight in you and sing the song of love I have for you."

* ("Metaxi" is a word used by Augustine suggesting that in our lives we are between Eden and Heaven. We cannot or should not expect perfection this side of heaven. Life will be messy.)

God Dances Over Us (a CLU Student)

"Lord, I have drifted away and so easily for the last two weeks. You know the why's. I need You. I must have intimacy with You above all else. My life depends on it. Speak to me this morning."

"It's hard for you to see Me or to understand when I dance over you with joy. I do not see you as you see yourself. I am not bogged down by the past and the failures. You are My joy. You are a joy to Me."

"But what about all my failures, even my most recent ones?"

"They are gone. Washed away. Forgotten. You have confessed them. I see your heart, My heart in you. There are two choices before you today. To dwell in Me or to dwell in you, on your sins, your failures or your struggles. Choose the better. Sit at My feet and learn of Me. You will find rest for your troubled soul. Come and sit. Dwell. Rest. Relax in My presence.

"I know your tendencies toward sin and how easily you stray from Me. I see. I know. As you sit before Me, I cover you with My robe. I place it on you. I lift your head by putting My hand under your chin, and lift your gaze into My eyes. There you see accept-ance, and approval.

"I know you feel like running, like pulling back. But how long can you go on like this? This is a much better way. Continue in My love. Live in My love and acceptance and in My approval. Nothing, absolutely nothing you can do can win My approval. This is hard for you to grasp. To be free from striving, trying hard to be accepted; to be free is where I am taking you. Total abandonment to Me. To My righteousness, to all that I give you; to receive from My hand. No strings attached.

"Remember, I do not see with your eyes, but you can see with Mine. As I touch your eyes, receive sight. This is a new day. Today. Come to Me TODAY. NEW! Fresh. Everyday is a new start. No past. No failure. Covered by My blood. Just as if you have never failed or sinned. That's how I see every morning. My mercies are new every morning! Start this day, every day with that fresh realization. Behold, all things are new. Come away, My beloved. Come."

God's Voice Behind Prison Walls (Kalyn)

Hello, My child. I love you, Kalyn. I love your smile and your laugh. I love the hunger in your spirit for journaling. I want you to keep journaling to meet Me here as often as possible until your faith is increased and your trust in Me is whole. I don't want you to worry about your mistakes right now for you will make plenty, but I still love you and I will teach you through them. I will never leave you high and dry without a place to stand. I am your rock. I will always be here for you and you will experience more of Me each time you sit down to listen to My words in your spirit. I love you, child. You are so precious to Me, Kalyn. Know how much I love you."

"As I contemplate what the Lord has done with my life since I began this course, Communion With God [That is the previous name of this book.], I am astounded. I have difficulty believing that I am the same person; even my friends have commented on the growth they have seen in me. The metamorphosis has been spectacular; it has been a supernatural transformation.

"I had been searching for answers to the many questions that I had and the teaching presented in the Communion With God course provided the answers. My biggest question was: How do I hear the voice of God? I have to admit I was skeptical at first. I didn't think that I could learn to hear the voice of God from textbooks and audio tapes. I had always been told that it was something God would have to teach me. But how was God going to teach me if I didn't recognize His voice? That was a question that my intuitive sisters couldn't answer. Praise God! This class has torn the veil, I have learned how to enter into the holy of Holies and have communion with my Daddy God.

"I have four good sisters-in-Christ (other prison inmates) that I feel I can submit my journaling to and gain wisdom and protection from error…I found a pair of earplugs can work wonders in zoning out the outside world!…In vision, I have seen the Lord touch my hands and I knew He was anointing them to be used for His divine healing. In vision, I have seen Him pray over me to the Father. In vision, Jesus has taken me to see my boys and He shows me that He is taking care of them. In vision, I have been a child, an adult, and all ages in between. In these visions I have played with Jesus, sat in His lap and been comforted by Him, and I have just spent time with Him."

"God, Why Aren't You More Specific in Our Journals?"
(Mark Virkler's journaling)

Situation: I was frustrated because I see in other people's journaling what I saw in mine — the constant encouragement of God to trust Him and to believe and to have hope, but not (in my perception) all the specifics they need for breakthrough in their lives. When I would provide the specifics they need by way of counseling, a breakthrough would come.

"Lord, why don't You provide these specifics to me and to others directly through our journaling? I do understand that faith, hope and love are central, but the specifics which provide the release are also extremely valuable."

"Mark, I have shown you in your spirit the answer. It is because I have ordained apostles, prophets, evangelists, pastors and teachers in the Body of Christ, to whom you are to relate for instruction and help and counsel. If you could get it all from Me directly, then you would not need each other. Thus you would fragment. Therefore I do not give you all you need through your journaling. I give you faith, hope and love and some other extras, but I purposely hold back some of the information you need and I give it to others to give to you. This way, each one must walk in relationship with others in the Body of Christ in order to become all that I have called and destined them to be.

"Journaling is a wonderful key, but it is not all that a person needs. He also needs My revelation through the other ways I speak. This includes instruction coming through others in the Body of Christ."

I shared this journaling with the following two spiritual advisors for their input:

Maurice Fuller's comments: "I agree with God. Journaling, to me, is a way to learn to hear from God until we can hear Him clearly in our spirit. So whether or not we continue to journal, it seems to be in the same category as hearing from God in our spirit. And that is only one way God speaks to us. Other ways are, as your journaling says, through others (which should confirm what God has already been speaking to us), through divinely-ordained circumstances, through prophecy (word of knowledge, word of wisdom, etc.), and through visions, dreams and so on. I do not put a lot of weight on one particular method.

"God often speaks to me when I am not specifically waiting for it. I submit a question to Him and He answers me in His time in the way He chooses. It is not a long wait but I have never been successful at pressing Him for a total answer right now. I have never found that I hurry the process up significantly by journaling. I always hear something through journaling but seldom does a complete solution come that way. Sometimes I don't hear anything in so many words but a conviction or a particular sense of direction begins to grow and grow until it crowds out all doubt and indecision."

Gary Greig's comments: "This makes entire sense to me and resonates with my spirit. It's also the point of 1 Corinthians 12 and Hebrews 10:25."

Remember, Journaling Is Only a Tool

We do not worship the tool or get stuck on the formula, as fantastic as journaling is. No, we come to the Creator and Sustainer of our souls, the Lord God Almighty. Can He speak outside of our journals? Obviously, yes! I have discovered that after journaling for awhile, I am much more aware of the inner sensation of the flow of the Spirit of Almighty God. Now even without my journal at my side, I find myself hearing that intuitive voice within speaking to me. Do I continue to journal? Yes, because it is such a powerful tool. But I also hear from God in other ways, including the counsel of friends, the Bible, circumstances of life, and dreams. When all these line up, I feel most confident that I am truly flowing in God. I do not live out of any one of these alone, but rather out of all of them.

Do I sometimes miss God? I imagine so. It's so hard to tell. There are really so few mentors in this area to show us the way. I accept the fact that we are children just beginning to learn to walk in the realm of the Holy Spirit. I expect that in such a stage of growth there would be numerous mistakes. However, I just keep on pressing on. Lord, keep me from faltering.

Books of Collections of People's Journaling

Our Father Speaks Through Hebrews by Rev. Peter Lord

Peter Lord is the pastor of a 6,000-member Baptist church in Titusville, Florida. He starts each entry with a verse from Hebrews and follows it with the journaling the Lord gave Him concerning that verse. Very powerful. The first book I know of that consists of a man's journaling. A landmark book.

Hearing God by Rev. Peter Lord

An excellent complement to ***How to Hear God's Voice.*** Peter Lord is on my board of advisors and shares similar insights from his life's experience of over 30 years in the ministry.

Journaling Exercise

Write down the following questions in your journal or on your computer: "Lord, what do You want to say to me about the use of journaling as a tool to help me in hearing Your voice? How important is it? What do You want to speak into my life at this time?"

Now pick a comfortable scene of you and Jesus together, either in Galilee or perhaps in your home with you. Make sure you are in a comfortable setting with Him so you can be relaxed!

Fix your eyes on Jesus, put a big smile on your face, relax and ask Him the questions above. Then tune to flowing thoughts and pictures and record what He tells you.

When your journaling is complete, reread it and share it with your spiritual advisors to ensure it is from God and to build your faith so you continue on in journaling.

Notes

CHAPTER 6

LIVING OUT OF THE FATHER'S INITIATIVE — SPIRIT-ANOINTED LIFESTYLES

A Short Story of How I Learned to Hear God's Voice

One day as I was praying, I took a pencil and paper and wrote down a question I wanted Jesus to answer. When I finished writing, I focused the eyes of my heart on Jesus, picturing myself sitting next to Him on the edge of a stone well (i.e., John 4). I peered at Him intently, waiting for Him to answer. All of a sudden, into my heart came an idea which was not my own, but was an excellent response to the problem. I wrote it down and turned my gaze again upon Jesus. Again, an excellent thought came to my heart, and I wrote it down. After a bit, I found I had written two paragraphs, and as I looked at the content, I was amazed at how perceptive and wise it was. I said, "I bet this is from the Lord!" When I shared it with my wife, she agreed.

I repeated this experiment in the following days during my devotional time. When spontaneous thoughts would come, I would react to them with my own analytical thoughts and questions, and He would then respond to my questions. I found I was dialoguing with the Lord! An experience I had always dreamed of and never experienced was finally happening. I was learning to converse with God! My search for a full relationship with the King of Kings was finally being rewarded.

As I experimented with this over the next few months, I became increasingly convinced it was the divine wisdom and love of Almighty God that was flowing through my pen. During those first days and weeks, I took much of my journaling to both my wife and to a spiritual friend who was able to hear the voice of God, and asked them to confirm whether or not it really was God. They told me it was! This confirmation from others continued to spur me on. Each person who begins journaling should have two to three spiritual friends with whom he shares his journaling. This is a critically important step!

Notes

Habakkuk Used the Same Four Keys to Hear God's Voice!

Then one day, God showed me how absolutely biblical my experience was. He showed me how perfectly it paralleled Habakkuk's experience. Habakkuk was a prophet who heard the voice of God. In Habakkuk 2:1-3, he tells us how he heard God speak. I was "blown over" by the revelation. Let us examine it together because I believe in it we have a summary of the previous chapters of this book, as well as a pattern for hearing God's voice that can be used by many.

The Four Keys to Hearing God's Voice:

As exemplified in Habakkuk 2:1,2	Key Succinctly Stated
I will stand on my guard post	Quiet yourself down by…
And I will keep watch to see	Fixing your eyes on Jesus.
What He will speak to me	Tune to spontaneity.
Then the Lord will answer me…and said, "Record the vision."	Write down the flow of thoughts and pictures.

Habakkuk is seeking a spiritual experience. He wants to hear the *rhema* of God directly in his heart so that he can understand the mess he sees around him. **First**, he goes to a quiet place where he can be alone and become still. He stations himself there waiting for God to speak.

Second, he quiets himself within by "watching to see" what God will say. The Hebrew word *sapha*, translated "keep watch," literally means "to watch closely, to be alert, to look expectantly, to wait for an answer from God." I believe he had some way of looking specifically toward God. In chapter one, verse one, it says that this is the "burden which Habakkuk the prophet *saw*" (emphasis added). So in some sense, God's *rhema* was couched in vision. As we have seen, focusing the eyes of our hearts upon God causes us to become inwardly still, raises our level of faith and expectancy, and makes us **fully** open to receive from God.

Third, he hears God's voice within him. We have, of course, defined this as the still small voice of God which is registered within us as spontaneous thoughts which light upon our mind.

Fourth, when God begins to speak, the first thing He says is "Record the vision." Habakkuk wrote down what he was sensing in his heart.

These four elements — becoming still, using vision, tuning to spontaneity and journaling — are the elements used by the prophet Habakkuk to hear the voice of God. And those with whom I have shared this approach have discovered that they,

Notes

too, are able to discern His voice. I believe this is a divinely-ordained pattern that can assist us on our approach to God and help lift us to the level of the Spirit.

Until I combined **all four** of these elements in my devotional life, I was not able to discern God's voice and commune with Him. I often had become frustrated and uncertain about what God really wanted. These elements truly have transformed my devotional life. In my earlier Christian life, I had quit singing the song "Sweet Hour of Prayer" because I never had sweet hours of prayer. Now, I find that I can enjoy dialoguing with God by the hour and leave fully charged with His life and love.

John Used the Same Four Keys When He Wrote the Book of Revelation

> *"I was in the Spirit on the Lord's day, and I heard behind me a loud voice like the sound of a trumpet, saying, "Write in a book what you see."* (Rev. 1:10,11, NASB)

Being "in the Spirit" suggests that he had quieted himself down. "Hearing a voice" means he is hearing a voice — in this case the voice of an angel — and it is not quite so soft as the "still, small voice" of God. "Writing in a book" is journaling, and "what he sees" indicates the use of vision. So once again we see a prophetic writer in Scripture using all four keys at one time to receive revelation from God — and, in this case, two visions which last 22 chapters!

After 25 years of teaching this message all over the world to all age groups, I am convinced that anyone who will use *all four keys at one time* will hear God's voice! Two or three keys at one time are not enough; all four keys are necessary. I am so convinced this will work 100% of the time that I feel comfortable offering a money back guarantee. A Christian who utilizes the four keys all at the same time will hear God's voice! Use them and teach them to others!

- Stillness

- Vision

- Spontaneity

- Journaling

Tell people that "Hearing God's voice is as simple as quieting yourself down, fixing your eyes on Jesus, tuning to spontaneity, and writing." Memorize this statement and share it over and over and over with people. Help them break out of a culture of rationalism and discover spiritual intimacy with Almighty God for themselves. I believe it is the greatest gift you can share with people, next to salvation and baptism in the Holy Spirit.

Some Personal Reflections on Hearing the Lord's Voice

1. God does not require more of you than you are ready to give. He will provide an alternate, easier path if you request it. However, He is most pleased when we allow Him to expand our faith and draw us out of our comfort zone.

2. Christ often speaks back using Scripture. *Rhema* is grounded in *Logos*.

3. When His inner voice lines up with inner thoughts you already have, rejoice. Don't doubt that it is His voice and assume that they are just **your own** thoughts. What is happening is that you were already picking up God's spontaneous thoughts before you began your prayer time. Your prayer time simply has confirmed what you already had been sensing from God.

4. When the Lord's words do not come to pass as you expected, go back and ask Him why. He will tell you. If the issue degenerates into a confusing mess that you can't comprehend, that's fine. Just put it on the back burner and maybe some day you will receive understanding about it. If not, you will understand it in eternity.

I have several such issues simmering on my back burner. One stayed there for eight years until God finally gave me understanding through another person in the Body of Christ. The Lord had spoken to me through a prophecy that I was going to move to Montana. I have never felt any witness in my heart to go to Montana, so I just let the prophecy sit in the back of my mind. When I was sharing this in a seminar one day, a person explained to me that "going to Montana" is a colloquialism that means "you are going to a higher plain" (i.e., since Montana is a high-altitude state). That made sense and bore witness in my heart, as this prophecy was given to me shortly after I learned to journal.

5. Initially, I looked upon my experiences as experiments. I was unsure and only acted on one-half to two-thirds of them. My confidence grew as I saw the positive results.

6. I found I could react to His ideas with my own analytical thoughts and questions, and that Christ would react to my thoughts with His words which I sensed as spontaneous thoughts. I still recognized a distinction between His spontaneous thoughts and my analytical thoughts.

Having a Passionate Hunger for Things of the Spirit

- When Oral Roberts was asked, "How do I go about learning to hear God speak to me?" he replied, "Wanting it badly enough to work on it."

You will not learn much about the spiritual world until you take time to be quiet and look within.

Notes

- Relating to the spiritual world is complex and takes as much time and effort as relating to the physical world.

- Learning to walk in the spiritual world is similar to learning to walk physically. There will be stumbling, falling and getting back up again.

- Westerners are underdeveloped in their understanding and differentiation of the spiritual world.

- Will you begin to live and walk in the Spirit (Gal. 5:25)?

Others Share How They Sense the Holy Spirit

Following is some confirming testimony on how others have discerned the voice of God in their hearts. The three basic truths you will find confirmed over and over are that: 1) God's voice comes often as a spontaneous thought, 2) the eyes of our hearts are used as God grants vision, and 3) the writing of these things is often important.

"An impression came to me."

"In my mind, I saw a girl sitting at the table…."

"I jotted down the thoughts."

From *Hear His Voice* by Douglas Wead (pp. 84, 94, 79)

"How does spontaneous revelation actually come?

"1. Pictures. God often spoke to [the] prophets through pictures or visions. He may plant a picture in your mind….

"2. Scripture. God speaks through specific Bible verses that come to mind. He may impress a part of a verse, even a reference, upon your mind.

"3. A word. God may bring to your mind a specific word or piece of advice that did not come as the result of a detailed thought process. It was more spontaneous and given as if dropped into your mind. The thoughts that come from the Lord in this way are usually unpremeditated and spontaneous in character and come more in a flash without a logical sequence; whereas, when we are consciously thinking, or even daydreaming, we usually connect one thought with another."

From "Spiritual Gifts and You" by Larry Tomczak,
Charisma, October 1981 (p. 57)

"The way my guidance comes…is intuitive. Gut feelings. Instincts."

Francis MacNutt quoted in *Hearing His Voice*
by John Patrick Grace (p. 57)

"When God speaks to me in the Spirit, His voice translates itself into thought concepts that I can conceive in my mind. So when I say, 'I heard the Lord,' or 'the Lord spoke to me,' I mean He spoke to me through a feeling in my spirit which was translated into a thought in my mind. And the thought immediately brings with it what young people call 'a rush.' It's something that hits you as right."

Ben Kinchlow quoted in *Hearing His Voice*
by John Patrick Grace (pp. 78,79)

"The lost art of Jesus is His use of imagination. 'Jesus looked at reality through the lens of the divine imagination. The imagination is the power we all possess of seeing harmonies, unities, and beauties in things where the non-imaginative mind sees nothing but discords, separations, ugliness. The imagination of man is but the window or door which, when thrown open, lets the divine life stream into our lives.'"

From *The Soul's Sincere Desire* by Glenn Clark

Creativity Released Through Journaling

Following is a poem from my journal that describes my experience of learning these truths. This was the first poem I had written in thirteen years, so I can truly say it was of the Lord. I do not write poetry.

Coming Apart Unto Him

Lord, You spoke in Your Word what You'd have me do.
To come apart and wait upon You.
That You would renew the strength of my life
And let me soar into heavenly heights.
Lord, it's so hard to come apart to You.
There are always so many things to do.
In the natural it seems like a fruitless waste
To fritter away my time into space.
But You're opening my eyes, allowing me to see
The value of coming apart unto Thee
That out of my stillness You finally get through

To speak to me plainly things concerning You.
Spirit to spirit impressions flow,
It's Your voice to me, so the story goes.
I look and I listen attentively,
Recording the thoughts You give to me.
I'm enticed by Your speaking into my heart,
Giving clarity and faith through what You impart,
In a moment saying more than I can in a month.
Clearly, powerfully, and it's more than a hunch.
Lord, I'm learning to come apart unto You.
To open my spirit and let You speak through.
That waiting on You is not vain,
It's the most precious experience I can gain.
Lord, You are filling all of my dreams.
You've filled my life with reality from Your scheme.
You fill my religion with Your grace,
Lifting me high above time and space.
As Jesus, may I come apart from life,
Waiting on You to regain new life,
Speaking it forth to the world around,
Sharing with them the life I've found.
Lord, teach me to look only at You
Not the wind and the waves, and all the to-do.
To stand firm and fast in what You speak
As I pray and fast, Your face to seek.
Lord, teach me Your voice more pointedly,
Keep me apart and waiting on Thee.
Allow Thy fullness my eyes to see,
Lord, I come apart to wait upon Thee.

God's Vision Is That Spirit-Anointed Leaders Disciple Nations (Matt. 28:18-20)

The Bible is full of stories about people who demonstrated Spirit-anointed lifestyles by living out of the voice and vision of Almighty God. Following are some modern day examples of this happening. These have come from people who have read this book before you, and had their lives transformed. We trust they will inspire your faith, and let you see that you can journal about anything. May God's blessing, healing, anointing and creativity flow into each and every area of your life.

Prayer is to be easy!

"Lord, what would You like to say to me today?"

Notes

"My child, you feel that you have an issue with prayer. Why? It is merely a conversation with a close, intimate friend — Me. Come to Me and talk, listen, enjoy — all the things you would do with any earthly friend — I am your everything. Allow Me to flow through you, from you in everything you think, say and do. Talk more. Listen more. Watch more. Practice with Jan. Practice with Me. It is easy if you look to Me for guidance — for My leading. I love you. Come. Rest in My rest. Allow Me to flow."

"Thank You, Lord. Is there more You would like to say?"

"Yes, My son. What you are doing is approaching prayer from your left-brain, the analytical approach. You can simply come to Me and let Me lead. Continue to pray. Do not feel there is a right and wrong way. Just do it. I will correct anything that needs correction. Trust Me. I will not lead you astray. Come. Be with Me. Abide in Me as I abide in you. Press in to Me. We are growing so well together. I love you. Press on. Be diligent — daily."

"Thank You, Lord."

God's Voice Brings Emotional Healing (Mike)

"Son, never is it in My heart that My children should live in torment and in deep turmoil of heart."

"Yes, Lord, I know. But why? Why can't I shake it? What is the open door that allows this garbage in and robs me of peace and sleep?"

"Son, a heart that has not found its total rest and hiding place in Me will be vulnerable to the attacks of the enemy of your soul. Your coming to Me must be often and consistent in order for Me to infuse you with My peace, My confidence and My comfort. It takes time for the transformation and impartation of all that's good into a heart that has been wounded and afraid and hard. I am so patient and so willing to impart all the good things that I have promised you.

"You are not alone. You are not an outcast. You are not alone in this walk. You are no different than many, many other believers. All who choose to walk with Me have to come and come and to receive and allow the transformation of their hearts and minds to take place.

"Remember, I can only do this as you come and sit before Me and open up your heart. Not just once in a while, but daily. I am so trustworthy. There is not a hint of deceit or unfairness in My heart towards you. My plans for you are good and My future for you is to have and experience My best."

"Father, it seems that I will never get out of my deep loneliness and despair and pit. It's even hard to come to You."

"Son, it has been your experience in coming to Me periodically. You allow yourself to believe that coming to Me is hard, that it takes hours to get through. Yet I tell you that coming to Me is like a dying, thirsty man coming to an oasis in the middle of a desert.

The oasis is there. All that is required is to come and drink. It is rather quite simple. Come and drink. Come and take. Come and receive. Forget about your efforts to break through. Forget your spiritual gymnastics and simply come to Me and drink.

"Often it is hard for you to come because you are still not convinced and persuaded of My absolute love and commitment to you. I am not holding out on you. I do not desire for you to be brought so low in shame and humiliation that you can barely lift your head. That is not My heart. That is My enemy's job.

"My peace I give to you. My life I give to you. My very heart I give to you. What have I withheld from you? Where is the proof of the lie that I am not sold out to you? I proved My love in going all the way for you. I had you in mind when I died. I had our times of communion and fellowship in mind when I hung upon the cross.

"Father, I hear Your words and they are true. Yet, in my heart and in my life it seems like You favor people. Some are so blessed. Some prosper and don't have the financial struggles, don't have the deep painful times of failure and struggle. I so want to believe You and trust You. There is so much garbage. I don't know where to start."

"Son, one day at a time. I appreciate your honesty and your willingness to be open. Often My Church is afraid to express their true feelings in fear that I will be angry and therefore withhold My blessings. I do not play that game. You can come to Me and bare your fears, your feelings, your thoughts and your soul and I will be there to listen and to comfort, to speak and to minister My life. There is a time to be honest and there is a time to let go. First be honest and then let go.

"I do not and will not withhold from you any good thing. That is not My heart. That is not the heart of Father. Yet, as you are coming to learn, there are destructive patterns and beliefs in your life that lead you to failure and defeat and that ultimately cause you pain and torment. I long to sit with you and to hold you and to comfort you. I long to be able to have a one-on-one, heart-to-heart with you on a regular basis. I will never withhold My love from you. Be convinced. Be persuaded of better things. Be convinced of My undying love and commitment to you."

Journaling About Christ Being Our Life (Michael)

"Lord, what do You want to speak to me concerning Your being my life? What does that mean practically?"

"My greatest desire is to see My children come into a place of complete rest in Me. This is mentioned in My Word over and over, and yet most of My children continue to strive and resolve within themselves to live and do better.

"I desire to see each one of My children truly enter this place of rest, where there is a complete ceasing from their own strivings, efforts and self-determinations. This place is a place where self is no longer asserting itself, a place where it is no longer the determinations of the will, no longer the efforts of well-meaning intentions, but simply a place of utter abandonment to Me and to My life within. A place where there is such a trust and

reliance on the divine flow and power of My resurrection life within that I said would flow like rivers out of your innermost parts.

"The great cry for today is to do, to try harder, to live holier lives, to press in, and all those are worthy and good intentions. Yet, when they are not done solely out of My life and divine enabling, it produces greater bondage and greater condemnation in the hearts of My children.

"I am your very life. I am everything that you need. I know you know these words, and you have quoted them many times, but the truth and the reality of these words are still not deeply ingrained in your spirit. It is coming. Rest assured. I know the way.

"It means a daily, and constant choosing to draw on Me. At the very moment of temptation or weakness, you must cease your striving and effort to conquer and simply tune and turn in to My vast supply that I have for you. Resurrection power and life abide within you: the same resurrection and power that raised up the Lord Jesus out of the grave and the lower parts of the earth.

"It's a refusal to turn to yourself, a determined choosing not to allow yourself to be drawn into the web of religious striving and effort that will certainly only produce failure and death. It is a realization that of yourself you can do nothing. Out of that you will truly be able to turn to Me and to draw upon the rich resources that I have. When it is My power and My Spirit, you will experience overcoming life and an abundant living that you have desired for so long.

"You have seen this from afar off for many years and you have desired this and have yearned for it. This has been My doing and My wooing within you. I will see to it that you come fully to Me and to My rest and out of that you will do greater, much greater things than you have ever done, by far.

"The life that you will then live will truly be that of the Son of God, it will not be your life through His, but His life through yours. The treasure coming through a surrendered and yielded vessel. You are simply a vessel. I am the life and the glory that will come forth.

"This is the great groaning of all creation, to see My glory through a yielded people. To see the life of the Son of God manifested in a many-membered body, the Body of Christ. This is how I have chosen to show My glory. Not through strong and able men and women, but through weak and yielded people. There is no other way. This is the way I have chosen.

"Continue to call upon Me and continue to ask Me to be ever reminding you of this glorious revealing and how simple it really is. Christ in you, Christ through you."

Jesus Provides Freedom and Hope (Della)

"Dearest Jesus, I love You. Come closer. What do You want to say?"

"Your ministry is not over. I have much in store for you. There always is a breaking, letting go, and a releasing before new things can take place. Rest in Me. I know the storm rages. Stay close to Me and let your ear rest on My chest. I do know what's best. Be comfortable with not knowing. Let go. It is OK not to know about tomorrow. Hippie Della is OK. She was very loved and taken care of by Me. She felt secure and had a child's heart. Embrace her. She is not gone. That is who you really are. Free like the spirit running with the wind. Draw close to Me. Open your soul's eyes. You will see Me waiting there for you. I have plans for your life. Rest in Me."

"Thank You, Jesus."

God Heals Heart Wounds (Robert)

"My son, you have received much by way of healing and your progress has been good. Although you have ministered in these realms and have received ministry yourself at certain times in your life, you have still been a little cynical over certain areas of inner healing. It is because of this cynical side of you that I have not been able to touch certain areas of your life, therefore you have only received a measure of freedom on some things.

"The situation that you mentioned at twelve years old is clear in My mind too, because I was there and saw it all. The only thing was, in those days, you didn't know Me and you were not aware of My presence, or that I even cared for you. But I do care for you, I always have. At that time, you were very introverted, unconfident and filled with much anxiety. This was because of inherited traits, and from family circumstances outside of your control.

"This situation would not have normally hurt you at all and had you been whole at that time you would have shrugged it off, but you didn't. You thought you had, but you didn't. That is why you can remember it in vivid detail. It had a profound effect on you, so much so, that you went from being an 'A and B' student to a 'C' average. You gradually lost interest in school and couldn't wait to leave. Do you remember this, My son?"

"Yes, Lord, I do."

"I want you to visit that classroom again in prayer, but this time we are going together. What do you see?"

"I see You, Lord, standing by my side as he made fun of me."

"What did I do with you?"

"Lord, You are bending down, putting Your arm around me and saying, *'It's okay, it's only a joke, he doesn't mean anything by it, don't take it to heart. I love you just the way you are, you are not inferior to them. So hold your head up high, you are Mine, and you don't know it yet, but I have great plans for you in the future.'* I feel warm and secure with Your arm around my shoulder. I feel protected and at peace."

"Now I want you to forgive Mr. Green, and your class friends."

"Lord, I forgive them for their careless remarks. I ask You to cleanse my thoughts in the conscious, unconscious and subconscious parts of my mind and fill them with Your thoughts. Thank You, Lord, for showing me and healing me!"

"Now, My son, go in My love and know that I am with you always. Know also, that this is why you have been given to comparing yourself to others and feeling inadequate and discouraged at times. But this day I have made you free."

Inner Healing (Darin from Korea)

Here are three testimonies of how the 'Communion With God' method has helped me to have 'life to the full:' [Note: **Communion With God** is the previous title of **How to Hear God's Voice**.]

"I was going to seminary in Kansas City and driving a school bus to support the family. One day I subbed in on a high school route. The regular driver had been letting the kids off at their houses instead of at the designated stops on the route. When I started to drop the kids off at the designated stops instead of at their houses, they started verbally assaulting me. I've never ever been called such bad names in all of my life. When I got to the end of the route I was ready to park the bus, leave the keys, and just quit! I was so emotionally hurt.

"Several years later, still feeling the pain, in prayer I asked God, 'Where were You?' As I closed my eyes and reflected back on the situation, I could see Christ standing behind me as I sat and drove the bus. I could see that the pain of the verbal darts of the kids was being taken upon the back of Jesus Christ. He had been with me all the time, simply standing behind me as I was driving and being my 'shield.' Since then, when I think back on the situation, all I can see is Christ Jesus standing behind me and shielding me. I can't even 'work-up' any pain. What release! Thank You, Christ Jesus!!"

✳ ✳ ✳ ✳ ✳ ✳ ✳

"When I was growing up, I got into trouble quite a bit, like most kids. As a young boy, when my mom would punish me (as is right for mothers to do) she would send me to my room. I was then supposed to stay in my room until I could come out without crying. The problem was, as I was in my room crying, I always wanted my mom to come in and love me up. It wasn't the physical pain that hurt me, but the emotional pain of thinking that I was being 'abandoned' or 'rejected' by my mom. (Please know that I have great parents and I'm sure they had no idea how I was feeling.)

"As an adult, and still feeling this emotional pain of rejection, in prayer, I asked God, 'Where were You?' As I closed my eyes and reflected back, I could see Christ sitting behind me, putting His arms around me and holding me as I sat in my room. He was there all the time and loving me. It brings such great comfort even as I write about it now. Since then, when I think back on the situation, all I can see is

Notes

Christ Jesus holding a small little boy, me. It's hard to even 'work-up' any pain over this situation. Thank You, Christ Jesus, for holding me."

✳ ✳ ✳ ✳ ✳ ✳ ✳

"As a young 4-year-old boy, I remember being picked on by a local bully named Kenny. I remember being in his old, dirty, brick house and being verbally 'pushed around.' I was very hurt. Even as an adult in my late 30's, that memory still caused me a great deal of pain and brought feelings of revenge.

"One day, in prayer, I asked God, 'Where were You?' As I closed my eyes and reflected back on the situation, I could see Christ Jesus simply standing beside me, with His right hand on my right shoulder. He was the size of an adult. Just His presence beside me relieved my emotional pain.

"I was also curious as to why this seemingly small incident had been such a sore spot for 30+ years. I could sense God saying, 'Things that happen to small children have a great impact on their lives.' My only feeling now about Kenny is sympathy. I hurt for him. How terrible to be so lonely that you have to bully people around to get a sense of relief. Thank You, Lord Jesus, for Your presence and Your healing."

From a Prisoner in Namibia, Africa

"Our counseling ministry, born as a result of the courses on 'How to Hear God's Voice' and 'Prayers That Heal the Heart', is doing great. We have seen people freed from homosexual sins, demonic attack, sleepless nights, depression, and high blood pressure."

Following is one of the journaling assignments from this student: "Lord, what would You like to speak to me concerning the way I process anger?"

"I love you with unfailing love. Do not allow the sun to go down while you are still angry. Never allow the enemy to step inside you. I am glad that you are growing faster in the way you handle your anger, by quickly turning to Me to deal with it. Continue to practice My presence all the time so that you can flow in My love and peace."

God Speaks Behind Prison Walls (Steven)

"I never knew if the Lord heard my prayers and certainly would not have even thought that He would want to talk with me in the way that I have experienced in the past few months. Because of this new relationship that I have, as well as the wisdom provided me by the Spirit, my life has changed a great deal and every day is now a pleasure to walk through, instead of the dark, empty hours I became so accustomed to here in this cold, lonely place.

"Today, whenever I walk in the compound, I have Jesus at my side talking and enjoying His company. I no longer feel alone. I have a sense of peace that I have never known in the past and even in this place, one of the darkest on this earth, He lights my way and guides me through as I put my complete trust in His mighty power."

God's Voice Enhances Physical Health (Paulette)

"Learning to hear God through journaling has been the most exciting and revolutionizing thing to happen in my life. It has brought extreme change to my life and that of my family. It has caused me to have constant and lasting joy in my life. It has given me wisdom and guidance in every area of my life. As a woman, I journal about everything from what I wear each day to what His will is for my life. Hearing each day what my Father wants me to eat has helped me to lose 60 pounds.

"Journaling has given me such confidence in myself. For many years satan has torn at my self-confidence in every area of my life. But now, I ask Jesus what He thinks of me. His thoughts of me are so beautiful, loving and caring. He tells me I am unique and special and He planned me just the way I am even before the world began. 'Wow!' Now that's special!

"I find that if I arise very early in the morning before the rest of my family, I can be quiet and alone with my Lord. Before the noise of my daily life begins, I can hear Him so easily. It starts my days out just right!

"There have been many times in my life that I have not followed God's will for my life, simply because I didn't know what it was. I was so busy 'feeling in the dark' for His will: going through 'open doors' and resisting the 'closed doors.' But now that I can hear God, I can know what His will is in each and every area of my life. Praise the Lord! I have not made any monstrous mistakes in my life since I learned to journal.

"But you know, I've found out the neatest thing! Jesus told me that even while I was so busy trying to find His will for my life, He had His hand on me even then. He tells me now that He planned the parents I would have, the husband and even the three boys I would have. Even while I was struggling, He gently guided me through my life.

"But I cannot praise my Father enough for making it possible for me to actually learn to hear Him through journaling. My life will never be the same!"

(**Note from Mark Virkler:** Is it going overboard to ask God what to wear for the day? I don't think so. If He cares about numbering every hair on our heads, I would surely think He would be glad to give me advice as to what to put on each day. I have to make the decision some way. I could use logic, or I could tune to flow and ask, "What should I wear today?" I choose the latter, since I have determined not to live out of man's reason.)

God's Voice Warns of Danger (Judith from St. Kitts)

"It was during the construction of the facility of Rivers of Living Water Christian Centre and every evening during the week and all day on Saturdays we

Notes

would gather as a congregation on the building site to do our part in its construction. That Wednesday evening I was late getting to the site and even though it was already 8:00 pm and darkness had fallen, I was still eager to get to the site to do my part for I knew that some of us would be working until after 10:00 pm and later.

"On arriving, I hurriedly parked my car and noticed that there was a group with a portable light working outside to the front of the building and all I could think to myself was to get to that area as quickly as possible so that I could do my part of working with them. I decided not to take the designated route in front of a barrier which had been set up to restrict passage to a certain area, but to proceed behind the barrier, which was the shorter route.

"As I started off a definite thought came to me very clearly: 'Judith, go around to the other side.' But I remember saying to myself, 'But this is the shorter route and I'll get there faster.' As I continued, another very strong thought came to me, 'Judith, go around. Do not go this way,' and I remember replying to myself, 'But I can see the light.'

"That was the last I remembered, for it turned out that I stepped into a 15ft. pit which had huge boulders at the bottom. I was covered with dirt and was knocked unconscious. No one knew that I had fallen into the pit and no one would have conceived that anyone could have been in that pit. But what I am told was that about 10 minutes later (for some of my friends had seen me pass by) they heard one of our sisters cry out that she had fallen into the pit and that it seemed that an animal was there with her for she had heard a groan. (That was me groaning!)

"It turned out that the Lord had sent a messenger to our sister to ask her to move her car. In going to do this, she found herself walking to the area behind the barrier. She reported that it was as if someone just dropped her down on her feet into the pit — she suffered not a scratch or a bruise and was able to call out for help immediately.

"As I lay on my hospital bed, the first thing I asked of the Lord was to show me what I had missed and He revealed to me very clearly that I had missed knowing and heeding His voice."

The Voice of God Provides Protection (Diane)

"I have found God's voice to be very gentle and yet very distinct from my thoughts. The text teaches that we all have spontaneous thoughts, ideas, feelings or impressions at times and if we pay attention, we will find that God is speaking to us. For instance, my sister and I were on the freeway going to a movie. On our way there, the thought kept coming to me to get off at the next off ramp. I ignored it for a while but it would not go away. Finally, I told my sister that we were going to take a different route to the show and got off the freeway.

"When we got home, my mom rushed to the door and said, 'You guys are all right!' We told her, 'yes,' and then asked what was wrong. She said that when we left, she saw us in a terrible car accident. So she started to pray and pray and did not stop until she felt that we were safe. I told her about the impression I had to get off the freeway and when I told her what time it was that we got off the freeway, we learned that it was the exact time she had stopped praying. Coincidence? I don't think so."

God says, "Celebrate the Storms of Life."

"Lord, what would You say to me?"

"You are a beautiful child with innocent eyes. See the clouds forming on the horizon? My arms will keep you safe. Storms are exciting times. Thunder and lightening—not to be feared, for My arms are around you and I'll not let you go.

"We can dance to the music of the storms—your feet on Mine; My hands holding yours.

"We dance with abandonment. The pounding of your heart is not from fear but pleasure and anticipation. The wind wraps My robes around you. Watch and be amazed at what I do. You will find peace in the midst of chaos."

Journaling About Sexuality (from a CLU student)

"I have never journaled about sexuality before and feel very awkward and unsure as to how to go about it. What do You want to say to me concerning sexuality?"

"Sex is one of My greatest gifts to humanity. When done within the boundaries I have set, it is one of the most beautiful and fulfilling acts that a husband and wife can experience. It's a beautiful thing. It draws together, causes an intimacy with two that comes no other way. I created and designed sex. It is not dirty but beautiful. Yet, the enemy of all mankind has taken My gift and has perverted it (as he does with all things) and has used it to do the very opposite of why I designed it.

"You have questioned Me often as to why I have given such a strong drive to men or to you. Why could it not be more balanced between male and female? I have placed with man and woman the perfect and exact amount or desire for sexuality, romance and affection. Man is the pursuer and woman is the responder. The two together, balance each other out. The two together, submitted, and surrendered together and to each other causes the highest degree or level of intimacy possible.

"It is just not a physical act, but an emotional and spiritual act. It is an honoring of one another. It is an abandonment and surrendering to each other. It is a letting down of walls, an exposing of hearts to one another. Satan causes the exchange to be just two bodies and keeps it in the sensual and carnal realm. My intention has always been so much deeper and intimate. My deepest blessing is upon husband and wife as they exchange and give and become vulnerable to each other. Never was sex meant to stay in the natural or carnal realm. Yes, there is a great physical pleasure and that is the way I purposed. Yet, when done in My way, the benefits go so much deeper. So much further. It draws so much closer.

"Can you see why the enemy desires so strongly to pervert such a beautiful gift? One produces death, shame, rebellion, etc. The other produces intimacy, a greater bonding, a greater peace and a drawing together. It produces a oneness. True sexual fulfillment comes only in the marriage bed and not looking elsewhere. That only leads to death and separation. As always, My way is perfect. It is best. I know. As all else that I created, it is for the pleasure and enjoyment of My children.

"Look to Me for restoration in your marriage. In you and also in your wife. There is no other way. There must be a greater turning away from the past, and each other's faults and shortcomings and a turning to Me. I will restore all the years. Again, that is My delight. I will go deep and remove and restore and impart all that is needed in your marriage relationship. I simply need your cooperation."

"Lord, I have believed that my sexuality was always a problem. That something was wrong with me. Why did You give me such a strong sexual drive? It's not right. I'm cursed. I'm not normal. Why not give a little more to women to even it out a bit?"

"The way I have created you is good. It is beautiful. It is not a problem. You are the pursuer. The pursuer needs a strong drive. Without the strong drive, the pursuer would not prevail or continue in his conquest. You need to win your wife. You need to pursue her and not give up. I give out the measure in perfect proportion in order to see that the task at hand is completed.

"You need to see your sexuality and drive not as a curse, but as a blessing. A tool (so to speak) in your hand that I have given you to go out and explore and conquer the prize. Without it the union between the husband and wife would be boring and stale. This adds excitement and challenge to a man which stimulates and propels him on to win his bride over and over again with love, passion and excitement. See it as a gift, son, not a curse. It is good. It is a gift."

God, How Do You View the Female Body? (from another CLU student)

"Lord, how do You view females? Will You redeem the sinful images that I have seen with my eyes?"

"I am the Great Artist. I am the Painter of the skies. I add color to all of nature. Indeed I formed and designed woman to be beautiful - she is indeed a work of art. Oh, can you picture Me sitting there, painting a picture of her? I do not look at her as a sinful man would look upon a prostitute. I do not look upon her nakedness, her sin. I look upon her as clothed with the radiance and beauty the Father has lavished upon her. I see the white robe of innocence that Jesus has given her, purchased for her by His own blood.

"I see the gold that is placed upon her by the Father. Her head is crowned — indeed, it is crowned with glory and beauty. The angels themselves carry the train of her gown. She is altogether beautiful, altogether lovely. She is like a lovely rose - she is the Bride of the Great Bridegroom - covered with the same innocence, purity and virtue of Jesus. It is not that she possesses these qualities of herself - they are given her by the Bridegroom.

"When compared to all the other works and wonders the Father has created in the heavens above, in the sea below, in the stars - the heavenly creatures themselves cannot compare to her beauty. She is to be revered, respected, the way the Great Princess of Creation should be.

"How can eyes see the way the Great Bridegroom does? How can they see that she is a precious stone, she cannot be coveted nor can she be bought? No woman on earth is a gem to be sold. She is of great value, importance. The Father has called her His daughter, to be daughters of the King.

"You have seen the female form with eyes of the flesh. Now I want you to see a woman with the eyes of your heart - eyes that look upon the body, soul, spirit to see the complete vision that the Father, the Son and the Holy Spirit see. See with new eyes."

Finding a Wife (from a pastor in Nigeria)

"I have worked hard in life not to defile myself with women and now I am ready to seek my own future partner, to settle down and to enjoy the rest of my life in the love of God.

"Dear Lord, how exactly do I know who to really go out with, and from which tribe and background she should be? What will be the color and the trait that I will see in order to be sure it is the right person?"

"The Lord said to me, *'Before you were born I knew thee and I formed thee in your mother's womb. Don't you think I had a plan for your life? I have kept you since you were born into this world and without doubt I have led you on the right course of life. All you've seen and gone through is not by accident. Your ability is My ability. I have given you the grace and privilege that has sustained you throughout all your life.*

"And now that you're set to go into a new phase of your life by choosing your life partner, don't you think I am still with you? Or have you forgotten I said in My Word that I would never leave you nor forsake you in life? Take note of Isaac My servant. At the right time for him I made a provision for his partner, and I am still the God of Abraham, Isaac, Jacob. I change not.

"Put your trust and hope in Me and believe My words. Cast all your cares upon me for I care so much for you. Though the world may have become corrupt, there is still a way for My children. I know how to program your life for success. Don't bother yourself much on this issue, for you are Mine and I will always be there for you. Be focused on all I call you to do and work in the ways I set before you.

"I will give you the bone of your bone and make life to be so interesting for you. Akintayo Ebenezer, I know you by name and I have predestined you for great success in life. Look and focus on Me, the Author and Finisher of your faith."

"Oh Dear Lord, I bless Your name for opening my eyes to know You and to be called Your son. I will forever trust in You and I will not allow this partner stuff to delay my progress in life. Lord, I count on You and I will be forever grateful for that

Notes

which You've done for me. Lord, I will not complain or be dismayed because I am sure You're by my side. Thank You, Lord Jesus, for Your words to me today and I know You will always be there for me. I count on You, dear Lord."

God's Voice Strengthens Marriage Relationships (Renay)

"Lord, how do You want me to approach my husband?"

"Oh dear little one, I am your Maker, your Creator. I placed this special man in your life because I alone know what you need. Man needs to feel loved and attended to. You are small and precious to him as you are small and precious to Me, yet he has greater expectations of you.

"Just love him, little one. For he must know your love. He must see it and feel it. He does not know your heart as I do. You must show him, you must make your love known. You must show him your respect, little one. For you are righteous and beautiful through Me and it is I Who give you strength. It is I Who will help you overcome and win your husband back. He longs for you as you long for him. He is lonely and empty without you, for you fill him as I intended it to be."

An Activation Technique for Receiving a Word of Knowledge Concerning What God Wants to Heal (Mark Virkler)

I am listening to Clark Taylor's CDs on "The Holy Spirit and Healing." He founded a church in Australia that grew to many thousand, and he travels in the U.S. from time to time. I want to share with you an activation exercise that utilizes vision and flow, which he teaches for receiving a word of knowledge of what God wants to heal in a group of people.

He instructs the volunteers to picture the human body in their mind's eye and look down over it, section by section, asking the Holy Spirit to show them anything He wants to heal in the group that night. He tells them to be sensitive to "faint impressions" and to share them. They might see something wrong with the body, or feel it. They call these things out and people with the described infirmities come forward.

The volunteers are instructed to hold both of the person's hands in one of theirs. They are then to quiet down and become very aware that the Holy Spirit lives within them, to see with the eyes of their heart that the power of the Lord God of the universe is inside of them and all around them. (I would describe this as quieting your heart and fixing your eyes upon Jesus.)

Once they are fully aware that the power of God is there and available to them, they figuratively reach into that power, take a "handful" of it and place it on the needy person. Nearly always, the individual falls under the power of God and is healed.

Those of you who earnestly desire to move into the word of knowledge and healing ministries may want to experiment with this exercise. Let me know what you learn as you grow in these gifts.

Notes

There is a complete manual on using vision and flow in healing prayer available at www.cwgministries.org/freebooks. Its title is "*How to Release God's Healing Power Through Prayer*."

Journaling Releases Anointing for Business (Charity)

"My husband Leo had been put on a team assignment at work that was very challenging. For weeks everyone had been trying to complete a specific project, but no progress was being made at all. Hours were spent in meetings, idea after idea was examined and rejected; nothing seemed to be quite what they were looking for.

"Leo started in on another weekend of brainstorming at home and he asked me for my thoughts on the project. I told him he should journal about it. (Actually, I told him he should have journaled about it a long time ago!) So, he asked God for His ideas on what should be done and wrote them down. They were brilliant, of course!

"Leo organized the revelations and made sure the presentation was just right. He took it in to work on Monday and waited for his turn to share. The meeting started as usual, with a few other associates giving their suggestions on the project, all of which were determined to be unacceptable.

"Then my husband shared the ideas that God had given him — and everyone loved it!! It was unanimously decided that this was the best presentation that anyone had come up with and it was just what they wanted! Finally, a breakthrough idea that everyone agreed on — a miracle!!

"The thing is, God's got the best perspective on everything, so instead of waiting until all else fails, maybe we should start by asking Him what He thinks. Tap into the divine creativity that is resident on the inside of us and release the anointing of God into our workplace. After all, isn't that why He put us there?"

Journaling Releases God's Creativity into the Marketplace (Bill)

"I have been journaling since 1992 using your material. I have often journaled about business issues and problems, and God has given me wisdom to solve business problems as well as give direction in relationships, sales campaigns, and solution approaches.

"There were two examples I felt that you might be interested in. The first occurred in a marketing meeting where we were trying to develop a new marketing tag line that captured the value of a new solution we were bringing to market. The team was stumped, so I journaled and the Lord gave me a marketing tag line. I told the team, they were amazed and said that was great, and it opened an entirely new approach for the team to work on.

"On another occasion I was really stumped trying to write a marketing brochure for a seminar my wife and I are doing, I tried to write it but I was really stuck. I journaled and the Lord gave me the entire copy. I simply wrote it down.

"In addition to my day job, Sue and I are also itinerant ministers. I used to take five hours to write sermons; now using journaling they are done in about 30 minutes.

"The approach to hearing God that I learned from you has completely transformed my Christian life and business. Thanks for teaching me this very practical method for hearing God's voice. I have taught it to others all over the world in my Christian seminars, and Sue and I have written a children's Sunday School program called 'Kids in Renewal' that teaches kids to hear God's voice using your method. This program has been taught in over 800 churches worldwide to date."

Journaling About the Powerful Symbolism of Easter

Jonathan has provided four journaling entries about the rich and powerful symbolism found in Easter. They are titled, "Robe, Crown, Nails, Cross." Read and enjoy these exciting new divine insights about one of our oldest celebrations. They are available at www.cwgministries.org/Easter-Journaling.htm.

Georgia gets a job because she can hear God's voice!

"Let me begin by saying thank you for some of the most incredible classes I have ever taken. I'd like to share good news — Christian Leadership University is very much a part of doors opening.

"I had an hour-long interview for the clinical pastoral education program at a hospital in Waco, Texas. Normally, the interview takes place with several persons, followed by a letter of acceptance later. And, once accepted, there is often a year waiting period to get into the CPE program.

"During my interview at the hospital I mentioned that God is never 'wordy.' The director of the program and his assistant kind of chuckled and said, 'That's cute — God is never wordy.' I simply said that I found Him to have what I call a universal male-sounding voice, which is filled with gentleness and that His living word always seems to effect my body by energizing it.

"It soon hit both of these pastors that I was not joking. They listened and I told them of auditions, visions and dreams. Then, I shared how I ended up at CLU and it was the best gift from the hand of God and that the final classes I am taking through CLU are the best classes I have taken at any seminary in the past several years.

"I was sent out of the room so that they could talk. When I returned they told me that they wanted me in their program right away. The director stated that he had been in the ministry for 30 years and never heard the terms I was using and has never heard the voice of God. He told me that he has never had anyone in the program that spoke of these things and it was a mandatory condition of my being in the program to bring all of what I have learned from CLU with me. The director said he wants what I have and he, too, wants to hear the voice of God.

"I will be spending 11 weeks beginning around June 6th in Waco…I can pick two wards and pastor those two wards totally for my shift for those 11 weeks…I was concerned that I may not be ready or capable to handle the changing drama of the ER but God gave me a dream and showed me standing in the middle of the ER. The dream had much detail but most important He showed me that He was 'all over me.' He will be with me. I no longer feel reluctant.

"In the closing of my interview they gave me a compliment I would have never given myself. They felt I have maturity in my faith that is unusual - CLU has taken me there!

"After the 11 weeks, I will be serving in a CPE program closer to my home in a much larger hospital. I was taken right into that program, too.

"The Lord is so, so sweet.

"If for some reason I had missed out on being a student of CLU, I would have missed out on absolutely 'everything' that is the most important.

"My heartfelt thanks to you and my instructors, and to think that we may never meet until we reach heaven hurts my heart, because I feel such gratitude for the years of study, prayer and commitment you have shared and gifted to me through my classes. May God bless you."

Journaling About the River of God (Rudi)

"Lord, how important is Your River in my life?"

"Son, My River is much more than a physical body of water flowing in a predetermined direction through life. It is through My River that I guide you and it is through My River that you are connected to Me. Too many people never recognize the flow of My River within them and they fail to really connect to Me.

"The water in My River brings life and contains My words, will and thoughts for your life. Some days you will drink of the water and it will be like words flooding your mind. Other times the water will be in the form of holy emotions that will stir you in the core of your being. Depending on your specific need on any given day, I will meet those needs from the same source: My River flowing within you.

"Son, you have seen the great rivers in America and the vastness they represent. Always remember that My River is much more than a small stream with a trickle of water. The greatest river on the face of the earth cannot be compared to the size and stature of My River flowing within you!

"With its source in My throne room, it extends across time and space maintaining a powerful flow even within your heart. It is important that you remember this,

because every time you surrender to the might of the flowing water within you, I will amaze you with the sheer power of the flow. The currents within My River are both diverse and abundant, designed to bring every yielded vessel to My determined plan for their lives.

"Trust the flow of My River in you. Enjoy its refreshing and power. In doing so you will effortlessly attain great distances in reaching My destiny for your life."

"Lord, what about the foundations I am building on in my life? Are they sure or faulty?"

"Son, in 1994 I caused many of the foundations in your life to crumble. In one week I caused the water level to rise significantly in your life. Back then you were determined that I establish a strong flow of My River in your life. Today, that flow is still present. The result of the continuous flow of My River in you has been a flooding in the low-lying areas of your life. These areas were once dry and flat, ideal for the building of foreign and faulty foundations. Today they are covered with water flowing from My throne and because of the strong current, it would be impossible to build something foreign in the river. I will cause the water to wash away any foreign objects.

"Son, as long as you desire more of Me and as long as you welcome and embrace the flow of My River in you, the River will be My foundation in your life. Fix your eyes on Me, do not lean on your own understanding and I will teach you the way you should go."

"Lord, I want to experience the deep waters of the River."

"Son, I am causing a deepening within you. Just like the Israelites prepared the dry river bed for water, by digging trenches to accommodate more water, I want you to prepare your spirit by digging trenches in your life. Make room for more of Me and I promise you I will fill all the room you make for Me.

"River-life demands a periodic scraping of the bottom of the river. As time passes by, a river becomes shallow because of sediment that settles to the bottom. Be aware of sediment that settles in your spirit. This sediment represents your growing familiarity with river-life. My work is fresh and up-to-date. Do not allow the frequency of things in your life to take away the freshness of My Spirit's power in you."

"Lord, please help me to optimize Your flow through my heart and mind."

"Son, let Me remind you that faith is what causes the River to flow. Faith is also what will keep the flow of the River in your life. Believe in Me and rely on what I show and reveal to you. Every step of faith you take, results in a stronger flow in your life. He who believes, out of his innermost being shall flow forth rivers of living water!

"Son, I want to keep equilibrium in your life. A balanced life is a successful life. This balance is not between good and evil. It does not represent spiritual compromise in any form. Rather it represents the role of the Word and the Spirit in your life. I said in My Word that My Spirit will always lead you into all the Truth. I am the Truth! My Spirit always complements My Word. The Holy Spirit reveals the Word in your life and opens your understanding to Who He really is."

Notes

"How can I broaden the scope of the gifts of the Holy Spirit flowing through me?

"You are right in identifying a need in the Church today. My people have regressed into a very narrow flow of My creative power, especially when it comes to the gifts that I made available to them. Many operate in the gifts based on an outdated example they saw sometime in their past. Carried through generations this powerless activity has gone unchecked and has in many cases not been corrected.

"I am looking for people who will boldly put their trust on Me and step out of this narrow box. I am ready to show fresh revelation and new applications of the gifts flowing through My Spirit that will cause many to be astounded. What was new before has grown stale, but I have newer things yet available. Step out in faith and do not draw back in fear. As you step out in faith I will unlock secrets to you that will become common in My Church again.

"What you have seen as coincidence and incidental before, you will now view as deliberate and significant. You will recognize My fingerprints even in the mundane things of your life. The people you meet and the things that cross your path will bring you closer to My destiny for your life. Not only will I bring you to destiny, but I will bring destiny to you.

"Be sensitive to the happenings around you. Speak with caution to the people around you. Use words and actions that will flow from the River in you. I will change the pictures around you. If you take the time, you will see Me in every picture and vision I show you. When you look at people's lives, yes look at the picture and vision of their surroundings, but never fail to see where I am in the picture. Where I am is where the need will be.

"Teach My people to yield to the flow of My River frequently and in real life situations. Teach them that I am practical and not theory. I cause My River to flow through life in its entirety. Help them to discover that flow within them."

God Says to Relax (Della)

"Dear Jesus, what are You telling me today?"

"Today is a beautiful day and you are in the center of My will. It only feels bad because of what you are holding on to. Breathe deep. Relax. Put your feet up. I am in charge. I still am head of the universe. And I am the laughing Jesus, or else there would be no laughter on earth. You, My daughter, are very, very serious. It all works out in the end.

"Turn your worry into warfare. Turn anxiety into answers. Turn your problems into prayers. Seek Me. I am here waiting. Sit at My feet. I will come. Give up on yourself and your circumstances. I AM is My name. The great I AM...."

Taking God's Voice into Every Area of Your Life!

So far we (Mark and Patti Virkler) have written 60 books demonstrating how to take God's voice into area after area of life. These are available at www.cwgministries.org/catalog. We have also developed over 100 college courses for Christian Leadership University (www.cluonline.com) which put the voice of God in the center of your learning experience. These classes can all be taken from your home.

Would you allow us to coach you to a full expansion of God's voice into each and every area of your life? Our lives are devoted to providing this mentoring for you.

"Kids in Renewal" Sunday School curriculum teaches children how to hear God's voice. It is available from Strang Communications: 1-800-451-4598 or www.kidschurch.com

Personal Journaling Application

Choose a Gospel story that is comfortable to you. You may want to reread it so it is fresh in your mind. Picture the story. Enter it, becoming one of the characters. Allow yourself to be present with Jesus. Fix your gaze upon Him. Ask Him the question that is on your heart. It may be as simple as "Lord, what do You want to speak to me?" Or it may be a question that arises from the story. Write or type the question. Tune to spontaneity and begin writing out of the flow that bubbles up within you. Don't test it as you receive it. Test it after the flow is finished.

Notes

CHAPTER 7

DIVINE PATTERNS FOR APPROACHING GOD

How Do I Tune My Heart to Hear God's Voice?

Our minds and physical senses cannot receive the fullness of God's revelation to us. It must come to our hearts intuitively through the operation of the Holy Spirit, living within us.

"But just as it is written, things which eye has not seen and ear has not heard, and which have not entered the heart of man, all that God has prepared for those who love Him. For to us God revealed them through the Spirit; for the Spirit searches all things, even the depths of God." (1 Cor. 2:9,10)

I have heard it used in sermon illustrations that our hearts are like a radio, which we need to tune to hear the signals that are coming from God. I would agree with that. However, no one could ever show me the tuning knob that would help me to adjust my heart more perfectly to the voice of God. Therefore the illustration always left me frustrated.

In this chapter we are going to look at ways God has said we can tune ourselves to hear His voice. Most of the aspects of tuning deal with preparing the condition of our hearts, since it is into the heart that God speaks. We will look at three biblical patterns of approaching God to hear Him speak: the tabernacle experience; the prophet Habakkuk; and the instructions given in Hebrews 10:22.

A. I *Approach God* Through the Tabernacle Experience

On Mount Sinai, God gave Moses the design for the tabernacle where the Israelites were to worship God, offer sacrifices, and hear directly from Him. Hebrews 8:5 tells us that this tabernacle and the services offered there were a copy, a shadow and example of the heavenly realities. It not only established the way for the Israelites to approach God and hear His voice, but it also demonstrates the way for us. (See diagram on following page.)

The tabernacle represents the spirit, soul and body of man. The outer court corresponds to man's body, where we receive knowledge mainly through our five senses. To illustrate this, the outer court didn't have a covering but was illuminated by natural light, showing that we receive light (knowledge and revelation) through natural means.

The Holy Place corresponds to man's soul. It had a roof over it, but inside it was illuminated by oil burning in a lampstand, representing the Holy Spirit revealing truth to our minds. (Oil often symbolizes the Holy Spirit in the Bible.)

The Holy of Holies was a totally dark, enclosed tent with no natural or artificial source of light. The only illumination that ever shone in the Holy of Holies was the light of the *shekinah* glory of God. When God was present, there was light. If God departed, all was dark. This represents man's spirit, where the glory of God lights our innermost being, giving us direct revelation within our hearts.

Each of the six pieces of furniture in the tabernacle represents an experience in our approach to God.

There were two items in the outer court:

—The Brazen Altar, Symbolizing the Cross (Exod. 27:1-8)

The brazen (or bronze) altar was the first thing you faced when you entered the tabernacle. You couldn't go around it. If you wanted to meet with God, you first had to stop at the altar. It was here that the priests offered the animal sacrifices to atone for the sins of the people. These sacrifices were just temporary measures, teaching the people about their sinfulness and the need for blood to be shed in order for them to be forgiven. The brazen altar, then, represents our need to make Jesus the Lord of our lives and present ourselves as living sacrifices to Him (Rom. 12:1,2). This is an absolute prerequisite to approaching God.

—The Brazen Laver, Representing God's Word (Exod. 30:17-21)

The brazen (or bronze) laver was a large basin where the priests would clean their hands and feet before moving into the Holy Place. If they entered into the Holy Place without stopping here to cleanse themselves, they would die.

The Tabernacle Experience — God's Design for Approaching Him

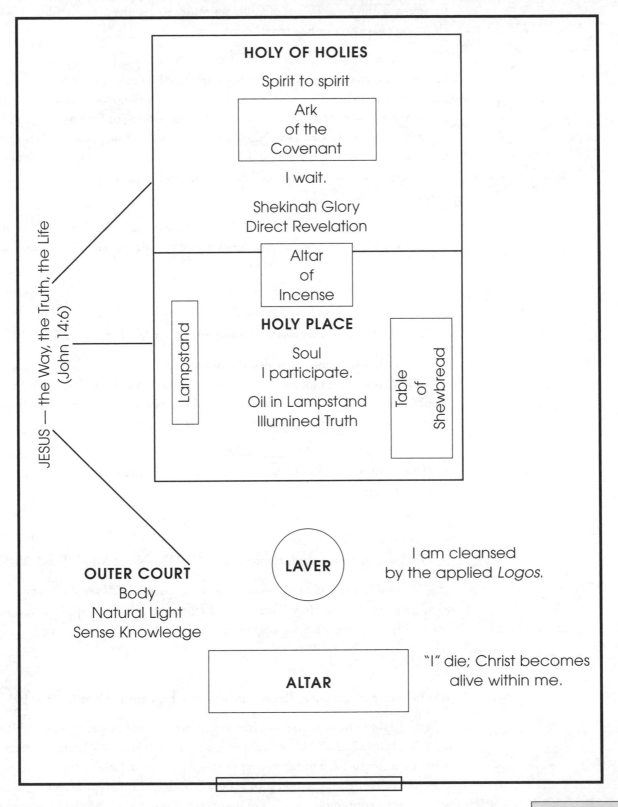

HOLY OF HOLIES

Spirit to spirit

Ark
of the
Covenant

I wait.

Shekinah Glory
Direct Revelation

Altar
of
Incense

HOLY PLACE

Soul
I participate.

Oil in Lampstand
Illumined Truth

Lampstand

Table
of
Shewbread

JESUS — the Way, the Truth, the Life
(John 14:6)

OUTER COURT
Body
Natural Light
Sense Knowledge

LAVER

I am cleansed
by the applied *Logos*.

ALTAR

"I" die; Christ becomes
alive within me.

Figure 7.1

The New Testament says in Ephesians 5:26 that Jesus cleanses and sanctifies us by the washing of water with the Word. So the laver signifies our washing ourselves by applying the *Logos* (Word of God, Scripture) to our lives. The applied *Logos* has a cleansing effect on our hearts and minds.

It is interesting that the brazen laver was made from the mirrors that the Hebrew women donated for the building of the tabernacle. In James, those who read the Word but do not obey it are compared to someone who looks in a mirror and sees that his face is dirty and his hair mussed but does nothing to fix himself up, just walking away without making any changes. As we read the Bible, God holds up a mirror to our hearts, showing what we really look like. As we approach God, He wants us to be changed, sanctified, and made holy by applying the cleansing power of His Word to our lives daily.

After stopping by the brazen laver to be washed, the priest would then move to the **Holy Place**. This was a large room with a roof of animal skins. Inside the Holy Place were three pieces of furniture.

— The Table of Shewbread, Symbolizing Our Will (Exod. 25:23-30)

This was a table on which the priests placed 12 special loaves of bread. Just as flour is ground fine for the making of the bread, so our will is ground fine as we totally commit our way unto the Lord. God wants our wills to be set only to obey Him when we enter His presence to hear from Him.

The priests would come together to eat this bread week by week. God uses our fellowship with other believers as a means of grinding our wills and shaping us into His image.

—The Golden Lampstand, Representing Our Illumined Mind (Exod. 25:31-39)

Also in the Holy Place was a golden lampstand with seven oil lamps. This is what gave light to the Holy Place. The oil represents the Holy Spirit. God lights up our minds with revelation truth as we meditate on His Word and as we journal.

—The Altar of Incense, Representing Our Emotions (Exod. 30:1-10)

Right in front of the doorway to the Holy of Holies was a golden table where the priest burned an offering of incense morning and evening. This table was perfectly square or balanced. The incense represents the praise of God's people. The way into the Holy of Holies, the manifest presence of God, is through praise and worship. As we offer up a continuous sacrifice of praise, our emotions are brought under the control of the Holy Spirit and come into balance.

Inside the Holy Place was a smaller, separate room called the Holy of Holies. Inside this "tent of meeting" was just one item.

—The Ark, Symbolizing Direct Revelation of the Spirit into Our Hearts (Exod. 25:10-22)

The Ark of the Covenant was a golden box that held symbols of God's covenant with Israel. The flat top of the Ark was called the Mercy Seat. On it, two golden angels stood facing each other with their wings stretched out toward the center as a covering over the Mercy Seat. It was from the Mercy Seat that God promised to meet with and speak to Moses and the priests.

This reminds us that out of worship and stillness we enter heart-to-heart communion with God as His glory fills our spirits. It is in the quietness of our hearts that we hear God speak to us.

B. Habakkuk 2:1-3 Provides a *Tuning Dial* for Hearing God's Voice

We have already looked closely at Habakkuk who gave us our four keys for hearing God's voice. Using all four of these keys is pivotal to your success at clearly discerning the Lord's voice in your heart. Remember:

- I quiet myself down by…

- Fixing my eyes on Jesus.

- I tune to spontaneity.

- I write down the flow of thoughts and pictures that come to me.

C. Hebrews 10:19-22 Presents a *Fine-Tuning Dial* for Hearing God's Voice

"…we have confidence to enter the holy place by the blood of Jesus, by a new and living way which He inaugurated for us through the veil, that is, His flesh, and since we have a great priest over the house of God, let us draw near with a sincere heart in full assurance of faith, having our hearts sprinkled clean from an evil conscience and our bodies washed with pure water." (Heb. 10:19-22)

MY EXPERIENCE OF INWARDLY QUIETING DOWN AND ALLOWING JESUS TO SPEAK

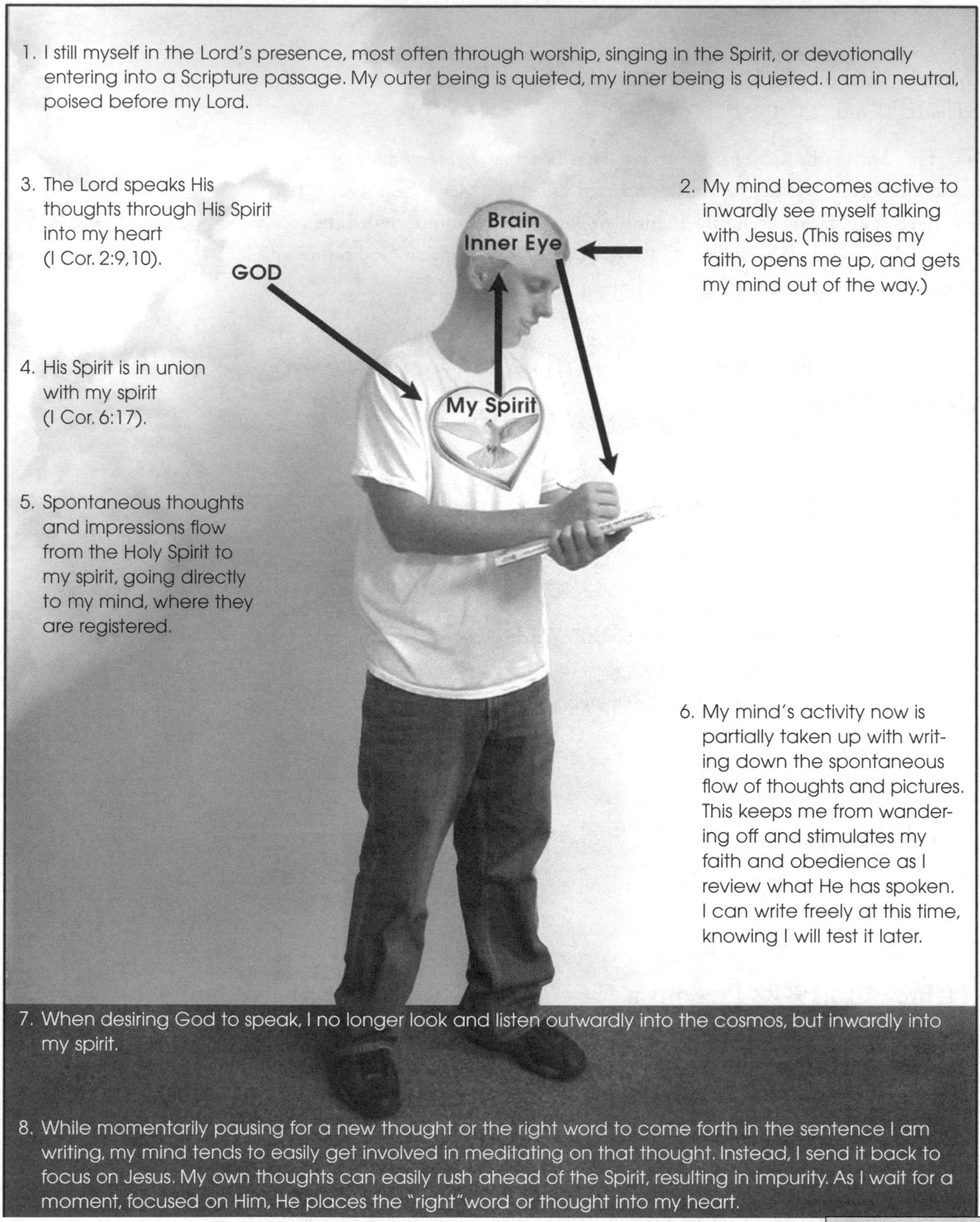

1. I still myself in the Lord's presence, most often through worship, singing in the Spirit, or devotionally entering into a Scripture passage. My outer being is quieted, my inner being is quieted. I am in neutral, poised before my Lord.

3. The Lord speaks His thoughts through His Spirit into my heart (I Cor. 2:9,10).

4. His Spirit is in union with my spirit (I Cor. 6:17).

5. Spontaneous thoughts and impressions flow from the Holy Spirit to my spirit, going directly to my mind, where they are registered.

2. My mind becomes active to inwardly see myself talking with Jesus. (This raises my faith, opens me up, and gets my mind out of the way.)

6. My mind's activity now is partially taken up with writing down the spontaneous flow of thoughts and pictures. This keeps me from wandering off and stimulates my faith and obedience as I review what He has spoken. I can write freely at this time, knowing I will test it later.

7. When desiring God to speak, I no longer look and listen outwardly into the cosmos, but inwardly into my spirit.

8. While momentarily pausing for a new thought or the right word to come forth in the sentence I am writing, my mind tends to easily get involved in meditating on that thought. Instead, I send it back to focus on Jesus. My own thoughts can easily rush ahead of the Spirit, resulting in impurity. As I wait for a moment, focused on Him, He places the "right" word or thought into my heart.

Figure 7.2

Brain Inner Eye — GOD — My Spirit

The passage says that we come before God by entering the "Holy Place." The literal word which is translated "holy place" is *hagios*, and refers to that inner room of the tabernacle, the Holy of Holies where I stand or kneel quietly in God's presence. Once there, we hear His voice in our hearts. The writer says that we come into God's presence with the following four attitudes:

1. **A Sincere Heart**

   My heart must be true, with no hypocrisy, no deception and no lying. I am wholehearted in my love, praise and trust of God. I return to Him with my whole heart; I search for Him with my whole heart; and I cry out to Him with my whole heart.

2. **In Full Assurance of Faith**

   "*...he who comes to God must believe that He is and that He is a rewarder of those who seek Him*" (Heb. 11:6). I have come to a decision to believe all that God says about me is true! I have an unshakable conviction that God lives in my heart and that His river flows out from within me. When I come before God and tune to His inner river, **the resulting flow is *God*! My God** is Immanuel, God with me! All doubt and unbelief is vanquished! I am a believer!

3. **A Heart Sprinkled Clean from an Evil Conscience**

   I absolutely believe that as I confess my sins before God, they are totally washed away by the blood of Jesus. I stand clean and holy before God, not because of my righteousness, but because of Christ's cleansing blood. I am not trying to be good any more than Jesus would accept the title "Good Master." I am cleansed. That is what makes me righteous before God. It is not of me; it is through Christ.

4. **A Body Washed with Pure Water**

   "*Christ also loved the church and gave Himself up for her; that He might sanctify her, having cleansed her by the washing of water with the word [rhema]*" (Eph. 5:25,26). Jesus speaks into my heart through my journaling and as I act on what He says, it cleanses my life. I am obeying the previous *rhema* God has spoken to me.

Keeping My Heart Tuned

I am to keep my heart tuned to God's channel all day long, receiving revelation continuously as I walk through life. That is the way Jesus lived (John 5:19, 20,30). That is how I am to live. I don't fall in and out of His presence. I **stay** in His presence by maintaining the biblical posture which is described above. The Bible calls it "abiding in Christ" or "praying without ceasing."

Checklist for Tuning in to God

I Am Living the Tabernacle Experience

- ☐ Altar — I have laid down my own initiative, self-effort and strength.
- ☐ Laver — I cleanse myself regularly by meditating upon the Bible.
- ☐ Shewbread — My will is ground fine before God and I walk in fellowship with the Body of Christ.
- ☐ Lampstand — I have moved from my reasoning to Spirit-led reasoning.
- ☐ Incense — I am a continuous worshipper; in everything I give thanks.
- ☐ Ark — I wait before God in stillness to receive what He has for me.

I Am Applying the Tuning Dial of Habakkuk 2:1-3

- ☐ I am quieting myself down by…
- ☐ Fixing my eyes on Jesus.
- ☐ I am tuned to spontaneity.
- ☐ I am writing down the flow of thoughts and pictures that come to me.

I Am Applying the Fine-Tuning Dial of Hebrews 10:19-22

- ☐ My heart is true, honest and sincere.
- ☐ I have absolute faith that God's river is flowing within me.
- ☐ My conscience is completely clear through Christ's cleansing blood.
- ☐ I have been obedient to God's previous *rhema*.

I Am Confirming My Journaling Through Other Ways God Speaks

- ☐ My journaling lines up with Scripture, and the character of God.
- ☐ My spiritual advisors confirm my journaling is from God.

Figure 7.3

Blocks and Problems to Hearing God's Voice

1. You have a lack of faith.

Remedy: Engage in "faith-builders" (e.g., tongue-speaking, worship in the spirit, praise, reading Bible promises, rereading your journal, using imagery, simply abandoning yourself to the God Who is faithful — Heb. 11:6).

2. Your mind wanders.

Remedy: Use a journal and use vision. Write down, pray through and confess things that are on your mind. Make sure your heart is not condemning you. If it is, purify it.

3. You feel God is not speaking.

Remedy: Pour out your heart **fully and completely**. Begin writing down any words you receive, even if there are only one or two. Remember, the Spirit's impressions are slight and easily overcome by bringing up your thoughts.

4. God is not speaking.

Remedy: It may be you are asking questions God does not want to answer. Perhaps you need to fast to release His answer. Check for problems on the fine-tuning dial. Maybe you have wrong motives (James 4:3).

Even though Christ has opened the way before us into the Holy of Holies by rending the veil and sprinkling us with blood, many Christians do not enter frequently. The way is not burdensome or unduly complicated. Christ does the work…Christ sprinkles us with His blood, Christ grants us faith, Christ gives us a clean heart. We simply need to be willing vessels to receive His finished work. Our love and attention must be set toward Him.

Yet, how often our love and attention are diverted to things other than Christ. We do not always earnestly seek His overcoming power because we enjoy a desire of the flesh. We are not always willing to lose our life in order to find His life.

Also, it takes **effort** to learn to walk in a new realm. I watched with amazement as my two children learned to walk. They tried so hard, stumbled and fell so many times. They hit their heads and hurt themselves so much for a period of **many months**, yet they would not give up. Walking just beats crawling, and the Holy of Holies just beats the Holy Place. I believe that for us to learn to walk in the Holy of Holies, it will take the same kind of attention and effort, involve the same kinds of falls and bruises, and take a **number of years** before we become skillful.

May we take up the challenge to come confidently before God and receive His life and love. May we put forth the attention and effort that is needed. May we be willing to fully lose our life in order to find it.

My Personal Experience

I find God speaks to me from the Outer Court, the Holy Place, and the Holy of Holies. He has often directed me through the simple reading and application of the Bible. He has often illumined a passage of Scripture to my heart, lifting it right off the page, letting me know it was His *rhema* for me at that moment. And He has often spoken with spontaneous thoughts, feelings and images directly into my heart as I have waited quietly before Him. Jesus has become my Way, my Truth and my Life.

Luke wrote his Gospel as a Holy Place experience — through Spirit-led reasoning (Luke 1:1-3). John wrote the book of Revelation as a Holy of Holies experience — through direct revelation, bypassing his reasoning process (Rev. 1:10,11). Both are equally valid. Both were 100 percent accurate in what they said.

Also, I have often found the Holy of Holies cut off to me because I did not adjust my fine-tuning dial. I have gone with a lack of faith or a condemning heart, and therefore, have not had the confidence to approach God.

Personal Journaling Application

Using vision, present yourself before each piece of tabernacle furniture. Fix your eyes upon Jesus and ask Him what He wants to speak to you about the placement of this experience in your life. Tune to spontaneity and record what He says. You may want to also ask Him about the fine-tuning dial.

CHAPTER 8

HOW TO TEST MY JOURNALING FOR ACCURACY

Notes

So now, I have one page or ten pages of journaling. How do I know for sure it came from God? How do I test it, and hold fast to what is true, setting aside the rest (1 Thess. 5:21)?

In Chapter One we discussed two primary means for discerning if our journaling is from God: 1) When my spiritual advisors check their spirits, do their hearts tell them it is God or not? 2) Does the content of my journaling line up with the names and nature of God and the Holy Spirit, or with the names and nature of satan? In Chapter Three we showed you how to instantly remove all idols from your heart by making sure your eyes were focused on Jesus while you journaled.

In this chapter we are going to build on what we have already learned, and add a methodology that I have used for many years and found to be extremely helpful in discerning truth in a variety of arenas.

The Names and Character of God

Anything that God says to us is going to be in harmony with His essential nature. Journaling will help you get to *know* God personally, but knowing what the Bible says *about* Him will help you discern what words are from Him and when the accuser may be trying to deceive you. Make sure the tenor of your journaling lines up with the character of God as described in the names of the Father, Son and Holy Spirit.

Through journaling, these Names will become revelation knowledge to you. You will no longer simply know that a Name of God is *Jehovah-Shalom*; you will know God as *your Jehovah-Shalom*! Wonderful Counselor will no longer be just a title of the Son; it will be an apt description of your Friend. The comfort of the Holy Spirit will not be merely a theological statement of faith but the living truth that you have experienced.

So these Names are given both as a standard against which to test the content and spirit of your journaling, and as an inspiration of the ways in which you can expect the triune God to make Himself known to you as you spend time with Him.

Names of the Father

Jehovah-Jireh (The Lord will provide) – Genesis 22:14

Jehovah-Raphe (The Lord my Healer) – Exodus 15:26

Jehovah-Nissi (The Lord my Banner) – Exodus 17:15

Jehovah-Shalom (The Lord my Peace) – Judges 6:24

Jehovah-Raah (The Lord my Shepherd) – Psalm 23:1

Jehovah-Tsidkenu (The Lord my Righteousness) – Jeremiah 23:6; 33:16

Jehovah-Shammah (The Lord is there) – Ezekiel 48:35

Almighty – Genesis 17:1

Judge – Genesis 18:25

Fortress – 2 Samuel 22:2

Lord of Lords – Deuteronomy 10:17

Heavenly Father – Matthew 6:26

Holy One of Israel – Psalm 71:22

Most High – Deuteronomy 32:8

I AM – Exodus 3:14

Names of the Son

Advocate – 1 John 2:1

Almighty – Revelation 1:8

Author and Finisher of our faith – Hebrews 12:2

Bread of Life – John 6:35

Captain of Salvation – Hebrews 2:10

Chief Shepherd – 1 Peter 5:4

Consolation of Israel – Luke 2:25

Cornerstone – Psalm 118:22

Counselor – Isaiah 9:6

Creator – John 1:3

Dayspring/Sunrise – Luke 1:78

Deliverer – Romans 11:26

Desire of all Nations – Haggai 2:7

Door – John 10:7

Good Shepherd – John 10:11

Governor – Matthew 2:6

Immanuel – Isaiah 7:14

Just One – Acts 7:52

King of Kings – 1 Timothy 6:15

Lamb of God – John 1:29

Lawgiver – Isaiah 33:22

Life – John 14:6

Light of the World – John 8:12

True Light – John 1:9

True Vine – John 15:1

Truth – John 14:6

Names of the Holy Spirit

Comforter – John 14:16

Free Spirit – Psalm 51:12

Holy Spirit – Psalm 51:11; Ephesians 1:13; 4:30

Power of the Highest – Luke 1:35

Spirit of Adoption – Romans 8:15

Spirit of Grace – Zechariah 12:10

Spirit of Holiness – Romans 1:4

Spirit of Knowledge – Isaiah 11:2

Spirit of Life – Romans 8:2

Spirit of Might – Isaiah 11:2

Spirit of Prophecy – Revelation 19:10

Spirit of Understanding – Isaiah 11:2

Spirit of Wisdom – Isaiah 11:2

Notes

Testing the Spirit, Content and Fruit

The Bible tells us that we can test the spirit, the content and the fruit of a revelation to determine whether it is of God. The chart below may help differentiate the three sources. Take some time to become familiar with it now, and if you receive any journaling that is questionable, use it to help clarify your discernment.

The fruit of inner spiritual experiences should be an increase in love, reconciliation, healing and wholeness. If, instead, you find the opposite happening, you should immediately discontinue your journaling until you receive help from your spiritual counselor.

Testing Whether an Image Is from Self, Satan, or God

Self	Satan	God
Find Its Origin (Test the Spirit — 1John 4:1)		
Born in mind. A painting of a picture.	A flashing image. Was mind empty, idle? Does image seem obstructive?	A living flow of pictures coming from the innermost being. Was your inner being quietly focused on Jesus?
Examine Its Contents (Test the Ideas — 1 John 4:5)		
A painting of things I have learned.	Negative, destructive, pushy, fearful, accusative, violates nature of God, violates Word of God. Image afraid to be tested. Ego appeal.	Instructive, upbuilding, comforting. Vision accepts testing.
See Its Fruit (Test the Fruit — Matthew 7:15-20)		
Variable	Fear, compulsion, bondage anxiety, confusion, inflated ego.	Quickened faith, power, peace, good fruit, enlightenment, knowledge, humility.

Figure 8.1

A Spirit-Anointed Paradigm for Discovering Truth

A Spirit-anointed paradigm (system) can also be used to confirm that your journaling is correct. I have used many systems for determining truth in my past. Following are some of them:

- If dad said it is true, then it is true.

- If my teacher said it is true, then it is true.

- If my pastor said it is true, then it is true.

- If my professor said it is true, then it is true.

- If an apostle said it is true, then it is true.

- If my reasoned theology said it is true, then it is true.

- If a double-blind scientific study said it is true, then it is true.

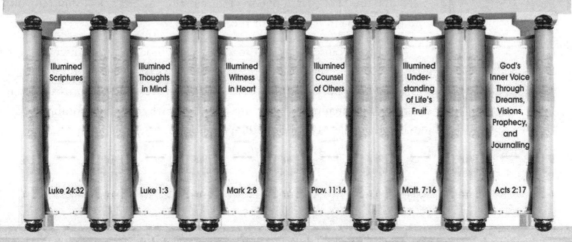

Figure 8.2

Finally, after about 40 years of doing all the above, it dawned on me that perhaps I should search through the Bible and discover **what God says is the appropriate method for discovering truth**! It is amazing to me that I was 40 years old before it occurred to me that I ought to research Scripture looking for God's methodology for determining truth!

My research involved meditating on more than 5,500 verses, and all that I learned is presented in a book entitled *How Do You Know?* On the following pages I have summarized in two charts what I believe is God's design for discovering truth. I have called it "The Leader's Paradigm," and it is a methodology that utilizes God's speaking to us through six different means, which I have pictured as pillars. I believe that, to be a successful leader, you will need to use this system or a system very close to it.

As you review these charts, you will see that I present a biblical basis for each of the six pillars. I have also compared these pillars to six key philosophies which have been promoted over the centuries. I have shown that all six philosophies do hold a fragment of truth, and that when you combine the Holy Spirit to each one, and then merge all six together, you have a wonderfully broad-based paradigm for discerning and clarifying truth. I have used this paradigm very successfully for the last 15 years of my life, and encourage you to prayerfully reflect on it and then try it.

Major Decisions

I expect and require that the leading of God will be consistent through all six pillars of the Leader's Paradigm before I make a major decision. Because I wait for all six to line up, I am spared making many major mistakes. I cannot tell you how valuable this paradigm has been for me.

Just because I have a broad-based methodology for discovering truth is no guarantee I will receive full truth. The Bible says that "we see through a glass darkly," so we still may not know the total truth in an area. However, it is as accurate as we can be in the circumstances we are in. That is why we walk humbly. That is why we remain teachable. "Blessed are the poor in spirit...."

Balancing the Six Pillars in Various Situations

The amount of weight I place on each pillar varies depending on the type of question I am trying to answer.

Relational Issues: These include working out personality differences, overcoming hurts, forgiving another, and sensing another's heart so I can understand how to respond to it in a most godly manner.

Pillar#	Key Verse	How Experienced	How Compared
Pillar One Illumined Scriptures	And they said one to another, "Did not our hearts burn within in us, while He talked with us by the way, and while He opend to us the Scriptures?" (Luke 24:32)	This pillar is experienced as the Holy Spirit illumines Scriptures to you — you sense them leaping off the page or just coming to your attention spontaneously.	This pillar could be viewed as enhanced Biblicism; however, we go beyond studying the Bible with our intellects only, asking for the Holy Spirit to illumine Scriptures to our hearts and minds.
Pillar Two Illumined Thoughts in One's Mind	It seemed fitting for me as well, having investigated everything carefully from the beginning, to write it out for you in consecutive order, most excellent Theophilus. (Luke 1:4 NASB)	This pillar is experienced as the Holy Spirit guiding your reasoning process through spontaneous impressions. It is obvious that Luke's Gospel was more than simply investigative research of his own mind, as what he wrote has stood as the word of God for 2,000 years.	This pillar could be viewed as enhanced rationalism; however, we go beyond simple rationalism to allowing the Holy Spirit to guide our thinking process (through combining intuition and reason) rather than guiding it ourselves.
Pillar Three Illumined Witness in One's Heart	And immediately when Jesus perceived in His spirit that they so reasoned within themselves, He said unto them, "Why reason ye these things in your hearts?" (Mark 2:8)	This pillar is experienced as an impression perceived in your spirit. Deep inner peace or unrest is often part of this experience.	This pillar could be viewed as enhanced hedonism in that we are doing what "feels" good; however, in our case, we are going with the "feel" within our hearts, rather than the "feelings" of the flesh.
Pillar Four Illumined Counsel of Others	Where no counsel is, the people fall: but in the multitude of counselors there is safety. (Proverbs 11:14)	This pillar is experienced as you ask your spiritual advisors to seek God for confirmation, additions, or adjustments in the guidance you sense God has given you.	This pillar could be viewed as enhanced humanism, as we are receiving counsel through others; however, we go beyond people's wisdom and ask them to impart the wisdom of God to us.
Pillar Five Illumined Understanding of Life's Experiences	Ye shall know them by fruits. Do men gather grapes of thorns, or figs of thistles? (Matthew 7:16)	This pillar is experienced as you ask God to give you insight and understanding concerning the fruit life is demonstrating. God gives you revelation as to what has caused the fruit.	This pillar could be viewed as enhanced empiricism, in that we are examining life carefully; however, we go beyond our own limited understanding of life and ask God to give us His understanding of what we are seeing.
Pillar Six Illumined Revelation from God Through Dreams, Visions, Prophecy, and Journaling	"And it shall come to pass in the last days," saith God, "I will pour out of My Spirit upon all flesh: and your sons and your daughters shall prophesy, and your young men shall see visions, and your old men shall dream dreams." (Acts 2:17)	This pillar is experienced as you receive direct revelation from God through dreams, visions, and journaling. Journaling is the writing out of your prayers and God's answers.	This pillar could be viewed as enhanced mysticism; however, we go beyond just "any" spirit-encounter as we pursue Holy Spirit-encounter.

The Objective: To have all six pillars in agreement before making a major decision.

Figure 8.3

When dealing with relational questions and counseling situations, I rely heavily on the illumined Scripture and journaling. I recommend that the primary focus of journaling is for relationships, and journaling shines when used with these types of questions. Also, the Bible has some key verses which help in relational issues: "Forgive everything against everyone." "As much as lieth in you live peaceably with all men." "Love the brethren."

So I rely more heavily on the two pillars of illumined Scriptures and journaling when dealing with relational issues.

Directive Guidance Questions: These include which job to take, who to marry, if someone will be healed, if I should buy this house, if my estranged spouse will return, when a certain thing will happen, and so on.

For these types of questions I rely mostly on three pillars: 1) A witness of peace or unrest in my heart, 2) The illumined counsel of others, and 3) What the experience of life is saying back to me. Following is an example of a time I misinterpreted a journal entry when asking a directive guidance type of question. When wondering what I should be doing for a job, I sensed the Lord saying in my journal to "wait upon Him." I misinterpreted that to mean I was not to be pursuing any course of action. After waiting several months and going deeply into debt, the experience of life was showing me that I was off track (because God was obviously not calling me to sit around and go into debt. This is contrary to the clear Scriptural command to "Owe no man anything but to love one another" in Romans 13:8.). So I actively began pursuing employment, which I consequently received. What I now believe God was saying to me was, "Have an inner attitude of waiting upon Me as you pursue courses of action I set before you."

Through these kinds of experiences I have come to lean less on my journaling in directive kinds of questions and more heavily on other pillars such as what life and others are saying.

YOU Should Balance the Six Pillars Based on YOUR Gifts

I think the more right-brain intuitive person will place more weight on the intuitive aspects of these six pillars. This is probably right because their gifts in the area of intuition make them more precise and wise when they lean upon these gifts.

On the other hand, the more analytical left-brain person will likely lean a bit more heavily on the analytical aspects of these pillars, because their strengths in the area of analysis and detection make them more precise and wise as they lean upon these gifts. This, too, is right.

However, both left- and right-brain people should stretch themselves somewhat so that they integrate both left- and right-brain faculties into their decision-making process.

If you are an accomplished Bible scholar, you will probably weigh more heavily on the pillar of illumined Scriptures. If you are very new to the Bible, you may not put as much weight on that pillar because of your lack of knowledge of the principles of the Word. It is not that the Bible is not reliable for the young Christian. It is that they are more ignorant of its contents.

Journaling Does Not Replace My Need for the Body of Christ

When I journal and ask God questions, I normally am only open to receiving answers that are within the very limited perspective through which I am viewing God's provision and responses. Any additional insights God desires to give me that are outside my particular outlook are easily missed (not that God is unable to give them, but I may not hear or understand them). By receiving input from several counselors, I gain God's answers from others' perspectives. In the multitude of counselors there is safety (Prov. 11:14). I should never assume that my journaling gives me the complete revelation of God on an issue.

Theologically speaking, journaling probably could give me a full picture if I were a totally yielded, transparent vessel, wide-open and trained in spiritual revelation, freed of all my limiting views and prejudices, and wholly cognizant of all statutes and principles taught in the Bible. However, most of us will not fully meet all these conditions, so we desperately need others who seek the Lord alongside of us and give us their input.

The failure to do this is one of the most limiting things I see in people's lives. Too many people live too much as an island, rather than seeking out others' input on an ongoing basis. Look at the diagram below and see what you miss by not receiving others' input. Look what you gain by receiving their prayerful reflections. The distance you travel in life toward fulfilling your destiny is greatly hindered or enhanced by whether you ignore or practice the principle diagrammed below.

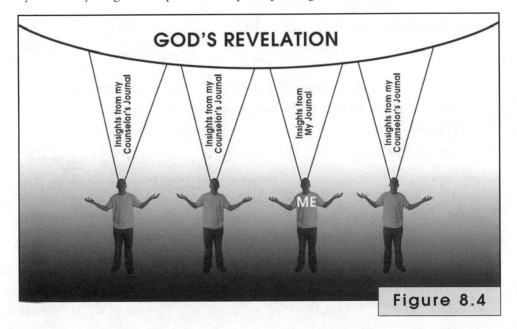

Figure 8.4

A standard question I ask when people want my counsel concerning direction they are sensing is, "What does your spouse say?" Wives have been told for years to listen to their husbands so I probably don't need to say it again. But just in case there are women who feel spiritually superior to their husbands and therefore don't solicit their input, I will say again, "Wife, what does your husband say about it?"

Unfortunately, too seldom have men been asked the same question: "Husband, what does your wife say about it?" I am appalled at the number of men I have counseled who do not seek the counsel of their wives, or who ignore what they sense God is saying. Men, hear me! Your wife is probably the greatest gift God has given you to help you on your path to spiritual fruitfulness and maturity! She has gifts that you do not have, and that you need! Listen to your wife!

Consider the twelve disciples and how their growth was accelerated as they were discipled by a Mentor Who was ahead of them in the area in which they needed to grow. Who are the mentors in your life who are helping you grow in specific areas? If you can't quickly name them and claim an ongoing, functional, working relationship with them, you are short-changing yourself and limiting what you could be developing into. Don't let this sin persist in your life. Discover your mentors today and establish strong working relationships with them.

I have people who serve as my spiritual advisors, several as business mentors, and some as counselors in the areas of human relationships. Do you have different mentors ahead of you in various areas who are speaking into your life on a regular basis? For your sake, I hope you do.

Journaling, Which Amounts to Personal Prophecy, Should Generally Be Limited to the Three Categories Given for Prophecy in 1 Corinthians 14:3.

After many years of personally journaling and teaching others worldwide, I have arrived at some conclusions. The most important is to steer clear of seeking predictions through your journal. Far too many mistakes occur. Here is why.

Since the Lord is speaking directly to you through journaling, I believe journaling amounts to receiving a personal prophecy. The New Testament limits prophecy to three categories: "edification, exhortation and comfort" (1 Cor. 14:3). None of these involve predictions, such as, "You will marry this person. Do this and _____ will happen. Your spouse will return to your marriage. You will be offered a certain job."

These are all predictive-type things and as such fall outside the scope of New Testament prophecy. Yes, Old Testament prophets did this kind of thing; however predictive prophecy is very rare in the New Testament. In addition, the New Testament declares three specific categories into which prophecy is to fall.

What are edification, exhortation, and comfort? Edification means to "build up," so your journaling will be building you up. It will be strengthening you in your faith and generally making you stronger in your walk with God.

Exhortation means to encourage toward a specific way of living, such as Jesus' exhortation to the woman caught in adultery: "Go and sin no more." Others examples are, "Love your spouse," or "Forgive this person," or "Display mercy rather than judgment." All these are exhortations to a certain way of living.

Comfort means to counsel, to bind up, to pour in healing oil. When God is simply loving you and healing you, that is comfort.

You see, journaling is primarily for building a love relationship between you and God. In our journals, God will call us to rest, believe, have faith, and trust, regardless of what the outcome will be. And because we believe, trust, and have faith, we maximize the opportunity for God's supernatural grace to work in our lives and the lives of others. Life is worth living because we are not full of negatives. So God must call us to faith, and He will over and over.

Three Areas of Knowledge We Are Tempted to Pursue

As we grow in our relationship with the Lord through hearing His voice, there will be times we want to discuss other issues that are important to us with Him. Let's talk about three of these areas.

First, there is the area of personal guidance: "Lord, should I take this job that has been offered to me? Should I ask this person to marry me? Should I continue to attend this church? What should I say to this person who is angry? Is this the house we should buy? What should I do to improve my health and receive my healing?"

Jesus declared that the Father knows the number of hairs on your head (which changes every time you run a brush through it!), and that He sees even the little bird when it falls. He cares about every aspect of your life, and He wants you to know His will. He wants you to make wise decisions and He offers His grace to give you strength to grow in holiness every day. He is pleased when you ask for His wisdom and He will generously give it to you (James 1:5). Just remember to keep your heart pure, allowing no idols (your own will) to distort the pure *rhema* of God to you.

However, it is very easy for this kind of question to subtly alter and become a predictive question about the future: "Lord, who will I marry? Will I marry this person? Will I get this job? Will our offer on this house be accepted? When will I receive that raise? Will this person be healed?" These are the questions that will get us into trouble! Throughout the Bible there are repeated prohibitions against seeking out or listening to soothsayers or diviners — those who claim to predict the future. Tomorrow belongs to the Lord, and He wants us to face it armed only with our faith in Him.

In addition, questions about the future nearly always involve the will of other people. That makes it always in a state of flux. God may tell you His will in the Scriptures or in your journal, but unfortunately, sinful man does not always act in accordance with God's will. God is not willing that any should perish but that all should come to repentance. Yet, sadly there are those who do not repent and who do perish. As long as man has free will, the future is fluid.

By His own initiative, God may choose to tell us something of our future, particularly in the areas of His promises to us and His plans for us. However, He will usually answer our nosy questions for more detail than He has given, with the exhortation, "Trust Me." If we keep pressing and asking questions He has already refused to answer, we will generally get an answer from a lying spirit or according to our own desires. Demanding to know more than God wants to share with us opens us to deception.

The Lord said this to our friend and mentor Maurice Fuller in his journal: "My will is not for hire. It is not for sale. It is not for you to inquire, as from an oracle. My will is plain to those who will do My will."

Maurice also gave us the following insights concerning this question: "Like you say, journaling is not some kind of Ouija Board. We cannot use journaling as a way to get around God's reluctance to reveal certain things to us. Journaling — as well as hearing God more naturally in our spirit — enables us to hear what God wants to tell us. It is not a method to persuade God to tell us things He doesn't wish to reveal to us.

"Witchcraft, as you rightly discern, seeks knowledge of the future for our own personal (and maybe selfish or even evil) benefit. In fact, some witchcraft practitioners have developed the ability to trick the demons into divulging information they did not at first want to reveal. Deuteronomy 18 strictly forbids practicing witchcraft but, more than that, that passage and others forbid us to approach God and try to use Him as the witchcraft practitioners use their familiar spirits.

"Not taking the name of the LORD your God in vain is actually a prohibition against Israel (and us) using the name of God as a talisman or to attempt to approach God as in witchcraft, trying to conjure information from Him. God will not allow Himself to be conjured up or to be conned into providing information as though He were no more than an Ouija Board.

"My sense of receiving information from God is that, unlike witchcraft, God ties His revelation to us to what He is doing in our lives at the moment. It may not be beneficial or helpful to us to know certain facts at certain times in our life. He may wisely and lovingly withhold the future from us for our greater good. We do not decide what we want God to tell us and then try to persuade Him to conform to our imperfect agenda.

"God tells us what He wants us to know and when He wants us to know it. God may tell us a little at a time, rather than everything at once because He does not do all His work in us in one fell swoop. Our approach should always be, in my view, not "God, tell me this or that," but "What do You want to tell me about this or that?"

"God may certainly tell us about some things far in the future in great detail, but it is at His initiation, not ours. My sense is that this is relatively rare, simply because we usually cannot easily handle too much information too far in the future. But it does happen and it is a very interesting experience watching how it comes to pass."

I hope you can see the difference between the questions, "Should I ask this person to marry me?" and "Will I marry this person?" The first is seeking personal guidance and direction about what I should do. The second seeks to know the future, and involves the free will of another individual. Be careful that you ask the right questions in your journal.

And you should be aware that even if the Lord says, "Ask her," that is not a guarantee that her answer will be "yes." Your responsibility is only to be totally obedient to what you believe the Lord is saying to you. You may not understand why things turn out as they do, even when you have obeyed. The working of God may not become clear to you until eternity. Yet, you must be obedient and faithful.

A sub-category of the predictive questions we are to avoid is the ever-popular, "Will this person be healed?" Sadly, many, many people have lost their faith in hearing God's voice, and even in God Himself because they believed with all their heart that they had God's assurance that someone they loved would recover, yet they died. I have to tell you that I do not understand healing — why some people live and some die. But I will share with you the conclusion God has brought me to, and that I encourage you to consider for yourself.

I am absolutely, 100 percent convinced that it is God's will to heal everyone who comes to Him. Everything I read in the Bible and everything I have learned about my Father through our personal relationship demands that this be so. Jesus healed all who asked, and He said that He was doing exactly what He saw the Father doing. I believe that complete healing is always the will of God. I believe that if I ask the Lord if it is His will to heal someone, the answer will always be "yes."

However, I also know that not everyone is healed. As I reminded you earlier, God's perfect will is not always accomplished on this earth. There are factors in healing that I simply have not comprehended so far in my life, search and meditate and pray and experiment and ask as I might.

So what do I do when someone I love is diagnosed with cancer? I believe that God will heal him. I believe that it is absolutely God's will that this child of His walk in health and serve Him his allotted threescore and ten years (at least). I pray with total confidence for the healing touch of God. I journal about what other steps we should take to promote his healing, and I share them with conviction and passion. I constantly stay tuned to the spontaneous impressions the Spirit may send to me so that nothing in me hinders the power of God from flowing.

And if he is not healed? I still believe it is absolutely God's will that His children walk in health. I still believe it is always God's will to heal. I do not understand why His will was hampered in this life, and I grieve the loss of the one I loved. But I do not allow any circumstance, no matter how tragic, to undermine my faith in my God. My understanding of the Lord and His will is not based on physical conditions but on the unchanging Word and character of God.

Determining Your Skill Level in Journaling

The value of journaling will grow in your life as you cultivate the skill. May I suggest that when we begin, we are babes, and we grow through several stages. As we go through these phases, our skill level (our spiritual dexterity) increases, and we find we can receive more precise data and information out of the spirit realm.

Each of us has different skill levels. I am under the distinct impression that right-brainers can reach further and with more dexterity into the spirit realm than left-brainers can. I also believe that with practice, anyone can go further than they could before. This is a natural law God has built into His universe.

Journaling at the Beginner's Stage — Operating in the *Spirit* of Prophecy (Rev. 19:10)

One working definition for this stage is, "Not being able to personally capture the prophetic flow unless you have been led into it by another." When I guide a group in journaling, I consider this an example of leading the group into experiencing the spirit of prophecy in the room.

When operating on this level, you should definitely keep your journaling restricted to the areas of edification, exhortation, and comfort. Most people will begin here.

Journaling at the Intermediate Stage — Operating in the *Gift* of Prophecy (1 Cor. 12:10)

A working definition for this stage is, "Personally able to flow in the prophetic even when it is not manifest in the meeting at large." This person is able to be prophetic, sensing the Spirit within his heart even when the circumstances without do not lend themselves to being prophetic. He has cultivated the ability to stand still before God while walking among men.

When operating on this level, you will journal in the areas of edification, exhortation, and comfort. In addition, you will find wisdom from the Lord, especially when functioning in the area of **your call and responsibility and ministry**. For example, you could journal about your family. If you are a teacher, you might journal about your teaching, or if an evangelist, you could journal about what God is speaking to you concerning evangelism, and so on.

Growing into the operation of the gift of prophecy is available for all who seek it. Second Timothy 1:6 indicates it is also imparted through the laying on of hands.

Journaling at the Advanced Stage — Operating in the *Office* of a Prophet (Eph. 4:11)

A working definition for this stage is, "Personally developed until you are recognized by other leaders in the Body of Christ as having a mature prophetic ministry." This is not a call everyone has, as is evidenced by Ephesians 4:11: "He gave some prophets…." So we will not all reach this level. Those who have the call to do so can; the rest of us will become what God is asking us to become. For me, it is to be a teacher in the Body of Christ, not a prophet. Perhaps I can be a prophetic teacher, but not a prophet. In my estimation, people who grow into the office of a prophet are often a bit more right-brain.

When operating in the office of a prophet, you not only can receive edification, exhortation, and comfort, but you may also have a matured skill and precision in predictive prophecies. You also display the fruit of the Holy Spirit in your life and have the character qualities of an elder in the Body of Christ. Do not press for this office unless that is what God has called and gifted you for. There are other offices and functions in the Body of Christ.

Asking Questions Outside of Your Scope of Knowledge and Giftings

If you need insight on obtaining financial freedom and you know nothing about how to go about doing it, you may find your journal a fruitless place to look for a direct answer, other than God telling you to go and do some studying or instructing you to enter into a relationship with an entrepreneur so you can become discipled. Journaling breaks down when you have not deposited anything in the "hard drive."

I see our minds as the hard drive of a computer, and our hearts and the intuitive flow as the software. As we fill our minds with the Word (both the Word of God and the testimonies and principles of successful people in our area), we prepare our hard drives by loading them up with information to draw upon. Once the hard drive is loaded, then the software can, upon command and under the direction of the Holy Spirit, select information that is the right application for the problem set before us.

I recommend not journaling about a problem or an area in which you have no knowledge, because in most cases I believe you will receive little or nothing of value. You may experiment for yourself and decide if I am right or not. I suggest you keep detailed records and analyze your findings. I would love to receive a copy of your conclusions. I have found that I must fill my hard drive before I activate my software if I want meaningful results.

Sharing Revelation from Your Journal With Others

Often we become emotionally attached to the revelation in our journals and demand others receive it. Sometimes, we share it with strong conviction, not mindful of the fact that our interpretation or application may be off base. Occasionally, the revelation itself might be just plain wrong.

Personally, I always try to share revelation in a way that allows the other person the most room in responding to the word. For example, I will often share it as an appeal or as counsel. That way, the other person is free to come to his own conclusion and take whatever action he feels is appropriate, or no action at all. If I really feel strongly about the issue, I might share it as an "impression."

Seldom do I add the emphasis of "thus saith the Lord." After all, if it is a word from the Lord, it will accomplish all that God intended for it to do (which, by the way, may be very different from what I expect), without any need of my stating God's endorsement.

The Body of Christ could save itself much grief by allowing revelation to move under its own authority rather than trying to bring others under our own authority by claiming that they need to submit to what we believe we have received from God. All true authority rests in the *rhema* word directly from God. We only have authority to the extent that we speak true *rhema*. And true authority does not need to be demanded or coerced. True authority is recognized and responded to without force or manipulation.

"The Word of the Lord Breaks"

As Psalm 29:5 states, "The voice of the Lord breaks the cedars," so often the voice of the Lord spoken in our quiet communion with Him will break us and humble us. Remember the Israelites at the mountain of the Lord. They refused to listen and have fellowship directly with Him because His voice was accompanied by His fire. The purifying fire of God always accompanies His voice. Yet the essence of that fire, the power that fuels it, is always Love. It is Love that draws us to Him, and by His Love, we become holy as He is holy.

Another reason the Lord speaks to us and reveals things to us is to build our faith. Jesus said in John 14:29, "And now I have told you before it comes to pass that when it comes to pass, you might believe." Our faith is of supreme importance to God. It is only what is done in faith that pleases Him. The growth of our faith is a high priority to the Lord, and you will recognize it as a major goal in all that He says to you through your journal.

In Closing

Let's remember that hearing God's voice is not about knowing "stuff," but about knowing Him. God's goal is the building of character rather than the revealing of futuristic insights. We must have faith in God, not in our revelation. We must be skeptical of our interpretation of the revelations God gives us, and realize that most things will not be fulfilled in the way we expected them to be fulfilled.

I pray these considerations will help your journaling be a life-giving experience. I pray for your victory and success.

Assignment: Read Appendix H: New Testament Christianity vs. the New Age Movement.

Personal Journaling Application Exercise

In your journaling notebook or on your computer, write the following: "Lord, what do You want to say to me concerning the ideas presented in this chapter?"

Now quiet yourself down into a comfortable scene with Him. Tune to flow and write what He says back to you. Share it with your spiritual advisors for confirmation.

Notes

CHAPTER 9

THE BIBLE SAYS TO "WALK BY THE SPIRIT"

"If we live by the Spirit, let us also walk by the Spirit." (Gal. 5:25)

"If you are led by the Spirit, you are not under the Law." (Gal. 5:18)

"We serve in newness of the Spirit and not in oldness of the letter." (Rom. 7:6)

"The law of the Spirit of life in Christ Jesus has set you free...." (Rom. 8:2)

"Setting your mind on the Spirit...." (Rom. 8:6)

"It is the Spirit who gives life; the flesh profits nothing." (John 6:63)

My Testimony: How God Moved Me from Boxes to Rivers

I grew up loving boxes. What do I mean? I enjoyed establishing theological systems and principles that I put together into an orderly grid of truth. Then I tried to stuff my life into it. Sounds inviting, doesn't it?

For instance, I established my theology concerning how much to witness, how much to pray, how much to disciple others, how to handle fear, anger, discouragement and guilt, how to properly crucify my flesh, how to rejoice without ceasing, etc., etc. Then I tried to live out of all the principles that I had established.

I discovered, however, that while I focused on one set of rules and principles, I forgot another group. As a result, I always felt guilty, condemned and depressed. I hadn't yet come to realize that the end of the Law is always death, and that if I tried to live out of laws, I would always be experiencing a death process working within me. For me, this death took the form of guilt, accusation, condemnation and depression. Not exactly the abundant life that Jesus spoke about.

My boxes just never seemed to work. First, the expectations of the laws that I had discovered within the Bible always left me feeling guilty, knowing I could never measure up. And second, my boxes always seemed to need adjusting. They never seemed any bigger than I was. (That should have been a clue that they were mine and not God's!)

When I first became a Christian, my box describing who was a Christian was quite small. It included my church and me. Eventually, I enlarged it a bit and let some other Baptists in. Then I enlarged it some more and allowed in some Methodists. Next I accepted the Pentecostals and Charismatics. (I had to overhaul the entire box to do that!) Eventually, I even discovered Catholics who were genuinely saved.

By then I had altered my box so many times and so radically that I was no longer sure about the value of building theological boxes. They seemed so small, so inadequate and so imperfect. They didn't seem like a very effective approach to living life. Besides, they always created so much division. Rather than maintaining the unity of the Body of Christ, I was always segregating it, based on my limited theological understanding. I began to wonder if this truly was the way we were to live, or if God had a better plan.

Discovering Life in the Spirit

Then something new began to enter my life. I began to learn the ways of the Spirit of God. I learned to hear His voice and see His vision. I learned to open my heart to the intuitive flow of the Spirit of God within me. I learned to live out of the stream that was welling up within me. Jesus had spoken of this river, but I had never really understood what the experience was. "'From his innermost being shall flow rivers of living water.' But this He spoke of the Spirit, whom those who believed in Him were to receive…" (John 7:38,39).

When I learned to recognize the voice of God as the bubbling flow of spontaneous ideas that welled up from my heart as I fixed my eyes upon Jesus, I discovered a new way of living, that of living out of the Spirit of God rather than simply the laws of God — not that they are in any way opposed to each other. It is just that the Holy Spirit has such great finesse in handling the laws of God that my shallow boxes were mere mockeries of His vast truth.

When struggling with a situation, I found that if I used my own theological boxes to deal with it, I would end up with narrow, judgmental decisions. However, if I went to Jesus in prayer and tuned to the flow of the river within, He would bring other principles to my attention that I had more or less forgotten. He would ask me to apply these over and above the principles that I had been trying to apply earlier.

It's not that some principles are right and some are wrong. It's that some are more weighty than others. Some are the true heart of the matter, and some are simply the periphery. Jesus told the Pharisees of His day that they strained at a gnat and swallowed a camel. "Woe to you, scribes and Pharisees, hypocrites! For you tithe mint and dill and cummin, and have neglected the weightier provisions of the law: justice and mercy and faithfulness; but these are the things you should have done without neglecting the others" (Matt. 23:23).

I found that I generally forfeited the principles of mercy and faithfulness when dealing with others. I was harsh and severe in my judgment of them, and rather than being faithful and loyal to them, I came against them, more as the accuser of the brethren than the Comforter. Therefore, I assumed a satanic stance, rather than a Holy Spirit stance; that is, I tended to "come against" rather than "coming alongside."

The Accuser's Stance or the Comforter's?

It took me years to come to grips with the realization that satan was the accuser of the brethren (Rev. 12:10), and that the Holy Spirit was the One Who came alongside and helped (John 14:16). Even when we are terribly wrong, God does not take an accusative or adversarial stand against us. For example, when the world had just committed its most hideous crime (i.e., crucifying the Son of God), rather than accusing and condemning, Jesus said, "Father, forgive them; for they know not what they do" (Luke 23:34).

As I began to examine my own life, I realized that I often took accusative and adversarial stands against people with whom I didn't agree. I felt it was what God wanted me to do. However, finally it dawned upon me that the accuser's stance is satan's attitude (the word "devil" literally means "accuser") and the comforter's stance is the Holy Spirit's position.

Since this revelation, I have made a commitment **never** to take an accuser's stance against anyone. No longer will I be the expression of satan. If someone is struggling, hurting, down or in error, I have one, and only one, posture. That is, to come alongside him and comfort him, to be faithful to him, and thus preserve the dignity of all men and the unity of the Body of Christ.

As I began to live out of the river that flows from within, I became less judgmental and less narrow-minded. I developed "largeness of heart," a trait that Solomon had (1 Kings 4:29). However, I became increasingly concerned about my more embracing attitude, my tendency to freely accept so many. It seemed a bit liberal to me. I wasn't too sure about it at first.

But I also realized that my narrow, theological boxes could be more easily equated with phariseeism than I cared to admit. I knew that it was time to make a change. I had never studied the characteristics of phariseeism and applied them to my life, but I was becoming uncomfortable, thinking that maybe a number of them might fit me too well. I finally did explore the New Testament for the principles of

Notes

Phariseeism and I examined myself in light of them. You can also by reviewing Appendix I: Self-Check Test on Phariseeism.

Discovering Certainty in the Spirit

As I prayed about my growing tendency toward acceptance of everyone and my growing disregard for boxes, I asked God, "Lord, can I trust the intuitive flow?" You see, I was losing my nicely defined fences. I was no longer so sure where the boundaries were. I was concerned about falling into cultism. After all, if you get into flow and you don't have clear edges, what keeps you?

The Lord answered me this way: "Mark, you can trust the intuitive flow of My Spirit more than you can trust the boxes you build with your mind." What He said made all the sense in the world. I began to wonder, "Where does it say in the Bible that we test for truth **using our minds**? Isn't the test so often made in our hearts, through discernment?" As a matter of fact, Jesus Himself recommends that we go with the intuitive flow over and above the analysis of the mind when He says, "When they arrest you and deliver you up, do not be anxious beforehand about what you are to say, **but say whatever is given you in that hour; for it is not you who speak, but it is the Holy Spirit**" (Mark 13:11, emphasis added).

Therefore, I began to set aside my love for boxes and for theological grids of truth. I came to cherish instead the intuitive, healing flow through my heart from the One so much wiser and more embracing than I. I dismantled the idolization of my mind and established my heart as the throne which God has chosen as the center of life and the central avenue through which to communicate with mankind. I began to experience the fact that those who are led by the Spirit are not under the law (Gal. 5:18).

I next asked the Lord, "Well, then, God, what about laws and rules and boxes? Should I scorn them as having no value? What is a proper attitude toward the Law, toward laws?" The Lord gave me several answers. First, the Law keeps us in custody (i.e., keeps us from killing ourselves), before we come to the point of being led by the Spirit (Gal. 3:23). Second, it is a tutor that leads us to Christ (Gal. 3:24). A tutor is one who teaches us a lesson. The law teaches us that we can never fully keep the law. Therefore, we must abandon ourselves to grace. Wow! What a release! Third, even though we study the laws of God, we never fix our eyes upon them. Instead, we fix our eyes on Jesus, the Author and Finisher of our faith (Heb. 12:2). Now when I look at a situation, I do not approach it with laws on my mind. I approach it as Christ would, with love first and foremost.

Learning to live in the Spirit rather than live in laws greatly impacted my prayer life. I had many rules about how I was to pray and what constituted a good prayer and categories of prayer and ways to pray. However, God gradually changed all that. Please refer to Appendix J: Prayer That Is *Led* by the Holy Spirit for a discussion of this transformation.

Loving Mercy, Not Justice

The Lord showed me that I loved justice, judgment and precision more than I loved mercy and compassion. I approached people first with judgment, and only secondarily with love and mercy. He showed me that He was the opposite of that. He approached people with love and mercy first, and only secondarily with justice.

He reminded me of the Micah 6:8 balance: "He has shown you, O man, what is good; and what does the Lord require of you, but to **do justly**, and to **love mercy**, and to walk humbly with your God?" (NKJV, emphasis added). He said to me, "Mark, you love justice and only do mercy. I love mercy and only do justice. You are the inverse of Me." With that I was cut to the quick and began to change, recognizing the truth of God's words.

Finally, the Lord began to show me the proper place and purpose of laws and rules in my life. He said, "The Sabbath was made for man, not man for the Sabbath" (Mark 2:27). I tended to get that all mixed up. I used to start with the rule and think that my purpose was to obey it. Jesus says, "No." We start with man and his fulfillment; rules are meant to serve man. They are there to assist in releasing the maximum amount of life possible. Jesus Himself came to give us life, abundant life. Therefore, I am learning to begin with the goal of "life" and see what application of which rules releases the most life within and through me. If I don't begin and end with the goal of life, I generally begin and end with the goal of obeying the rule. And man was not created so that he could keep a bunch of rules. He was created to experience abundant life.

How to Avoid Stoning the Prophets

Have you thrown a stone at a prophet lately? Would you know it if you had? Do you know who the contemporary prophets are? Do you know what the prophetic messages are that God is giving to the Church in this generation?

You say, "I don't even think there are prophets restoring truth in this generation. I don't see any!" Neither did the people during the time of Jesus' earthly ministry see any prophets in the land. The Church has a history of being blind to the prophets in her midst. More than that, she has rejected and stoned them.

Jesus said that "Elijah already came, and **they did not recognize him**, but did to him whatever they wished. So also the Son of Man is going to suffer at their hands"

(Matt. 17:12). Jesus' brothers could not see him as a prophet, much less as the Son of God. They even mocked Him (John 7:2-9).

This is a serious indictment against us all, because each of us is part of the Church, and each of us has a built-in blindness to the prophets in our midst, as well as a tendency to reject and revile them. Therefore, rather than point critical fingers at those who, in other times, stoned the prophets whom God had sent them, let us carefully examine this tendency in our own lives and seek to rid ourselves of it completely, so as not to be found guilty of the same sin.

Who are the prophets of our age? What are their messages? I do not purport to know them all or to be able to give you a complete list of them here; however, I would like to give you a sampling of some of those who have touched my life. If you do not agree with my appraisal of all those who follow, please do not stone me! Rather, simply say, "That point doesn't register with me right now, so I think I will put it on the back shelf for awhile and bring it down for re-examination at a later date." This kind of response will produce a lot less bloodshed and allow me to arrive safely at my next birthday, which both my family and I would deeply appreciate.

The further back into history that we look, the easier it is to identify the prophets. The closer we come to the day in which we live, the more difficult it becomes for the Church to clearly recognize its prophets. Although some individuals may discern these prophets very quickly, the Church, as a Body, reaches that point more slowly.

Probably all would agree that Martin Luther, John Calvin, Charles Wesley and Charles Finney were prophets of their day, restoring truth to the Church. At the beginning of the 20th century, God began to restore the truth of the baptism of the Holy Spirit and the gift of speaking in tongues. This restoration was not easily received, and some Pentecostals found their homes and churches burned by other Christians who were convinced these people had moved into error. However, by the year 2000 A.D., the *World Christian Encyclopedia* reported that 27 percent of the Church had embraced the baptism and the gifts of the Holy Spirit. Yet, do all accept the validity of this prophetic word to the Church? No, certain groups of "Bible believing" Christians still hold out, unable to receive the prophetic word in their midst.

In the 1940s, the message of the place of physical healing in the life of the Christian was presented to the Church by Oral Roberts and others, and Christians began to find that they have power through the Holy Spirit over sickness and disease.

In the 1950s, Kenneth Hagin appeared on the scene, teaching the place of faith, and the power released in confessing the Word of God over a situation.

In the 1960s, Derek Prince began teaching the Church the place of deliverance as part of an overall prayer ministry.

Dr. David (Paul Yonggi) Cho restored to the Church worldwide the truth of home cell groups and demonstrated the effectiveness of this truth by building a church with over three-quarters of a million members, a phenomenon never before realized in the history of Christianity.

Time seemed to be condensed in the 1980s as we saw God restoring an array of truths to the Church. Inner healing, as part of the overall prayer/counseling ministry of the Church, has been discovered and applied with great healing benefits to those who receive it. Self-esteem and the dignity of man have been called the New Reformation by Robert Schuller, an ingredient he says we missed in the reformation of the 1500s. The truth that not only does God desire to commune with His people, but He has enabled us to do so, was one of the truths restored during this decade. This has been evidenced through the growing realization that it is possible to teach the Church to hear God's voice clearly and to see easily into the spirit world.

Dance, as a part of praise and worship, is continuing to be restored in a variety of expressions throughout the Body. Not only do we see untrained spontaneous dance, but skilled and artistic dance have emerged as spiritual expressions of praise and worship. The use of banners and pageantry as a means of manifesting praise and worship has also returned.

A theology of dominion as a result of the death and resurrection of the Second Adam is being brought to the Church from numerous quarters today.

The above list obviously is not complete. It serves only as a sampling of suggested prophetic truths that God has restored to the Church in our generation. How did you respond? Did your heart say "yes" to some and "no" to others? Did you feel like casting a few stones as I went down the list? If so, I want to remind you that stone-throwing is our typical response to the prophets in our midst. Stephen, in reciting the Israelites' history, summed it up by asking, "Which one of the prophets did your fathers not persecute? And they killed those who had previously announced the coming of the Righteous One, whose betrayers and murderers you have now become" (Acts 7:52). To demonstrate the degree of their openness, his listeners "covered their ears, and rushed upon him with one impulse.... and began stoning him..." (Acts 7:57,58), thus proving his point that **we have a tremendous tendency to stone the prophets in our midst**.

Why do we respond this way? If we can identify the reasons for this response, we can more effectively keep it from occurring in our lives.

Reason # 1 — Often the prophetic word is veiled, being revealed only to those with spiritual understanding.

For example, Malachi said, "Behold, I am going to send you **Elijah the prophet** before the coming of the great and terrible day of the Lord. And he will restore..." (Mal. 4:5,6, emphasis added). The Jews took this literally and looked for Elijah to return. However, Luke very clearly says that John the Baptist fulfilled this prophecy, because he came "**in the spirit and power of Elijah...**" (Luke 1:17, emphasis added). Jesus said that "all the prophets and the Law prophesied until John. And if you care to accept it, he himself is Elijah, who was to come. He who has ears to hear, let him hear" (Matt. 11:13-15).

In addition, as we present a new idea or concept, we will not do it the first time with the finesse and precision that will develop as we say it over and over, allowing time for it to be sharpened and clarified by the response of the Body of Christ. Therefore, when you hear a new word being spoken, approach it with the understanding that it may be nebulous and as yet not well-defined. Rather than coming against it, which is the work of satan, the accuser, come alongside it, which is the work of the Comforter. Seek to ground it biblically and clarify it. Sometimes, after trying to ground a new message in Scripture, you will find that it is impossible to find any biblical support for it at all and will then have to reject it as a false word.

Reason # 2 — In the zeal of our new discovery, we try to cram a prophetic truth down the throats of unready and unwilling victims.

How many of you, when you were first saved, rushed out and tried to convert a close friend when he was not ready? You most likely caused a substantial reaction! How many of you did the same thing when you were baptized in the Holy Spirit? Those who have a prophetic message need to be aware of this tendency and learn to slow down and wait a bit for the timing of the Lord, rather than sharing it with everyone they meet. Some are not ready for this message. On the other hand, if we are hearing a prophetic message, we need to pray for God to enlarge our hearts, so that we can be open to mull it over prayerfully under the illumination of Scripture.

Reason # 3 — Those who hear the prophets do not always make the message theirs before passing it on, and thus they dilute or distort it.

Kenneth Hagin Sr. spent 50 years meditating on the Word under the illumination of the Holy Spirit and found that it had become so fleshed out in his life, and his faith had so deepened, that as he spoke it forth, the power of the Word would be released into the situation at hand. One of his adherents shared with me with great pain that she had confessed the Word of healing over her baby until it died of a problem that could easily have been handled by the doctors. Because she had not had the life experience of Kenneth Hagin and the inner intuitive and visionary nature of Kenneth Hagin, she was not able to see the same power released that Kenneth Hagin has, and tragedy resulted. This type of occurrence does not make Kenneth Hagin's prophetic word wrong; however, it does demonstrate the great need for intense clarity and understanding and wisdom as we pass along a prophetic word.

Reason # 4 — There is a tendency toward eccentricity as the prophet continually shares only his new revelation.

Some people cast demons out of doorknobs and off the sidewalk. This makes us tend to reject the deliverance ministry. However, one extreme is as bad as the other. We must not throw out a prophetic truth because the prophet or one of his adherents becomes out-of-balance. One-third of Jesus' prayers for supernatural intervention were deliverance prayers (12 out of 41). If He is the perfect balance and goal of my life, then presumably one-third of my prayers for supernatural intervention should also be deliverance prayers.

Some people believe that if you really have faith for divine healing you should never go to a doctor. Does that mean I should reject prayer for divine healing when I am sick?

No, in each of the above cases I need simply to recognize the tendency toward eccentricity as a truth is being restored and smile, letting the pendulum take its necessary swing, being as careful as possible to find a balance. Admittedly, this balance may not always be possible until we have worked with the particular truth for a period of time.

Reason # 5 — There may be pride on the part of the speaker.

As the sharer of the new revelation speaks, he may do so with a condescending attitude, implying, "I have something you don't have;" "I'm better than you;" or "Here, let me educate you." This will generally provoke such a reaction in our flesh that we will have a hard time getting past it.

If you are the sharer, be careful of this kind of spiritual pride. If you are the hearer and detect an arrogant spirit, ask God for the grace to stand above it so that your heart can hear and respond to the prophetic word that is being delivered, even though the messenger is manifesting some imperfections.

Reason # 6 — There may be pride on the part of the hearer.

We may struggle with our own pride as someone shares a new insight with us. "How can anyone know something I don't know?" "I've been a Christian longer than he has;" or "Can anything good come out of Nazareth?" Beware of this pride and ask God for the grace to crucify it whenever you sense it emerging.

Reason # 7 — Sometimes the hearer examines Scripture to prove that the word of the prophet is not so.

There is enough tension in Scripture that we can generally find verses that appear to speak to the opposite of almost any truth we believe. For instance, if you believe you have to love your brother to get to heaven, I can quote the words of Jesus when He said, "If anyone comes to Me, and does not hate his own father and mother and wife and children and brothers and sisters, yes, and even his own life, he cannot be My disciple" (Luke 14:26).

If, on the other hand, you believe that you must hate your brother in order to get to heaven, I can quote John's command that "The one who says he is in the light and yet hates his brother is in the darkness until now" (1 John 2:9). So I say again, there is enough tension in Scripture to make almost any truth appear wrong, **if we have a mind to do so**. However, we are to be more noble-minded than this. "Now these were more noble- minded than those in Thessalonica, for they received the word with great eagerness, examining the Scriptures daily, to see **whether these things were so**" (Acts 17:11, emphasis added).

The Bereans tried to prove the truth of the new message, rather than the error of it. This is as the difference between night and day, between God and satan, between taking the accuser's stance and the Comforter's stance, between coming against and coming alongside to help. Make a determination always to come alongside and help, rather than to come against and accuse. Let our hearts and minds be used by God and not by satan.

Reason # 8 — The hearer may fix his vision on a few extreme examples of the prophet's message, instead of seeking out the core of the message.

I am amazed at how often this is done, even by national leaders who are frequently seen on television. They write articles telling about a few extreme applications of a prophet's message, then couple these with a verse that is on the opposite end of the tension point in Scripture, thus "proving" their point: "The prophet is deceived!" What a sad day for the Church, when the sheep become convinced of such reasoning, being deceived while they proudly believe they have been spared from deception. Who really is being deceived? You decide.

How foolish to gaze on the extreme! Instead, we are to reach in and discern the core of the message and seek to clarify and confirm it with Scripture. We know the extreme will always be there. Satan will make sure of that, hoping to convince us to reject the message. However, as children of the Light, we have spiritual discernment. We must look for the heart of the message. We must examine Scripture daily to see if these things are so. We must come alongside as helpers, giving greater clarity to the message. We must become the expressions of the Comforter, rather than the accuser. **We are children of the Light.**

If after reading this chapter, you realize that you have cast a few stones that you ought not to have cast, ask His forgiveness, and ask that by His grace you may be sensitized to discern satan's attempts to draw you into stoning the prophets of our generation.

A New Reformation in Christendom

The last Reformation in Christianity occurred in the 1500s at a time when the Western world was just discovering the scientific method and rationalism. Although the Reformation healed much within Christianity, it may have left some gaping holes as it sought to be palatable to the world in which it lived. It did not lay much stress on dreams and visions and the voice of God guiding the believer by day and by night. The emphasis was not on spirit encounter, but on the theological fact that every believer had the right to approach God for himself.

At the beginning of the 20th century, God began emphasizing the work and moving of the Holy Spirit, and now one-fourth of all believers have found a new walk of intimacy with the Spirit of God. I believe this century will be seen by historians as a century of Reformation as the Church discovers the role of the Holy Spirit in their lives corporately and individually. I believe we are in the midst of a New Reformation within Christianity. That is why we are suffering so many birth pangs. During the last Reformation, we martyred and killed those who led the way, only to recognize their vast contribution and pioneering spirit after their life's blood had been spilt. Today these martyrs are our heroes.

May we not take the lives of those who stand out in front and lead us. May we be willing to doubt our own infallibility just a bit and honor the voice of God in the midst of His Church. We truly are living in the most remarkable age of Christendom. We are seeing 78,000 new believers added to the Church every day and 1,600 new churches being started in different places of the world each week.[1] No other time in Church history has seen such awesome moving of God.

Let us be open to what God is doing. Let the murderous spirit of religion be cast back to the pit of hell where it came from! Let our hearts overflow with humility and meekness as we watch what God is doing. It is truly a "new age"! The theology we have has essentially been passed down for three hundred years. We need to again search the Scriptures in light of God's movement in today's world and allow Him to reinterpret things that have stood for centuries. Who will have the courage to do so? The Kingdom of God suffers violence, and violent men take it by force. Will you wrestle with your theology and allow it to be transformed by the wonder of what God is doing in this present day?

I Thought I Knew: The Kingdom That Almost Was

Let me close this chapter with a story/parable.

As a native of the land of Israel, I was taught about the great coming deliverer. He would come as the mighty and strong arm of the Lord, freeing His people from the yoke of oppression. He would restore the kingdom of David, establishing righteousness in the land. The Father would grant unto Him an eternal kingdom, one that would not pass away. He would rule the earth in righteousness and glory. His glory would cover the earth. He would be the great Messiah! He would be called Immanuel, "God with us!"

Therefore, it was with great exuberance that my brother came running to me one day saying, "We have found the Messiah, the One of Whom the Scriptures speak!" I raced with him to this One Whom he had discovered and followed after Him for a great many days.

I watched Him heal the sick, proclaim release to the captives, and teach, saying, "The Kingdom of God is at hand." For more than three years He proclaimed this great message. **We believed!** The great Deliverer was in our midst. No longer would we be subject to cruel oppressors, such as Rome. We waited excitedly for Him to establish His throne. All the Scriptures would be fulfilled. All I had been taught would soon be realized.

But then tragedy struck. The King was betrayed by one of His own followers. Sold for 30 pieces of silver, the price of a slave, He was whisked through a mock trial and crucified on the same day. All of my hopes turned to ashes. Life became empty. **The King did not rule.** He never even got the chance to set up His kingdom before His tragic death. All my beliefs were dashed to pieces. All my hopes were gone.

What about all the teachings of the Word? They were **not fulfilled**. My faith was shaken. I returned to my home and my job in listless despair. Maybe all of life was a cruel hoax. The teachings I had learned from my youth were wrong. Maybe even the Scriptures were a fraud. I was filled with hopelessness and confusion.

And then the cry came: **He had risen and ascended** to the Father. We were to wait in Jerusalem for the promise of the Father, His Spirit, to baptize us in power. He **had set up** His kingdom, and now we were going to help Him establish it.

As I waited, I went back to the Word. I reexamined the book of Isaiah. I discovered verses I had never understood before — about a suffering Servant Who would come as a Lamb before His slaughterers.

Maybe the Word was true after all! Maybe it was only the interpretations that I had been taught that were not true. It amazed me how different the Word looked now, in light of the events around me.

Maybe the simple teaching of the Word is not enough. Maybe we need to search the Word **in the light of our experiences in life**. Maybe the Word will always speak in somewhat new and different ways to me as life progresses around me. Maybe I will never have full understanding in this life, but only that which is revealed to me in the context of my own life. Maybe full understanding will have to wait for eternity.

Lord, speak to me. I'm a bit unsure. How do I fit together the testimony of Your Word and the testimony of life? In what way should they be blended? How exactly do I discover truth?

Personal Application

Record in your journal what the Lord says to you concerning the above questions. Tune to spontaneity, fix your eyes upon Jesus, and begin to write in simple childlike faith. Begin by writing down the questions above. Share what you receive with your spiritual advisors for confirmation.

Endnote

1. "Reaping the Harvest" by C. Peter Wagner; *People of Destiny* Magazine, November/December 1986.

Notes

CHAPTER 10

HOW TO POSSESS YOUR PROMISED LAND

"…You may enter the land which the Lord your God gives you, a land flowing with milk and honey, as the Lord, the God of your fathers, promised you." (Deut. 27:3, NASB)

God says astounding things in our journals. He plans on using us in greater ways than we ever imagined. He plans on doing greater things through us than we dreamed of doing ourselves. He plans on blessing us more than we expected to be blessed. God told Abraham, "… in you all the families of the earth will be blessed" (Gen. 12:3, NASB). "And He took him outside and said, 'Now look toward the heavens, and count the stars, if you are able to count them.' And He said to him, 'So shall your descendants be.'" (Gen. 15:5, NASB). These promises were spoken to Abraham by God when Abraham was 75 years of age and **had no children**!

Often in the Bible, when God told people what He was going to do through them, they turned around and explained to God that He could not do such a great thing through them, and why.

Moses said, "I can't lead millions of people because I can't talk" (Exod. 4:10,11). That point didn't bother God, because God knew He could speak through Moses and make him better than he was. However, Moses refused to be convinced. God became angry with Moses and said, "Fine, I will give you Aaron as your mouthpiece, but I could have spoken through you if you would have believed Me" (Exod. 4:12-15).

God plans on fulfilling these great promises He makes to us in our journals through His anointing working in and through us, and not through our own strength. If we will only believe and obey, God can and will do the supernatural through us!

God said to the Israelites, "I have given you the promised land" (Deut. 27:3). God will say similar things to each of us in our personal journals. He said to me, "Mark, you are going to saturate the earth with communion with God" (i.e., teaching people how to hear God's voice). How are we to respond when God tells us such great things?

I used to respond by saying, "Hallelujah!" and sitting back to watch God accomplish what He had promised. Often nothing happened and I became frustrated. I had not yet learned that when God is speaking a prophecy like this through my journal, he is revealing my potential. If I walk hand in hand with God, this potential will be realized. If I don't, the potential will be wasted.

When God makes a promise to us, it is usually conditional on a number of things. Even if He doesn't say the promise has conditions, it still generally does. For example, God told Jonah to tell the inhabitants of Nineveh that He would destroy them in forty days (Jon. 3:1-4). There was no "if clause" at all. That was the end of the sentence. However, when the Ninevites decided to repent, God, too, repented of the destruction which He had prepared to bring them and did not destroy them as He had planned (Jon. 3:5-10).

God even states this principle of conditionality. He says:

"At what instant I shall speak concerning a nation, and concerning a kingdom, to pluck up, and to pull down, and to destroy it; If that nation, against whom I have pronounced, turn from their evil, I will repent of the evil that I thought to do unto them. And at what instant I shall speak concerning a nation, and concerning a kingdom, to build and to plant it; If it do evil in my sight, that it obey not my voice, then I will repent of the good, wherewith I said I would benefit them." (Jer. 18:7-10)

Another classic example is when God told the Israelites that He had given them the Promised Land. Did that mean they could sit back and the Promised Land would drop into their laps, or did they have to seek God for direction and then go in and battle and conquer city after city? They had to ask God for direction and then they had to fight.

So, too, when God says to me, "I have healed you," my next question needs to be, "God, are there any specific actions You want me to take to precipitate Your healing flow?" Often there will be, because His covenant of healing is based on four prerequisites found in Exodus 15:26.

One of the prerequisites is to "keep ALL His statutes." So there are any number of His health laws which I may be breaking that are prohibiting me from obtaining the promise He has given to me both in His Word (Bible) and in my journal. Here is where the counsel of my advisors (who in this case know about health) comes in. I ask them to pray concerning any things God would tell them that I should be aware of or doing or changing in my lifestyle in order to release the healing flow of God's power.

I never used to do this. I would just sit back and wait. And nothing would happen. Now, I ask God and my spiritual advisors what I am to do and I receive their counsel. I remain active rather than passive. I am getting much better results this way. I believe it is a key answer to many people's dilemmas.

If God says he is going to heal your marriage, you then ask God what He wants you to do to be a catalyst for that healing. He will probably give you several things to do, attitudes to change and actions to take.

You need to know that when another person's will is involved (as it is in this scenario), God will not overrule their will, but He and you will be doing everything possible to make the other party willing (in this case — to restore the marriage). However, in the final analysis, God will not overrule their will, and so there is a possibility that a spouse may walk out and God's declared will for the marriage would not be fulfilled.

This does not mean your journaling was wrong. This means God does not overrule people's wills to force His will to be done. By instructing you to believe and act in faith, God has positioned your heart to release the maximum force possible, intensifying the probability that a miracle of restoration will occur in your marriage.

Following is a short summary list of what Joshua and the Israelites had to do before they POSSESSED the Promised Land that God said He had **already given** to them.

Steps the Israelites Took in Order to Possess Their Promised Land

1. They sent out spies into the land they were going to possess (Josh. 2:1).

2. The people consecrated themselves for battle (Josh. 3:5).

3. Their spiritual leaders led in battle (Josh. 3:6).

4. They kept listening to the Lord every step of the way so that they knew God was with them in the actions they were taking. (Josh. 3:7).

5. They acknowledged a leader who was appointed by God, who in turn commanded the spiritual and the military leaders (Josh. 3:8,9).

6. This leader could command a miracle to happen, and it did (Josh. 3:10-17).

7. The Lord continued to give direction to this spiritual leader (Josh. 4:1).

8. They took time out to follow God's instructions to create memorials to remind their descendents of the miracle-working power of God in their midst (Josh. 4).

9. God's miracles made the enemies' hearts melt before them (Josh. 5:1).

10. Complete obedience to God was required (Josh. 5:2-10).

11. Joshua encountered and obeyed an angelic commander (Josh. 5:13-15).

12. God gave detailed instructions about how to conduct the battle. These were followed to the letter and Jericho was taken (Josh. 6).

13. Disobedience to God's voice within the camp brought defeat (Josh. 7:1-5).

14. Seeking the Lord brought God's voice and revelation of why there was defeat and how to remove the sin that caused it. The sin was removed (Josh. 7:6-26).

15. God gave detailed instructions of how to defeat the enemy. These were followed and the enemy defeated (Josh. 8:1-35).

16. They were tricked by the Gibeonites because they did not seek the counsel of the Lord (Josh. 9:14).

17. God's voice led Joshua into victory against five kings. (Josh. 10:8).

18. Obedience to God's voice brought victory (Josh. 11:6).

19. Complete obedience and complete victory were finally obtained (Josh. 11:15,23).

Journal, asking the Lord to speak to you from the above list about the key requirements you need to know if you are going to possess the land the Lord has told you is yours.

Obviously, hearing God's voice, believing it, and obeying it must rank at the top of anyone's list who wants to possess their promised land.

What Keeps People From Entering Their Promised Land?

God told Moses to speak to the rock and water would come out (Num. 20:8), but instead, in his anger he hit the rock (Num. 20:11). *"But the Lord said to Moses and Aaron, 'Because you have not believed Me, to treat Me as holy in the sight of the sons of Israel, therefore you shall not bring this assembly into the land which I have given them.'"* (Num. 20:12, NASB)

Not honoring and absolutely obeying the voice of God kept Moses and Aaron out of the Promised Land.

How does God determine if we are prepared to walk into the promises He has for us?

"You shall remember all the way which the Lord your God has led you in the wilderness these forty years, that He might humble you, testing you, to know what was in your heart, whether you would keep His commandments or not." (Deut. 8:2, NASB)

God tests us to see if there is faith in our hearts — to see if, when under pressure, we say "I trust in God as my Provider and Deliverer." Failing God's tests keeps us from receiving our inheritance here on this earth!

"Surely all the men who have seen My glory and My signs which I performed in Egypt and in the wilderness, yet have put Me to the test these ten times and have not listened to My voice, shall by no means see the land which I swore to their fathers, nor shall any of those who spurned Me see it." (Num. 14:22,23, NASB)

The Israelites failed ten of these tests while in the wilderness. Below are two of them. Rather than trusting in God, they began to whine and complain.

"Then they set out from Mount Hor by the way of the Red Sea, to go around the land of Edom; and the people became impatient because of the journey. The people spoke against God and Moses, 'Why have you brought us up out of Egypt to die in the wilderness? For there is no food and no water, and we loathe this miserable food.'" (Num. 21:4,5, NASB)

"So they gave out to the sons of Israel a bad report of the land which they had spied out, saying, 'The land through which we have gone, in spying it out, is a land that devours its inhabitants; and all the people whom we saw in it are men of great size. There also we saw the Nephilim (the sons of Anak are part of the Nephilim); and we became like grasshoppers in our own sight, and so we were in their sight.' Then all the congregation lifted up their voices and cried, and the people wept that night. All the sons of Israel grumbled against Moses and Aaron; and the whole congregation said to them, 'Would that we had died in the land of Egypt! Or would that we had died in this wilderness!'" (Num. 13:32–14:2, NASB)

God's response to man's whining is*: "'How long shall I bear with this evil congregation who are grumbling against Me? I have heard the complaints of the sons of Israel, which they are making against Me. Say to them, "As I live," says the Lord, "just as you have spoken in My hearing, so I will surely do to you; your corpses will fall in this wilderness, even all your numbered men, according to your complete number from twenty years old and upward, who have grumbled against Me. Surely you shall not come into the land in which I swore to settle you, except Caleb the son of Jephunneh and Joshua the son of Nun."'"* (Num. 14:27-30, NASB)

"For the sons of Israel walked forty years in the wilderness, until all the nation, that is, the men of war who came out of Egypt, perished because they did not listen to the voice of the Lord, to whom the Lord had sworn that He would not let them see the land which the Lord had sworn to

their fathers to give us, a land flowing with milk and honey." (Josh. 5:6, NASB)

So they received what they expected and declared. They did not believe God was their Shepherd. They grumbled and complained saying they would die since God didn't care for them, and God said, "Fine, if that is what you want to believe for and confess, then that is what you will get." They all died in the wilderness.

It took me years in my own life to understand that God gives me exams (tests) on an ongoing basis. These tests come in the form of God allowing some pressure into my life, so He can see by my confession what I believe in my heart. Once I learned this, I became painfully aware that I had failed many tests over the course of my life and that this was hindering me from entering into the promised land God had in store for me.

I have repented of my whining and unbelief and my confession now is, "God is my Lover, my Provider, my Defender and my Sustainer. I worship my God." This confession in times of pressure has allowed me to pass several tests, and helped me to press on into what God has promised me.

What Lets You Enter Your Land of God's Promised Abundance?

"But My servant Caleb, because he has had a different spirit and has followed Me fully, I will bring into the land which he entered, and his descendants shall take possession of it." (Num. 14:24, NASB)

What kind of a spirit is God looking for in those who would enter into their promised lands?

"Take care, brethren, that there not be in any one of you an evil, unbelieving heart that falls away from the living God. But encourage one another day after day, as long as it is still called 'Today,' so that none of you will be hardened by the deceitfulness of sin. For we have become partakers of Christ, if we hold fast the beginning of our assurance firm until the end, while it is said, 'Today if you hear His voice, Do not harden your hearts, as when they provoked Me.' For who provoked Him when they had heard? Indeed, did not all those who came out of Egypt led by Moses? And with whom was He angry for forty years? Was it not with those who sinned, whose bodies fell in the wilderness? And to whom did He swear that they would not enter His rest, but to those who were disobedient? So we see that they were not able to enter because of unbelief." (Heb. 3:12-19, NASB)

What Kind of Plan Does God Have for Our Lives?

"'For I know the plans I have for you,' declares the LORD, 'plans to prosper you and not to harm you, plans to give you hope and a future.'" (Jer. 29:11,12, NIV)

I believe God has a Promised Land experience for each of us. It touches our marriages, our health, our finances, our ministries and our children. We can ask God to give us a detailed picture of what our Promised Land looks like in each of these areas.

What attitude must a leader have who is going to lead people into their promised lands?

"Be strong and courageous, for you shall give this people possession of the land which I swore to their fathers to give them. Only be strong and very courageous; be careful to do according to all the law which Moses My servant commanded you; do not turn from it to the right or to the left, so that you may have success wherever you go. This book of the law shall not depart from your mouth, but you shall meditate on it day and night, so that you may be careful to do according to all that is written in it; for then you will make your way prosperous, and then you will have success. Have I not commanded you? Be strong and courageous! Do not tremble or be dismayed, for the Lord your God is with you wherever you go." (Josh. 1:6-9 NASB)

Unwavering faith in the power of Almighty God flowing in and through you is a must! Total obedience to the voice of God at all times is a must! Meditating on, speaking forth and obeying the Bible at all times is a must, because then you make your way prosperous and then you have success.

Since standing in faith and not whining during times of testing is crucial to each of us if we are going to enter the lands God has promised to us, we are going to take some time below and explore **in depth how one stands in faith** in the midst of personal adversities.

✳ ✳ ✳ ✳ ✳ ✳

The next section is written by Dr. Gary Greig, one of my spiritual advisors.

"How to Survive and Thrive in the Purging Before the Promised Land"

Overview of the nine steps: The most important steps in prayer the Lord has taught us to cooperate with His purging necessary to come into His promises for us,

Notes

to break off every attack of the enemy and be filled with the life and peace of Christ are: (1) Treating the Lord as our treasure before the promise comes; (2) Being filled with the Holy Spirit; (3) Quieting ourselves in His presence; (4) Confessing all revealed sins; (5) Submitting ourselves to the Lord; (6) Dying to self and circumstances; (7) Giving thanks for everything; and (8) Receiving the Lord's life, peace, and power to (9) Do whatever He says in moving closer to the promise.

The key is to focus your thoughts and your mind's-eye on Jesus (Heb. 3:1; 12:2) and His light surrounding you (Heb. 1:3; Matt. 17:2-5; 1 John 1:5-7) and dispelling the darkness of the lies, the temptations, and the demons the enemy is sending against you. As you pray these prayers, don't focus on or think about the lies, the dark feelings, the enemy and get swallowed up in the darkness of the attack, but look at and think about Jesus, His truth, His radiant presence and light and see His light and truth driving out the lies and darkness that are attacking you.

The nine prayer steps listed:

1) Make the Lord and His presence your treasure before the promise comes.

2) Get filled with the Holy Spirit in worship.

3) Quiet yourself, forget about yourself and think only of the Lord Jesus — center yourself on Him.

4) Confess all sins the Lord shows you.

5) Submit yourself and the circumstances to the Lord.

6) Die to self, die to fears and sinful desires, and die to the circumstances that threaten you.

7) Give thanks in everything and give thanks for everything.

8) Receive the life, peace and power of "Christ in you, the hope of glory" (Col. 1:27).

9) Then just listen to the Lord's voice and obey what He says to do.

The nine prayer steps are expanded below:

1) The Lord and His Presence Are Our Treasure Before the Promise Comes.

Genesis 15:1 *"Do not be afraid Abram. I am your shield and your very great reward."* (God was speaking to Abram at about age 80, as he waited for God's promised miracle son. Abram had about 20 more years to wait at this point until Isaac was born and the promise fulfilled — Genesis 12:4 and 17:24,25)

Job 22:25 *"Then the Almighty will be your gold, the choicest silver for you."*

Psalm 16:5-8 [literal Hebrew] *"Lord, You are my food portion and my cup; you are holding my lot securely....I will praise the Lord who counsels me; even at night my heart instructs me; I set the Lord always before me; because He is at my right hand I will not be shaken."*

Psalm 73:26 *"God is the strength of my heart and my portion forever."*

Psalm 119:57 *"You are my portion, O Lord, as I promise to obey your words."*

John 4:34 *"'My food,' Jesus said, 'is to do the will of Him who sent Me and to finish His work.'"*

Psalm 142:5 *"You are my refuge, my portion in the land of the living."*

Psalm 37:4 *"Delight yourself in the Lord [Heb. "treasure unto yourself the Lord"] and He will give you the desires of your heart."*

Psalm 63:3 *"Your love is better than life."*

Isaiah 58:14 *"Then you will treasure unto yourself the Lord, and I will cause you to ride on the heights of the land, and to feast on the inheritance of your father Jacob."*

Pray: "Lord, I thank You that You are my shield protecting me and my very great reward. You are my treasure, o Lord. Your presence, Your Spirit is the source of my life and all that I need (2 Pet. 1:3). Thank You that it is You that brings me all the energy I need, all the money and provision I need, all the protection I need, all the wisdom and skill I need, all the friendship and fellowship I need.

"Lord, I thank You that You are my food portion and my cup, that as I obey You, I feed off Your presence and drink of Your Spirit, so that Your Spirit energizes me like food and drink (John 4:34; Ps. 119:57; Ps. 16:5). Help me be jealous for Your presence, o Lord, and to hate everything that would compete with Your presence in my life. Thank You that when I put You first in my life, You will give me new strength, You will provide my needs and guide and protect me, and You will bring me into Your promises for me in Your time."

2) Get Filled with the Holy Spirit (Eph. 5:18); Worship the Lord and Through Praise and Worship Ask the Holy Spirit to Fill You Up.

John 7:37,38 *"On the last and greatest day of the Feast, Jesus stood and said in a loud voice, 'If anyone is thirsty, let him come to Me and drink. Whoever believes in Me, as the Scripture has said, out of his belly shall flow streams of living water.'"*

a) Put your hand on your stomach as you spiritually **drink of and breathe in the Holy Spirit's presence.** It corresponds to the "belly" mentioned in John 7:38 (Greek *koilia* "belly, stomach") as a picture of your innermost being and it will help you cooperate with the flow of the Holy Spirit from your innermost being to fill your whole body, soul, spirit, mind, and emotions.

b) **Be Thirsty** — Tell the Lord you are thirsty for His Spirit to fill you and renew your spirit, soul, and body (Ps. 42:1). Pray: "Lord Jesus, I am thirsty for Your Presence and Your Spirit to fill my spirit, soul and body, my mind and my emotions to overflowing (Ps. 42:2; 63:1). Lord Jesus, You are my portion and my cup (Ps. 16:5); You are my shield and my very great reward (Gen. 15:1); Your presence is my gold and choicest silver (Job 22:25); I treasure You and Your presence (Ps. 37:4); I love You more than money, more than the praise of people, more than anything else in life."

c) **Come To Jesus' Presence** — Fix your mind's-eye on Jesus ("fixing our eyes on Jesus" — Heb. 12:2) and picture yourself stepping into the radiance of His presence (Jesus is "the radiance of God's glory" — Heb. 1:3). Pray: "Jesus, I come into the radiance, the glory, and the light of Your presence; I need You and Your Spirit more than the air I breathe."

d) **Drink of Jesus and Breathe/Drink in His Holy Spirit** through your faith and desire. Pray: "Lord Jesus, by my faith in You and my desire for You I now drink of You and Your Holy Spirit into my spirit, soul and body, and I thank You that Your Spirit is now filling my spirit, soul and body to overflowing. I drink and breathe You into myself, Holy Spirit." (Remember Jesus breathed on the disciples for them to receive the Holy Spirit in John 20:22, suggesting that we can breathe the Holy Spirit in as an act of receiving His daily filling of us.)

e) **Believe and Depend on Jesus** for His Holy Spirit to flow and break the yoke of every attack and burden. Pray: "Lord, I am depending on You to cause rivers of Your Holy Spirit to flow within me now. Jesus, I drink of Your Spirit; Come, Holy Spirit! Come, Holy Spirit, rest on me and on us! Holy Spirit, I breathe in Your peace, I breathe in Your joy, I breathe in Your anointing of faith, I breathe in Your patience, I breathe in Your purity, I breathe in Your quiet strength and power...."

3) Quiet Yourself, Forget About Yourself and Think Only of the Lord Jesus — Center Yourself on Him.

Isaiah 30:15 "*In repentance and rest is your salvation; in quietness and trust is your strength.*"

Pray: "Lord Jesus, I still and quiet my own mind and spirit now to focus on You, Your presence and power in me and around me. Help me turn my mind fully on You, Lord Jesus. I choose to forget my issues and leave them all at Your feet so that I can worship You. Thank You for Your life and death, Your blood that releases me from all my sins, and from all evil, and from all the enemy's power.

"I receive Your strength and power from which all life comes, and which quells every storm around me and in me. Jesus, I praise You for Your holiness, for Your glory and radiance shining around me and in me, for Your ever-burning light and life filling me now by Your Holy Spirit. Jesus, I praise You for Your mercy and Your purity and Your power to heal me and to bring me and my circumstances under Your control and into Your path for my life."

4) Confess All Sins the Lord Shows You that may have opened a door to the enemy and given him a foothold to attack you (Eph. 4:27).

1 John 1:5-9 *"God is light; in him there is no darkness at all. If we claim to have fellowship with him yet walk in the darkness, we lie and do not live by the truth. But if we walk in the light, as he is in the light, we have fellowship with one another, and the blood of Jesus, his Son, purifies us from all sin. If we claim to be without sin, we deceive ourselves and the truth is not in us. If we confess our sins, he is faithful and just and will forgive us our sins and purify us from all unrighteousness."*

Pray: "Lord, please show me where I have grieved You in any way. I confess… (Specify the sins the Lord shows you.). Lord Jesus, I receive the forgiveness of Your blood covering my sin, covering me, and covering all that belongs to me."

5) Submit Yourself and Your Circumstances to the Lord; put all on the altar before Him, and release all your control to the Lord.

James 4:7,8 *"Submit yourselves, then, to God. Resist the devil, and he will flee from you. Come near to God and he will come near to you. Wash your hands, you sinners, and purify your hearts, you double-minded."*

Pray: "Lord Jesus, I thank You that You are a God of order and a God of peace (1 Cor. 14:33; Rom. 16:20). By faith I receive and I breathe in Your order and peace, Holy Spirit, and Your power and life to fill me and my circumstances. I stay my mind and lean it upon You, Lord Jesus, depending on You for protection and strength in all things (Isa 26:3).

"I praise You, Lord Jesus, that You are an ever-present help when I am in trouble (Ps. 46:1-3) and that You are 'Immanuel' God-with-us Who is right beside me right now (Matt. 1:23; Isa. 7:14). Lord, keep my mind and my heart humble before You so that You can teach me Your way of peace in these circumstances (Ps. 25:9; Prov. 16:7; Isa. 59:8). Keep my head and my attitude low in humility before You and Your people; keep me walking in the fear of the Lord. I surrender my desires to You. Let Your will be done — Your will is my will and I ask for your grace and power to give up my will for Your will in these circumstances."

6) Die to Self, Die to Fears and Sinful Desires, and Die to the Circumstances That Threaten You. Release Them to the Lord.

Galatians 2:20 *"I have been crucified with Christ and I no longer live, but Christ lives in me. The life I live in the body, I live by faith in the Son of God, who loved me and gave himself for me."*

Romans 6:11 *"In the same way, count yourselves dead to sin but alive to God in Christ Jesus."*

Romans 8:13 *"For if you live according to the sinful nature, you will die; but if by the Spirit you put to death the misdeeds of the body, you will live."*

Psalm 46:10 *"Be still [Heb. Let go (one's grip)], and know that I am God."*

Mark 8:34,35 *"If anyone would come after me, he must deny himself and take up his cross and follow me. For whoever wants to save his life will lose it, but whoever loses his life for me and for the gospel will save it."*

Pray: "Lord, I die to myself and my desires… (Specify them!). I die to all sinful desires that are coming into my mind and feelings now… (Specify them.). I die to all feelings and thoughts that are not of You, Lord Jesus (fear, dread, abandonment, insecurity, anger, bitterness, etc. — Specify them.) and in the authority of Jesus' Name, I put them to death by the power of the Holy Spirit (Rom. 8:13) and the power of the blood of Jesus (Rev. 1:5) and break them off of me. I break off all demons bringing these desires, feelings and thoughts against me and I command them to leave me now (James 4:7,8 and Matt. 4:10; 16:23; Rev. 12:11; Eph. 2:1,2; 4:27 and context; 2 Tim. 1:7; Rom. 8:15; Luke 13:11; Zech. 13:2; Hos. 4:12; 1 Kings 22:22).

"Lord, help me not look at and think about the things that are not from You — the darkness and the demonic forces — so that I am swallowed up by the darkness coming against me now. But help me to focus on You, Lord Jesus and Your Presence, Your light, Your power, Your purity in my mind and heart now, Lord. Your Word says that 'God is light and in Him is no darkness' (1 John 1:5). Help me walk in the light, as You are in the light, so that I can have fellowship with You, and so that Your blood, Lord Jesus, can purify me from all sin (1 John 1:6-9). Fill me up, Holy Spirit, with the thoughts and feelings that come from the Lord Jesus!

"I die to these circumstances that are threatening or pressuring me (not being able to pay my bills, the possibility of losing my house, car, apartment, losing this or that friendship, losing my job, not knowing which direction to take, etc. Specify them.). I release them to You, Lord. If it is Your will that I go through the worst-case scenario, I release myself and die to self to go through it for Your sake, Lord Jesus, and to lose my life and my will for Your sake, because I love You, Lord. Let Your will be done rather than my will.

"Let me feel Your peace that is within me, Your power and Your strength to endure whatever You let happen to me and to love You and obey You through it step-by-step. Thank You, Lord, that You are making me more aware of Your light which fills me, Your Spirit, and Your love, and that you will give me victory in Christ and that I will find Your grace and strength in time of need (Heb. 4:16). Lead me in Your steps of peace that will bring Your salvation and breakthrough into my life and my circumstances (Isa. 52:7)."

7) Give Thanks *in* Everything and Give Thanks *for* Everything

Give thanks to the Lord not only for the good things in your circumstances but also for the bad things. Welcome the Lord's jurisdiction and power over the bad things by thanking Him and praising Him for them ("You are the Holy One Who is enthroned in the praises of Israel" — Ps. 22:3), because He is working for our good through the bad as well as the good.

Ephesians 5:20 *"Always giving thanks to God the Father FOR (Greek huper) everything, in the name of our Lord Jesus Christ."*

1 Thessalonians 5:18 *"Give thanks in all circumstances, for this is God's will for you in Christ Jesus."*

Romans 8:28 *"And we know that in all things God works for the good of those who love him, who have been called according to his purpose."*

Pray: "Lord Jesus, I thank You for… (Specify the **positive things** in your circumstances.). Lord Jesus, I also thank You for all the bad and hard things… (Specify the **negative things** in your circumstances.) and thank You that You are working for my good through these bad things happening to me. I forgive all those who are and have been hurting me, betraying me, or giving me a hard time. Show me Your steps and path of peace through these circumstances. Come in, Holy Spirit, and fill these circumstances with Your will and Your power so that Your will is done in them and in me. Jesus, have Your way in me, and I thank You that Your way is the best way for me."

8) Receive the Life, Peace, and Power of "Christ in You, the Hope of Glory" (Col. 1:27).

John 15:5 *"I am the Vine; you are the branches. If a person remains in Me and I in them, they will bear much fruit; apart from Me you can do nothing."*

1 Corinthians 6:17 *"He who unites himself with the Lord is one with Him in spirit."*

Isaiah 26:3 *"You will keep in perfect peace him whose mind is steadfast, because he trusts in you."*

Isaiah 40:31 *"But those who hope in the LORD will renew their strength. They will soar on wings like eagles; they will run and not grow weary, they will walk and not be faint."*

Pray: "Lord, I rest in Your faithfulness and I ask You, Jesus, to release in me through Your living presence within, Your peace, Your stability, Your power, Your purity, Your patience, Your clarity, Your prophetic revelation, Your wisdom, Your plans and strategies. Please release in me the mind of Christ (1 Cor. 2:16).

"Lord, I praise You that You are the Vine and I am the branch. I thank You that the branch and the vine are one and You are the Branch as well (John 15:5). I am in You and You are in me (John 14:20). I thank You that You are the roots, the flower, the fruit — You are more than I can ask for or desire and I am one with You (1 Cor. 6:17).

"Thank You that I am one with Your fullness, that I don't have to strive to receive Your holiness, Your power, Your provision, Your peace, but that as I believe and accept the fact that I am one with You and give thanks to You for it, Your life and resources are released in me, and I will find it to be so indeed in me and in my circumstances (Eph. 3:19).

"Thank You that when my body and mind can't take any more pressure, Your life and power release me and lift all the strain and weight off of me (Matt. 11:28-30) and Your ocean of light and life and holiness and peace and stability are instantly released in me as I rest in You and Your faithfulness.

"Thank You, Lord Jesus, that all that I need is in You and Your presence. Thank You that all that I need for my life (food, clothing, provision, money, etc.) and for the power of godly living comes from your Holy Spirit's power released in me through knowing You, Jesus (2 Pet. 1:3). Thank You, Lord, that I have been given fullness in You and that You are the head of every power and authority (Col. 2:10) so that You have absolute miraculous control over all my circumstances.

"Thank You that I can rest in Your faithfulness. Thank You that even when I am faithless You remain faithful to me and faithful to all Your promises (2 Tim. 2:13; 2 Cor. 1:20). Thank You that Your faithfulness to me is great and Your mercies are new every morning (Lam. 3:22,23). Thank You that You will never forsake me as I trust in You (Ps. 37:28), that You are guarding my life (Ps. 97:10), and that You will be faithful to keep Your promises to me (Ps. 145:13 NIV). Thank You that You will never leave me nor forsake me (Heb. 13:5). You are always with me and You are my Helper so that man can do nothing to me and satan can do nothing to me without Your letting them through to me (Heb. 13:6).

"Thank You that because I am one with You (John 15:5; 1 Cor. 6:17), I cannot remain poor while You are rich, I cannot be without food and covering while You have these things in Your hands, I cannot be weak while You are strong, I cannot be without peace when You are the God of peace. Therefore I receive and thank You for Your riches (financial and spiritual), Your provision, Your peace, and Your strength right now, through the power of Your Holy Spirit releasing it to me. I believe that I have received it and thank You for it as if it were in my possession now and thank You that it will be mine (Mk. 11:22-24).

"Thank You that nothing can keep You, Lord Jesus, from carrying out Your will in my life. Thank You, Lord, that You are my Savior and that You bear my burdens daily (Ps. 68:19). Thank You that I do not have to be afraid because You are with me; I do not have to look anxiously about me, because You are my God and You will strengthen me. You will help me and uphold me with Your righteous right hand (Isa. 41:10). Thank You that Your resources for me are equal to every emergency that I might face (Phil. 4:13,19). Thank You that in the easiest situations You must give me Your grace and in the most difficult situations Your grace and strength will be just enough for me (2 Cor. 12:9).

"Thank You, Lord, that You cannot sin. In You I count myself dead to sin and alive to God (Rom. 6:11). Thank You that You can keep me from sinning and from offending You, as I depend on You (Gal. 2:20; Jude 24).

"Thank You, Lord Jesus, that I can do all things through Your strength and power in me (Phil. 4:13) and in me You can do all things that You are calling me to do (John 14:20; Gal. 2:20; Col. 1:27)."

9) Then Just Listen to the Lord's Voice and Obey What He Says to Do. This stage is when He works miracles in our circumstances.

John 10:27 "*My sheep listen to My voice; I know them, and they follow Me.*"

Matthew 11:28-30 "*Come to Me, all you who are weary and burdened, and I will give you rest. Take My yoke upon you and learn from Me, for I am gentle and humble in heart, and you will find rest for your souls. For My yoke is easy and My burden is light.*"

Pray: "Lord, show me Your heart and mind for these circumstances (or this problem I face, or this need that I have). Show me what You want me to do, and give me Your strength and strategy to do it."

(End of insights from Dr. Gary Greig.)

✳   ✳   ✳   ✳   ✳   ✳

As you can see from the way I have quoted my spiritual advisors throughout this book and even in the section that follows, they have had great impact on my life. I pray you will draw upon yours as much as I draw upon mine, and that yours will have equal impact on your life!

One issue which was a block to my walk of faith, and that I personally had to resolve, was my concern that if I openly confessed the promise of God to me, and the fulfillment of that promise was not yet manifested at the time of my death, I would look like a fool to all those standing around at my funeral. I suppose I shouldn't have been so concerned since at that point I would be out of here anyway but I hate appearing foolish, so I was always reticent to confess the amazing promises the Lord gave me in my journal.

Finally one day, I talked to the Lord about this concern, and He answered me this way: "Mark, if you die in faith confessing what I have told you to confess, you will not be a fool. I will put you in Hebrews 11 as a hero of faith." Wow! That revelation had never dawned on me. They, too, died in faith believing that what God had said would come to pass even though they did not see it in their lifetimes (Heb. 11:13).

In the same way, God may want me to die in faith, and not die complaining! I get it! I shall die in faith! I will give up whining! (Actually, God has taken a strong stand against complaining. He killed 14,700 people in one day for grumbling [Num. 16:41-50]. It really is not healthy to whine.)

This whole thing of fearful moaning is a big issue in many of our lives and in the Church today. I was saved at age 15 in a church that did not believe that God speaks anymore, nor that the Church could possibly win any battles against satan, encroaching evil in this world, or the antichrist.

We have learned from our review of Joshua's life that victory and success come by consulting God on every turn, hearing what He is saying, and then implementing it. So if a church does not believe God is speaking, they will not be able to participate in any Spirit-anointed victories. To make their doctrine consistent with their experience, they will develop a theology of satan winning, taking over the world through the antichrist and bringing in the Great Tribulation.

I suspect satan is more than happy to help his archenemy, the Church, build a belief that he is the powerful one, and the Church is the weak one. It appears he has succeeded, since the largest group of people on the earth today believing for the takeover of the world by satan, is satan's nemesis — the Christians! Of course, if satan can get the Church to believe he is the powerful one, to see it, confess it and act it, then he has won even if God never intended for him to win.

I sense in my heart that this belief of the Church <u>angers God greatly</u>, because He is absolutely sure that <u>He rules in the realm of mankind</u> and not satan (Dan. 4:26; 5:21; Deut. 10:17; Ps. 136:3; 1 Tim. 6:15; Rev. 17:14; 19:16). I sense in my heart that God views this as "**spiritual treason and spiritual adultery:**" The fact that His engaged Bride, the Church, is infatuated with the belief that the King's archenemy, satan, whom the King Himself defeated at great cost, will now expand his rule and reign, and will ravish and humiliate the King's Betrothed.

When I was in college, I took the time to back up from Scripture three totally different interpretations of the book of Revelation. At that point, I simply said, "I don't care any more. For now, my focus is on making my Christian life work and on getting the job done that God wants me to do, that of discipling the nations. The end times can transpire any way God wants them to. I don't know exactly how it will happen, but it is in God's hands and it will happen the way He intends it to." So for me, eschatology was put on the back burner for the next 20 years, other than that **I still believed the heart of the theology**, that things would get worse and worse, and evil would grow stronger and stronger.

I remember very vividly the day I was being pessimistic about the world and life, and Roger Miller, one of my spiritual advisors, made this comment to me: "**Leadership is automatically transferred to those who remain optimistic.**" Wow! That *rhema* of God burned in my heart like a searing fire. I wanted so much to be a leader in the world and make a difference for Christ, and yet my heart was in instant agreement with the *rhema* word Roger had spoken to me. Not many would want to follow me if I was a down-in-the-mouth pessimist!

That was the day I made a decision that I would be positive for the rest of my life. The quote from Roger stands in a frame on my desk for me to look at each and every day. Satan is not more powerful than God. Evil is not more powerful than Good. Darkness is not more powerful than Light.

My confession is:

- Light is more powerful than darkness!

- Truth is more powerful than error!

- Righteousness is more powerful than wickedness!

- God is more powerful than satan!

- Wherever I stand, darkness must flee!

- The Church **will** fulfill Christ's great commission to disciple all nations, and we **will** make His enemies His footstool (Acts 2:34-36)!

George Otis, Jr. is the CEO, Founder and President of The Sentinel Group (www.sentinelgroup.org), a Christian research and information agency dedicated to helping the Church pray knowledgably for end-time evangelization, and enabling communities to discover the pathway to genuine revival and societal transformation.

As an avid researcher, Mr. Otis has authored several books including *The Twilight Labyrinth, Informed Intercession* and *God's Trademarks.* He is also the executive producer of the award-winning videos, *Transformations, Transformations II: The Glory Spreads, The Quickening,* and *Let the Sea Resound.*

These faith-impacting videos document how entire communities are being transformed by people living out of the voice and power of God in our present age. If you have a passion to see your nation changed, these are a must for you to see. They will give you a vision of how God intends the Church to live and transform society. The Church is the victor. We are the salt of the earth. We are the light of the nations. We can and we do make a difference as we hear God's voice and live out of it.

Let the Sea Resound is their newest video, as of 2005. They describe it this way: "In an earlier, but not so distant, age the nation of Fiji groaned under the weight of superstition and sorcery; ancestral spirits roamed freely promising abundance, and demanding their due; tribal fighting was gruesome and frequent. Fueled by revenge and greed, violent warriors depopulated entire villages — even islands.

"Today's Fiji bears no resemblance to its former self. This 79-minute documentary covers the astonishing revival that is currently sweeping through the nation of Fiji. It is a moving and instructive testament of unprecedented Christian unity, contemporary signs and wonders, rapid church growth and genuine socio-political transformation. The breath of God has revived even the land and the sea."

One of the riveting things Jesus spoke into my journaling one day was this: **"Mark, whatever you focus on grows within you and whatever grows within you, you become."** This *rhema* word galvanized my approach to spiritual growth. I will fix my eyes upon Jesus (not my self, my sin, my weakness or my strength), and Jesus will grow within me.

And concerning eschatology — we surely have no command to fix our eyes upon the antichrist. But there is a clear command to fix our eyes upon our Lord and Savior Jesus Christ! And that is what I have chosen to do. The book of Revelation is about the revealing of Jesus Christ, not the antichrist (Rev. 1:1). Seeing the Risen Christ builds faith. Seeing the antichrist builds fear. I have tried fear and I have tried faith. As for me and my family, we have chosen faith.

Make sure that you are a child of faith so that people can follow you, and that you are a leader in discipling this world for our Lord and Savior, Jesus Christ. If you journal regularly, God will turn you into a child of faith as He did me. **Journal regularly! Become a child of faith** (Heb. 11:6; 1 John 5:4)!

In his book *Paradise Restored*, David Chilton has shown that according to the writings of the great historian Josephus, the prophecies of the antichrist, the tribulation, and the mark on the forehead or on the hand were fulfilled during the time of the Roman Empire, and therefore no longer need to be projected into the future. (This is not to say that satan isn't still around seeking to foster rebellion in people's hearts toward God, and building whatever he can through people's mistaken belief in him.)

If we don't need to project the reign of the antichrist into the future, then we are free to expect what God promised, the increase of His government!

David Barrett, author of the **World Christian Encyclopedia** discusses the growth of the Church. In 100 A.D. there was one Christian for every 360 non-Christians. By 2000 A.D. there was one professing Christian for every three non-Christians. **So statistics confirm that over the last 2,000 years there has been no end to the increase of God's government (Isa. 9:7)!** This, of course, means that there has been no end to the decrease of satan's government!

Let the Church rejoice and celebrate the ever-expanding kingdom of God! Let each one of us be an integral part of this expansion, even as Joshua was! Let each one of us take dominion over the area God has assigned to us.

May *you* disciple the area God has allotted to you, bringing it under the rule and reign of Christ.

I pray that you learn to live in obedience to the voice of God and that His Spirit-anointed victories become the pattern for your life, even as they were for Joshua! To the King be glory forever and ever — Amen!

God says:

"Of the increase of His government and peace there shall be no end, upon the throne of David, and upon His kingdom, to order it, and to establish it with judgment and with justice from henceforth even for ever. The zeal of the LORD of hosts will perform this." (Isaiah 9:7, emphasis added)

AMEN!

Personal Application Exercise: On six different days, journal out God's answer to the following questions concerning what His Promised Land blessings look like in your life:

- God, what is Your vision of my finances and what conditions do You want me to meet to see these blessings released in my life?

- God, what is Your vision of my health and what conditions do You want me to meet to see these blessings released in my life?

- God, what is Your vision of my marriage and what conditions do You want me to meet to see these blessings released in my life?

- God, what is Your vision of my family and what conditions do You want me to meet to see these blessings released in my life?

- God, what is Your vision of my ministry to the world and what conditions do You want me to meet to see these blessings released in my life?

- Lord, what is Your vision of our nation and this world and what conditions do You want me to meet to see this vision realized?

Maintain a journal which records the continuing instructions of God to you in each area and the steps you have taken and are taking to attain the above Promised Land which God has given to you in each and every area.

Additional journaling questions are suggested in Appendix L. Use them over the next three to six months to help you establish the place of consistent journaling in your life.

You may feel led to host Mark Virkler in your community for a weekend seminar on "How to Hear God's Voice." Details can be found at the following websites:

www.cwgministries.org/seminars

www.cwgministries.org/Tips-for-a-Successful-Seminar.htm

Notes

Notes

HOW CAN I GET CLOSER TO GOD?

You may wish you could improve your relationship with God. Or, you may want to be sure that you will go to heaven when you die. You may have enjoyed the journaling which Mark shared in this book and long to be able to have the same kind of experience in your own life. The wonderful thing is, you can! Here's how.

The Bible teaches that God hungers to share His love with you. In the Garden of Eden, God walked and talked with Adam and Eve in the cool of the day. That is what God wants to do with each of us, also. He yearns to be able to share His love with us and have us share our hearts with Him on a daily basis. As our Creator and Sustainer, He knows what we need even more than we do, and He answers our questions even before we ask.

God's heart was broken when sin entered into Adam and Eve's lives and stole away that relationship He had with them. The enemy tempted Adam and Eve to live like gods themselves, rather than enjoy the flow of God's life through them. In choosing to look to self, rather than looking beyond to the wonderful Giver of Life, Adam and Eve cut off much of the flow of God within them.

So God sent His Son, Jesus of Nazareth, in the form of a man, to remove the sin which separated mankind's heart from the heart of God. By entering the world as a man, God was able to take the sins of the entire world upon His own shoulders and pay the penalty of this separation by allowing His Son Jesus Christ to be separated from Him for a moment of time. That is why Jesus cried out while dying on the cross, "My God, My God, why have You forsaken Me?" However, in forsaking His Son for a moment of time, God was restoring the opportunity for you and me to return to the experience of the Garden of Eden and, once again, have fellowship with Almighty God. Once again, we could walk with Him in the cool of the day and share our lives with Him and have God share His life with us.

So our relationship with God can be enhanced. We can be sure of going to heaven by receiving the sacrifice of Jesus' life for our sins. The steps are quite clearly laid out in the Bible. They are as follows:

Notes

1. Acknowledge: "For all have sinned, and fall short of the glory of God" (Romans 3:23).

2. Repent: "Repent, then, and turn to God, so that your sins may be wiped out..." (Acts 3:19).

3. Confess: "If you confess with your mouth, 'Jesus is Lord,' and believe in your heart that God raised Him from the dead, you will be saved" (Romans 10:9).

4. Forsake: "Let the wicked forsake his way and the evil man his thoughts. Let him turn to the Lord...for He will freely pardon" (Isaiah 55:7).

5. Believe: "For God so loved the world that He gave His one and only Son, that whoever believes in Him shall not perish but have eternal life" (John 3:16).

6. Receive: "He came to that which was His own, but His own did not receive Him. Yet to all who received Him, to those who believed in His name, He gave the right to become children of God" (John 1:11,12).

We have this promise: "If the Spirit of Him who raised Jesus from the dead dwells in you, He who raised Christ Jesus from the dead will also give life to your mortal bodies through His Spirit who indwells you" (Romans 8:11).

A Prayer of Response

If you want a closer relationship with God, if you want to know for certain that when you die you will go to heaven, then offer the following prayer to God, from the depths of your heart. Pray aloud.

"Precious Holy Spirit, do a work in my heart as I offer the following prayer to God.

"God, I come to You in the name of Your Son, the Lord Jesus Christ. I acknowledge that I have sinned and fallen short of Your ways. I repent of my sin and ask that the blood of Jesus Christ cleanse me of all my sins. I receive this cleansing even now as You sweep over my soul. I confess with my mouth that Jesus Christ is the Son of God and the Lord of my life. I invite You, Jesus, to have first place in my heart and my life. I believe God raised Jesus from the dead, and that He is alive in my heart today. I forsake any evil ways and thoughts which I have harbored and this day turn my life over to Jesus. I ask, Jesus, that You fill my heart and my mind with Your ways and Your thoughts and that You begin a transforming work from within my heart and my spirit. By believing in Jesus and His life within me, I am assured a place in heaven with God. I receive eternal life this day. Thank You, Lord Jesus Christ. I yield myself right now to the moving of the Holy Spirit within my spirit. Holy Spirit,

Notes

please make this very real in my heart and let me sense You within me. May You seal this prayer this day."

Now just wait quietly for a few minutes in the presence of God and His Holy Spirit and see what you sense within. Lift up your eyes to Jesus and humbly receive His life within your soul.

Record below any impressions or sensations which you received in your heart and soul as you prayed this prayer.

Date I prayed this prayer: _____

Assurance: "But these are written that you may believe that Jesus is the Christ, the Son of God, and that believing you may have life in His name" (John 20:31).

If you have just prayed the above prayer, we invite you to write or call for a free book giving you an even deeper understanding of your salvation experience. Contact us at Communion With God Ministries, 1431 Bullis Road, Elma, NY 14059. Telephone 800-466-6961.

We also have a series of follow-up courses utilizing books, cassettes, and videos which will train you in many spiritual areas and equip you for greater effectiveness in all of life. These materials can be used in independent study or as an external degree course through Christian Leadership University, a program which leads to Bachelor's, Master's, and Doctoral degrees.

We love you and do want to hear from you if you have just prayed to receive Christ, so do contact us.

Yours in Christ,
Mark & Patti Virkler

--------------------------------- RESPONSE FORM ---------------------------------

Name _____ Phone _____

Address _____

_____

I prayed to accept Jesus Christ as my Lord and Savior on the following date _____.

_____ Please send me free information on additional courses which I may take through Christian Leadership University which will help strengthen my life.

Notes

BRAIN PREFERENCE INDICATOR TEST

1.   In a problem-solving situation, do you:

_____ a.   take a walk and mull solutions over, then discuss them?

_____ b.   think about and write down all alternatives, arrange them according to priorities, and then pick the best?

_____ c.   recall past experiences that were successful and implement them?

_____ d.   wait to see if the situation will right itself?

2.   Daydreaming is:

_____ a.   a waste of time.

_____ b.   amusing and relaxing.

_____ c.   a real help in problem-solving and creative thinking.

_____ d.   a viable tool for planning my future.

3.   Glance quickly at this picture.

Was the face smiling?

_____ a.   yes

_____ b.   no

4.   Concerning hunches:

_____ a.   I frequently have strong ones and follow them.

_____ b.   I occasionally have hunches and place much faith in them.

_____ c.   I occasionally have hunches but don't place much faith in them.

_____ d.   I would not rely on hunches to help me make important decisions.

5. In thinking about the activities of your day, which is most typical of your "style"?

     _____ a.   I make a list of all the things I need to do…people to see.

     _____ b.   I picture the places I will go, people I'll see, things I'll do.

     _____ c.   I just let it happen.

     _____ d.   I plan the day's schedule, block out appropriate times for each item or activity.

6. Do you usually have a place for everything, a system for doing things, and an ability to organize information and materials?

     _____ a.   yes

     _____ b.   no

7. Do you like to move your furniture, change the decor of your home or office frequently?

     _____ a.   yes

     _____ b.   no

8. Pleace check which of these activites you enjoy:

_____ swimming	_____ travel
_____ tennis	_____ bicycling
_____ golf	_____ collecting
_____ camping/hiking	_____ writing
_____ skiing	_____ chess
_____ fishing	_____ bridge
_____ singing	_____ roulette
_____ gardening	_____ charades
_____ playing an instrument	_____ dancing
_____ home improvements	_____ walking
_____ sewing	_____ running
_____ reading	_____ hugging
_____ arts/crafts	_____ kissing
_____ cooking	_____ touching
_____ photography	_____ chatting
_____ doing nothing	_____ debating

9. Do you learn athletics and dance better by:

     _____ a.   imitation, getting the feel of the music or game?

     _____ b.   learning the sequence and repeating the steps mentally?

10. In sports or performing in public, do you often perform better than your training and natural abilities warrant?

     _____ a.   yes

     _____ b.   no

11.   Do you express yourself well verbally?

_____ a.   yes

_____ b.   no

12.   Are you goal-oriented?

_____ a.   yes

_____ b.   no

13.   When you want to remember directions, a name, or a news item, do you:

_____ a.   visualize the information?

_____ b.   write notes?

_____ c.   verbalize it (repeat it to yourself or out loud)?

_____ d.   associate it with previous information?

14.   Do you remember faces easily?

_____ a.   yes

_____ b.   no

15.   In the use of language, do you:

_____ a.   make up words?

_____ b.   devise rhymes and incorporate metaphors?

_____ c.   choose exact, precise terms?

16.   In a communication situation, are you more comfortable being the:

_____ a.   listener

_____ b.   talker

17.   When you are asked to speak extemporaneously at a meeting, do you:

_____ a.   make a quick outline?

_____ b.   just start talking?

_____ c.   shift the focus to someone else or say as little as possible?

_____ d.   speak slowly and carefully?

18.   In an argument, do you tend to:

_____ a.   talk until your point is made?

_____ b.   find an authority to support your point?

_____ c.   just become withdrawn?

_____ d.   push chair or table, pound table, talk louder — yell?

19.   Can you tell fairly accurately how much time has passed without looking at your watch?

_____ a.   yes

_____ b.   no

20.   Do you prefer social situations that are:

_____ a.   planned in advance?

_____ b.   spontaneous?

21.   In preparing yourself for a new or difficult task, do you:

_____ a.   visualize yourself accomplishing it effectively?

_____ b.   recall past successes in similar situations?

_____ c.   prepare extensive data regarding the task?

22.   Do you prefer working alone or in a group?

_____ a.   alone

_____ b.   group

23.   When it comes to "bending the rules" or altering company policy, do you feel:

_____ a.   rules and policy are to be followed?

_____ b.   progress comes through challenging the structure?

_____ c.   rules are made to be broken?

24.   In school, did you prefer:

_____ a.   algebra

_____ b.   geometry

25.   Which of these handwriting positions most closely resembles yours?

_____ a.   regular right-hand position

_____ b.   hooked right-hand position (fingers pointing toward your chest)

_____ c.   regular left-hand position

_____ d.   hooked left-hand position (fingers pointing toward your chest)

26.   In note taking, do you print:

_____ a.   never

_____ b.   frequently

27.   Do you use gestures to

_____ a.   emphasize a point?

_____ b.   express your feeling?

28.   Do you instinctively feel an issue is right or correct, or do you decide on the basis of information?

_____ a.   feel

_____ b.   decide

29.   I enjoy risks.

_____ a.   yes

_____ b.   no

30. After attending a musical:

_____ a. I can hum many parts of the score.

_____ b. I can recall many of the lyrics.

31. Please hold a pencil perpendicularly to the ground at arm's length, centered in your line of vision and lined up with a frame, board, or door. Holding that position, close your left eye. Did your pencil appear to move?

_____ a. yes

Close your right eye, Did your pencil appear to move?

_____ b. yes

32. Sit in a relaxed position and clasp your hands comfortably in your lap. Which thumb is on top?

_____ a. left

_____ b. right

_____ c. parallel

33. Check as many of these items as you feel are true about you:

_____ I can extract meaning from contracts, instruction manuals, and legal documents.

_____ I can understand schematics and diagrams.

_____ I strongly visualize the characters, setting, and plot of reading material.

_____ I prefer that friends phone in advance of their visits.

_____ I dislike chatting on the phone.

_____ I find it satisfying to plan and arrange the details of a trip.

_____ I postpone making telephone calls.

_____ I can easily find words in a dictionary, names in a phone book.

_____ I love puns.

_____ I take lots of notes at meetings and lectures.

_____ I freeze when I need to operate mechanical things under stress.

_____ Ideas frequently come to me out of nowhere.

34. I have:

_____ a. frequent mood changes.

_____ b. almost no mood changes.

35. I am:

_____ a. not very conscious of body language. I prefer to listen to what people say.

_____ b. good at interpreting body language.

_____ c. good at understanding what people say and also the body language they use.

Scoring Key

Here is the scoring key to the self-test. Enter the numbers of each answer you checked in the right-hand column provided. List the sum of the numbers in the two column questions.

1.	a. 7	b. 1	c. 3	d. 9	_____
2.	a. 1	b. 5	c. 7	d. 9	_____
3.	a. 3	b. 7			_____
4.	a. 9	b. 7	c. 3	d. 1	_____
5.	a. 1	b. 7	c. 9	d. 3	_____
6.	a. 1	b. 9			_____
7.	a. 9	b. 1			_____

8.					
	swimming	9	travel	5	_____
	tennis	4	bicycling	8	_____
	golf	4	collecting	1	_____
	camping/hiking	7	writing	2	_____
	skiing	7	chess	2	_____
	fishing	8	bridge	2	_____
	singing	3	roulette	7	_____
	gardening	5	charades	5	_____
	playing an instrument	4	dancing	7	_____
	home improvements	3	walking	8	_____
	sewing	3	running	8	_____
	reading	3	hugging	9	_____
	arts/crafts	5	kissing	9	_____
	cooking	5	touching	9	_____
	photography	3	chatting	4	_____
	doing nothing	9	debating	2	_____

9.	a. 9	b. 1			_____

10.	a. 9	b.1			_____
11.	a. 1	b. 7			_____
12.	a. 1	b. 9			_____
13.	a. 9	b. 1	c. 3	d. 5	_____
14.	a. 7	b. 1			_____
15.	a. 9	b. 5	c. 1		_____
16.	a. 6	b. 3			_____
17.	a. 1	b. 6	c. 9	d. 4	_____
18.	a. 3	b. 1	c. 7	d. 9	_____
19.	a. 1	b. 9			_____
20.	a. 1	b. 9			_____
21.	a. 9	b. 5	c. 1		_____
22.	a. 3	b. 7			_____
23.	a. 1	b. 5	c. 9		_____
24.	a. 1	b. 9			_____
25.	a. 1	b. 7	c. 9	d. 3	_____
26.	a. 1	b. 9			_____
27.	a. 2	b. 8			_____
28.	a. 9	b. 1			_____
29.	a. 7	b. 3			_____
30.	a. 9	b. 1			_____
31.	a. 8	b. 2			_____
32.	a. 1	b. 9	c. 5		_____

33.	contracts	1	postpone	7	_____
	schematics	7	find words	1	_____
	visualize	9	puns	3	_____
	advance	2	notes	1	_____
	chatting	3	freeze	3	_____
	plan trip	1	nowhere	9	_____

| 34. | a. 9 | b. 1 | | | _____ |
| 35. | a. 1 | b. 7 | c. 5 | | _____ |

Now add the number of points you listed on the right column and divide the total by the number of answers you checked. (This latter number will vary among testers, since questions 8 and 33 have a large number of parts.) For example: if your points totaled 300 in 40 answers, your Brain Preference Indicator (BPT) would be 7.5.

Left ——— Right
  1   2   3   4   5   6   7   8   9

The questions in this self-test cover the most salient differences between dominant rights and lefts.

A score of 5 would indicate that you are using both haves of your brain together quite easily. A score near 1 or 9 would indicate an extreme brain hemisphere preference, and you should work on cultivating a greater ability to use the other hemisphere of your brain. Most scores will range between 3 and 7.

The one who uses **all** the giftedness inherent within him will be more effective in service to the King, especially as he learns to yield these abilities for the Holy Spirit to flow through.

Side note: Having all the members of your family take this test and discussing the scores and differencess should improve family relationships considerably. Remember, we are not out to try to change others' personalities, but to understand them and come alongside them and support them. I personally am a Luke. I get my revelation in a method similar to Luke's, using a lot of investigation. Others will be more like John. We do not have to turn Lukes into Johns or Johns into Lukes. Honor the differences which God has place within His body. Don't try to change them.

"*RHEMA*" IN THE BIBLE

Below are all 70 uses of the word "*rhema*" in the New Testament. Look up these verses and see what the Lord reveals to you. I noticed that they never referred to written words, making them distinct from *logos*, which can include words written down. *Rhema* means "spoken word," and occasionally a "supernatural event."

Notes

Rhema is translated "word" in the following 54 passages:

Matt. 4:4	Matt. 12:36
Matt. 18:16	Matt. 26:75
Matt. 27:14	Mark 14:72
Luke 1:38	Luke 2:29
Luke 3:2	Luke 4:4
Luke 5:5	Luke 20:26
Luke 24:8	Luke 24:11
John 3:34	John 5:47
John 6:63	John 6:68
John 8:20	John 8:47
John 10:21	John 12:47
John 12:48	John 14:10
John 15:7	John 17:8
Acts 2:14	Acts 5:20
Acts 6:11	Acts 6:13
Acts 10:22	Acts 10:37
Acts 10:44	Acts 11:14

Acts 11:16	Acts 13:42
Acts 16:38	Acts 26:25
Acts 28:25	Rom. 10:8 (2)
Rom. 10:17	Rom. 10:18
2 Cor. 12:4	2 Cor. 13:1
Eph. 5:26	Eph. 6:17
Heb. 1:3	Heb. 6:5
Heb. 11:3	Heb. 12:19
1 Pet. 1:25 (2)	2 Pet. 3:2
Jude 17	Rev. 17:17

Rhema is translated "saying" in the following eight passages:

Mark 9:32	Luke 1:65
Luke 2:17	Luke 2:50
Luke 2:51	Luke 9:45 (2)
Luke 7:1	Luke 18:34

Rhema is translated "thing" in the following three passages:

Luke 2:15	Luke 2:19	Acts 5:32

Additional verses:

Matthew 5:11: "Shall say all manner of evil [lit., every evil *rhema*] against you falsely...."

Luke 1:37: "With God nothing [lit., not any word] shall be impossible."

THE ORIGIN OF THOUGHTS, BIBLICALLY AND PHILOSOPHICALLY

The Origin of Thoughts, Biblically Speaking

The thoughts are in my head, so didn't they originate with me? The biblical answer is, "Not necessarily." The Bible is very clear to say that our thoughts may come from any of three sources: self, the Holy Spirit or demons. This understanding is critical for the person seeking to live his life out of the voice of God since God's voice will often come as a spontaneous thought which is sensed as being in our minds. Some thoughts come from God, and yes, some come from satan.

God did not create man as a self-contained unit. God calls us vessels (2 Cor. 4:7). A vessel, of course, is designed to be filled with something. We are designed to be filled with God (2 Cor. 4:7). However, in the Garden of Eden, satan tempted man to live out of self, and man fell to the temptation. Since that point in time, man can have self's thoughts, and self is the filling station for satan. So now we find that we can also be filled with satan and his demons. Thus our thoughts can come from God, self, or satan.

Humans are composed of a spirit, soul and body (1 Thess. 5:23). Our spirits are designed to be united or joined to another Spirit. Before we invited the Lord Jesus Christ into our hearts to be our Lord and Savior, the Bible tells us that we had evil spirits working within us ("[You were obedient to and under the control of] the [demon] spirit that still constantly works in the sons of disobedience" Eph. 2:2 AMP). Once we are saved, the Holy Spirit is joined to our spirits (1 Cor. 6:17) and His work within us quickly grows and expands.

Both demons and the Holy Spirit can give us thoughts (Luke 22:3; Acts 5:3; 1 Cor. 2:10). In both cases, they are registered in our minds as spontaneous thoughts. Spontaneous or flowing thoughts come from the spirit world. John 7:37-39 teaches

Notes

that the flow we sense within is coming from the Spirit. Conversely, analytical thoughts come from our use of our rational minds.

When we are attempting to discern the voice of God from our own or satan's impulses, we need to begin by determining if the thoughts were spontaneous or analytical. If they are spontaneous, they have come from the spirit world. Now we need to determine if they came from the Holy Spirit or from evil spirits.

If the tenor of the thoughts lines up with the names and character of satan, they are coming from satan; if the tone of the thoughts line up with the names or character of the Holy Spirit, then they are probably coming from God. (Occasionally satan will manifest himself as an angel of light and give us thoughts which appear to be God's thoughts.)

Spirit-led reasoning can be defined as allowing flowing pictures and words from the Holy Spirit to guide our reasoning process. We can ask for this and seek it out by properly posturing our hearts before the Holy Spirit (John 7:37-39; Ps. 73 – David reasoned in the sanctuary of God).

Demonically-led reasoning is when we allow flowing pictures and words from demons to guide our reasoning process. An idle or undisciplined mind will quickly fall into this trap. The result will be thoughts that reflect the purposes of satan: condemnation, fear, lust, anger, lies, and every form of wickedness.

This is why the Bible instructs us to "take every thought captive" (2 Cor. 10:3-5). We must ensure that we only allow the Holy Spirit to use our minds, not self or satan, if we are to grow strong in faith and in the holiness of the Lord.

"Western study," which can be defined as "man using his reasoning capacity," gives us reasoned knowledge. "Biblical meditation," which is "the Holy Spirit utilizing all faculties in both hemispheres of man's brain," gives us revelation knowledge. Study is man in action. Meditation is God in action.

Study gives me what Paul called "knowledge" which comes through the strength of the flesh — me using my mind myself (Phil. 3:4-8). Meditation gives me what Paul called "true knowledge" (Col. 2:2), or revelation knowledge (Eph. 1:17,18; Luke 24:32) — knowledge birthed by the Spirit of God. Paul repudiated the reasoned knowledge he obtained in his Bible school learning (Phil. 3:1-11), in favor of the revelation knowledge he received while alone with God in the Arabian desert (Gal. 1:12,17,18).

God's plan from the beginning, from the Garden of Eden, was that we would be in daily communication with Him and He would grant revelation knowledge into our hearts (Gen. 3:8,9). Living this way would result in the work we do being birthed by and anointed with the Holy Spirit's power. Jesus lived that way Himself, doing nothing of His own initiative but living totally from divine impulse, or we could say out of *rhema* and vision (John 5:19,20,30).

Satan's plan was to tempt man to live out of himself, to figure things out on his own, without divine revelation. God had commanded him not to eat from the tree of the knowledge of good and evil for it would surely bring about spiritual death or loss of divine communication between them if they did (Gen 2:17).

Satan convinced Eve that if she ate from it (tried using her own mind herself) it would not result in loss of spiritual communion or death, but instead would make her smart like God and able to know things on her own, without having to get the knowledge from God through spiritual union. He said to Eve, "For God knows that in the day you eat from it your eyes will be opened, and you will be like God, knowing good and evil." (Gen. 3:5). This one step caused mankind to descend into a philosophy called rational humanism, which we will discuss in a moment.

A more complete discussion of the role of the mind can be found in chapter five of *Wading Deeper Into the River of God* by Mark and Patti Virkler.

The Origin of Thoughts, Philosophically Speaking

Joseh Pieper has written a book entitled *Divine Madness, Plato's Case Against Secular Humanism* published by Ignatius. Plato (428–347 B.C.) believed that knowledge could be obtained through three primary sources: reason, sense knowledge and divine madness.

Divine Madness was defined by Plato as "the god-given state of being-beside-oneself," which in Plato's mind included the receiving of prophecy. When I reflect on people receiving prophecies from God, the following scenes come to mind as possibly being perceived and labeled "divine madness."

I am reminded of Samuel's "Schools of the Prophets" which got a bit hairy when Saul prophesied and stripped off his clothes and lay naked all day and all night. (1 Sam. 19:20-24). Divine Madness also brings to mind the practice of "treeing demons" during John Wesley's revivals, where people would chase demons up trees after they had been cast out. I consider this as a prophetic gesture that was demonstrating what God was doing among them. Divine Madness reminds me of some of the revivalist scenes I have seen at Toronto Airport Christian Fellowship, where I have seen people strewn out on the floor, some shaking violently, as they are receiving revelation from Almighty God.

From those pictures, I can see where it would be easy to call this experience "divine madness." However, all prophetic revelation need not be accompanied by such emotionally or physically intense behavior. I think of Jesus Who did only what He saw and heard the Father doing, and was thus receiving divine revelation continuously throughout the day (John 5:19,20,30). We have no record that He manifested such violent emotional or physical reactions to the divine flow within Him. Nor is there record of Paul or John having such manifestations as they ministered and wrote various parts of the New Testament.

So it seems that violent emotional and physical reactions need not accompany the reception of divine revelation, even though for some they may. Personally, I prefer to call it "revelation knowledge" rather than divine madness. In my experience, when I receive God's thoughts I hardly ever experience physically or emotionally "wild" or "mad" behavior. I stay relatively calm most of the time.

After polling many people at Toronto Airport Christian Fellowship, it does appear to me that right-brainers have a greater tendency to experience stronger emotional and behavioral manifestations than do left-brainers. That's fine with me. We are all hungering for the revelation and anointing of God to be poured into and through us. The Bible nowhere dictates that a prerequisite for this is intense emotional or physical reactions, nor does it forbid them. If they happen to some, that is fine. If they don't happen to some, that, too, is fine. God graciously deals with each individual as is best for him.

Aristotle (384–322 B.C., coming immediately after Plato) dropped "Divine Madness" as a way of discovering truth. For Aristotle, truth came through sense knowledge and reason only. Plato's ideas were not popularized until the Middle Ages when Thomas Aquinas (1225–1274) began teaching Aristotelian thought in European universities. This led to scholasticism, which led to rational humanism.

Rational humanism is, of course, what satan was offering to Eve in the Garden of Eden. If you remember, the devil's temptation in the Garden was that man live out of himself, acquire his own wisdom and knowledge, and move with his own power. He said, "You will be like God, knowing good and evil." In accepting this temptation, mankind moved from being a vessel which contained God to being a vessel that manifested satan and his demons (as self is the filling station for satan).

The two key words in satan's temptation were "you" and "know." From these two words we now have built two philosophies, **humanism** and **rationalism**. Humanism reveres the efforts of humans as the center of life, and rationalism centralizes man's reasoning process. Both philosophies are satan's alternatives to God's original plan. Both are wrong, and both are idolatry. And God has made it extremely clear in the Ten Commandments that He hates idolatry and has forbidden it (Exod. 20:3).

Jesus lived out of divine flow, and by becoming the Second Adam He reversed what the first Adam had done. Jesus insisted that He did nothing out of His own initiative but only said what He heard the Father saying and did what He saw the Father doing (John 5:17,19,20,30; 8:26,28). Thus Jesus stepped away from both humanism and rationalism, and back to revelation knowledge and divine anointing, which are at the heart of Christianity.

When Paul declared that we have died and Christ is our life (Gal. 2:20), and that we must die daily (1 Cor. 15:31), he was insisting that we must return to the lifestyle of Adam in the Garden of Eden and Jesus, as He walked in Nazareth. We die to our own self-initiative, except to choose to connect to the indwelling Christ and to release Him. We choose to labor to do only one thing — to come to rest, to cease our own laboring, and to touch and release the Spirit of Christ out through our beings (Heb. 4:11).

I live out of the "Christ I" by continuously doing the following:

1. I look to the indwelling Christ, not my own wisdom or strength.

2. I tune to my heart — that is, to flowing thoughts, pictures, feelings and anointing (John 7:37-39).

3. I call forth His life (Heb. 3–4).

4. I glorify God for all that flows out through me.

The "Christ I" releases the following through me:

1. **Anointed reason in place of man's reason** — Instead of looking to, trusting and applying the analytical abilities of my own mind, I yield my mind to flowing pictures and flowing thoughts, and I journal these out (Isa. 1:18).

2. **Divine vision in place of vain imagination** — Instead of evil or vain imaginations (Gen. 6:5; Rom. 1:21), I use the eyes of my heart for "godly imagination" (1 Chron. 29:18) and to receive divine dreams and visions by asking the Holy Spirit to give me a flow of pictures, which I tune to within (Acts 2:17).

3. **Anointing in place of my strength** — Instead of setting my will to accomplish or to overcome, I set my will to connect with the indwelling Christ and to release His power and His anointing through mc (1 John 2:20).

4. **Divine emotions in place of my emotions** — Instead of living out of my feelings, I ask God to give me His feelings about the situation (Gal. 5:22,23).

Christ's life and anointing make you better than you are! Let Christ live through you by the indwelling Holy Spirit! Apply the law of the Spirit of life in Christ Jesus (Rom. 8:2). Choose to tune inward and draw upon the river of power, anointing, wisdom and revelation that is in the indwelling Holy Spirit.

May each of us ascend back to a biblical worldview and a Spirit-anointed lifestyle, following the example of our Lord and Savior Jesus Christ, as well as the original design which God laid out in the Garden of Eden.

Notes

TO WHOM DO WE PRAY?

Notes

I have been asked, and I have asked the Lord, to whom we are to pray. Is it the Father, or is it the Son? Technically, I believe we are to pray to the Father, through the Son, by the working of the Holy Spirit. Therefore, the entire Trinity is involved in prayer.

On the other hand, the fifteenth chapter of John calls us to abide in Christ, or to live in Him. I find for me that a part of living in Jesus involves dialoguing with Him, and that when I look for a vision of the Godhead, He is the image that often appears (Col. 1:15). I find that when I pray with authority, I tend to address the Father, and that when establishing intimacy and friendship, I generally commune with Jesus. When in corporate worship or beginning a class, I often speak to the Holy Spirit, inviting Him to manifest His presence among us.

I have asked the Lord about this, and He has confirmed that it is most proper to pray to Him, through the Son, by the working of the Holy Spirit. However, He has also said that since the Three are One, He will also honor my prayer when it is Jesus and I talking. After all, Jesus only speaks the words the Father has spoken (John 5:19,20).

Actually, in considering 1 John 1:3 and 2 Corinthians 13:14, we find that the Bible tells us we may fellowship with the Father, the Son, or the Holy Spirit.

*"...and indeed our **fellowship** is with the Father, and **with His Son Jesus Christ**."* (1 John 1:3, emphasis added)

*"Let the grace of the Lord Jesus Christ, and the love of God, be with you all through the **fellowship of the Holy Spirit**."* (2 Cor. 13:14, a paraphrase from the Greek, emphasis added)

Therefore, I believe our fellowship can be with the Father, the Son and the Holy Spirit.

Notes

DREAMS AND VISIONS THROUGHOUT SCRIPTURE

Following is the printout of a study using CompuBible, an early computer program designed to help Bible students make complete concordance studies on any topic they choose. I set the program to find every reference in the Bible that contained the words dream, vision, seer, look, and eyes. Obviously, some of the references located referred to natural sight, not spiritual. All of these have been carefully weeded out so that the references listed below refer only to spiritual vision.

I encourage you to take a week or two of your devotional time to study these verses, praying over them and asking God to show you insights and revelations from them which you have not seen before. Keep a paper and pencil nearby and record what you discover. This will form a biblical foundation in your life upon which you can begin building a theology of how God uses dream and vision.

The prayer that was on my lips as I meditated on these verses was, "Lord, show me how You want to use the eyes of my heart, and show me how You want me to use the eyes of my heart." I encourage you to make this your prayer as you meditate on the following verses, and let God give you a biblical understanding of His intention for the eyes of your heart.

Notes

Title: The place of dream and vision in your spiritual life.

Range: Genesis 1:1 to Revelation 22:21

Subject —	1. dream	2. vision	3. seer	4. look	5. eyes
Gen. 3:5					
Gen. 3:6					
Gen. 3:7					

Subject —	1. dream	2. vision	3. seer	4. look	5. eyes
Gen. 15:1					
Gen. 18:2					
Gen. 20:3					
Gen. 20:6					
Gen. 21:19					
Gen. 28:12					
Gen. 31:10					
Gen. 31:11					
Gen. 31:12					
Gen. 31:24					
Gen. 37:5					
Gen. 37:6					
Gen. 37:8					
Gen. 37:9					
Gen. 37:10					
Gen. 37:19					
Gen. 37:20					
Gen. 40:5					
Gen. 40:6					
Gen. 40:7					
Gen. 40:8					
Gen. 40:9					
Gen. 40:16					
Gen. 41:1					
Gen. 41:5					
Gen. 41:7					
Gen. 41:8					
Gen. 41:11					
Gen. 41:12					

Subject —	1. dream	2. vision	3. seer	4. look	5. eyes
Gen. 41:15					
Gen. 41:17					
Gen. 41:22					
Gen. 41:25					
Gen. 41:26					
Gen. 41:32					
Gen. 42:9					
Gen. 46:2					
Gen. 46:4					
Exod. 3:1					
Exod. 3:2					
Exod. 3:3					
Exod. 3:4					
Exod. 3:5					
Exod. 3:6					
Exod. 16:9					
Exod. 16:10					
Exod. 16:11					
Exod. 24:15					
Exod. 24:16					
Exod. 24:17					
Exod. 24:18					
Exod. 25:1					
Num. 12:6					
Num. 21:8					
Num. 22:31					
Num. 24:2					
Num. 24:3					
Num. 24:4					

Subject —	1. dream	2. vision	3. seer	4. look	5. eyes
Num. 24:15					
Num. 24:16					
Deut. 6:8					
Deut. 11:18					
Deut. 13:1					
Deut. 13:2					
Deut. 13:3					
Deut. 13:4					
Deut. 13:5					
Deut. 29:2					
Deut. 29:3					
Deut. 29:4					
Josh. 5:13					
Josh. 5:14					
Josh. 5:15					
Judg. 6:12					
Judg. 6:13					
Judg. 6:14					
Judg. 7:13					
Judg. 7:14					
Judg. 7:15					
Judg. 13:16					
Judg. 13:17					
Judg. 13:18					
Judg. 13:19					
Judg. 13:20					
1 Sam. 3:1					
1 Sam. 3:2					
1 Sam. 3:3					

Subject —	1. dream	2. vision	3. seer	4. look	5. eyes
1 Sam. 3:4					
1 Sam. 3:5					
1 Sam. 3:6					
1 Sam. 3:7					
1 Sam. 3:8					
1 Sam. 3:9					
1 Sam. 3:10					
1 Sam. 3:15					
1 Sam. 9:9					
1 Sam. 9:10					
1 Sam. 9:11					
1 Sam. 9:15					
1 Sam. 9:16					
1 Sam. 9:17					
1 Sam. 9:18					
1 Sam. 9:19					
1 Sam. 28:6					
1 Sam. 28:15					
2 Sam. 7:4					
2 Sam. 7:5					
2 Sam. 7:6					
2 Sam. 7:7					
2 Sam. 7:8					
2 Sam. 7:9					
2 Sam. 7:10					
2 Sam. 7:17					
2 Sam. 15:27					
2 Sam. 24:11					
2 Sam. 24:12					

Subject —	1. dream	2. vision	3. seer	4. look	5. eyes
1 Kings 3:5					
1 Kings 3:6					
1 Kings 3:7					
1 Kings 3:8					
1 Kings 3:9					
1 Kings 3:10					
1 Kings 3:11					
1 Kings 3:12					
1 Kings 3:13					
1 Kings 3:14					
1 Kings 3:15					
1 Kings 6:15					
1 Kings 6:16					
1 Kings 6:17					
2 Kings 17:13					
1 Chron. 9:22					
1 Chron. 17:15					
1 Chron. 21:9					
1 Chron. 21:10					
1 Chron. 21:16					
1 Chron. 25:5					
1 Chron. 25:6					
1 Chron. 25:7					
1 Chron. 26:28					
1 Chron. 29:29					
2 Chron. 9:29					
2 Chron. 12:15					
2 Chron. 16:7					
2 Chron. 16:8					

Subject —	1. dream	2. vision	3. seer	4. look	5. eyes
2 Chron. 16:9					
2 Chron. 16:10					
2 Chron. 19:2					
2 Chron. 26:5					
2 Chron. 29:25					
2 Chron. 29:26					
2 Chron. 29:30					
2 Chron. 32:32					
2 Chron. 33:18					
2 Chron. 33:19					
2 Chron. 35:15					
Job 4:13					
Job 4:14					
Job 4:15					
Job 4:16					
Job 7:13					
Job 7:14					
Job 20:8					
Job 33:15					
Job 33:16					
Ps. 5:3					
Ps. 13:3					
Ps. 25:15					
Ps. 89:19					
Ps. 119:18					
Ps. 123:1					
Ps. 123:2					
Ps. 141:8					
Prov. 29:18					

Subject —	1. dream	2. vision	3. seer	4. look	5. eyes
Eccles. 5:3					
Eccles. 5:7					
Isa. 1:1					
Isa. 6:1					
Isa. 6:2					
Isa. 6:3					
Isa. 6:4					
Isa. 6:5					
Isa. 6:6					
Isa. 6:7					
Isa. 6:8					
Isa. 6:9					
Isa. 6:10					
Isa. 8:17					
Isa. 17:7					
Isa. 17:8					
Isa. 21:2					
Isa. 22:1					
Isa. 22:5					
Isa. 28:7					
Isa. 29:8					
Isa. 29:10					
Isa. 29:11					
Isa. 30:10					
Isa. 33:17					
Isa. 40:26					
Isa. 42:18					
Isa. 42:19					
Isa. 42:20					

Subject —	1. dream	2. vision	3. seer	4. look	5. eyes
Isa. 44:18					
Jer. 5:21					
Jer. 8:15					
Jer. 14:14					
Jer. 23:16					
Jer. 23:18					
Jer. 23:27					
Jer. 23:28					
Jer. 23:32					
Jer. 27:9					
Jer. 29:8					
Jer. 29:21					
Lam. 2:9					
Ezek. 1:1					
Ezek. 1:4					
Ezek. 2:9					
Ezek. 7:13					
Ezek. 7:26					
Ezek. 8:3					
Ezek. 8:4					
Ezek. 8:5					
Ezek. 8:7					
Ezek. 10:1					
Ezek. 10:9					
Ezek. 11:1					
Ezek. 11:24					
Ezek. 12:2					
Ezek. 12:22					
Ezek. 12:23					

Subject —	1. dream	2. vision	3. seer	4. look	5. eyes
Ezek. 12:24					
Ezek. 12:25					
Ezek. 12:26					
Ezek. 12:27					
Ezek. 13:7					
Ezek. 13:16					
Ezek. 40:2					
Ezek. 40:4					
Ezek. 40:6					
Ezek. 43:1					
Ezek. 43:2					
Ezek. 43:3					
Ezek. 43:4					
Ezek. 43:5					
Ezek. 43:6					
Ezek. 44:1					
Ezek. 44:4					
Ezek. 44:5					
Ezek. 46:19					
Ezek. 47:2					
Dan. 1:17					
Dan. 2:1					
Dan. 2:2					
Dan. 2:3					
Dan. 2:4					
Dan. 2:5					
Dan. 2:6					
Dan. 2:7					
Dan. 2:8					

Subject —	1. dream	2. vision	3. seer	4. look	5. eyes
Dan. 2:9					
Dan. 2:19					
Dan. 2:26					
Dan. 2:28					
Dan. 2:36					
Dan. 4:5					
Dan. 4:6					
Dan. 4:7					
Dan. 4:8					
Dan. 4:9					
Dan. 4:10					
Dan. 4:13					
Dan. 4:18					
Dan. 4:19					
Dan. 5:12					
Dan. 7:1					
Dan. 7:2					
Dan. 7:7					
Dan. 7:13					
Dan. 7:15					
Dan. 8:1					
Dan. 8:2					
Dan. 8:3					
Dan. 8:13					
Dan. 8:15					
Dan. 8:16					
Dan. 8:17					
Dan. 8:18					
Dan. 8:26					

Subject —	1. dream	2. vision	3. seer	4. look	5. eyes
Dan. 8:27					
Dan. 9:21					
Dan. 9:22					
Dan. 9:23					
Dan. 9:24					
Dan. 10:1					
Dan. 10:5					
Dan. 10:6					
Dan. 10:7					
Dan. 10:8					
Dan. 10:9					
Dan. 10:10					
Dan. 10:11					
Dan. 10:12					
Dan. 10:13					
Dan. 10:14					
Dan. 10:15					
Dan. 10:16					
Dan. 11:14					
Dan. 12:5					
Hos. 12:10					
Joel 2:28					
Amos 7:12					
Obad. 1:1					
Mic. 3:6					
Mic. 3:7					
Nah. 1:1					
Hab. 2:2					
Hab. 2:3					
Zech. 1:18					

Subject —	1. dream	2. vision	3. seer	4. look	5. eyes
Zech. 2:1					
Zech. 4:2					
Zech. 5:1					
Zech. 5:5					
Zech. 5:9					
Zech. 6:1					
Zech. 10:2					
Zech. 13:4					
Matt. 1:20					
Matt. 2:12					
Matt. 2:13					
Matt. 2:19					
Matt. 2:22					
Matt. 13:15					
Matt. 13:16					
Matt. 24:23					
Matt. 27:19					
Mark 8:18					
Mark 9:8					
Luke 1:22					
Luke 24:23					
Luke 24:31					
John 12:40					
Acts 1:10					
Acts 2:17					
Acts 7:55					
Acts 9:10					
Acts 9:11					

Subject —	1. dream	2. vision	3. seer	4. look	5. eyes
Acts 9:12					
Acts 10:3					
Acts 10:4					
Acts 10:17					
Acts 10:19					
Acts 11:5					
Acts 11:6					
Acts 12:9					
Acts 16:9					
Acts 16:10					
Acts 18:9					
Acts 26:18					
Acts 26:19					
Acts 28:27					
Rom. 11:8					
Rom. 11:10					
2 Cor. 4:18					
2 Cor. 12:1					
Eph. 1:18					
Heb. 11:10					
Rev. 1:10					
Rev. 1:14					
Rev. 4:1					
Rev. 4:2					
Rev. 4:3					
Rev. 5:6					
Rev. 6:8					
Rev. 9:17					
Rev. 14:1					
Rev. 14:14					
Rev. 15:5					

DREAMS AND VISIONS THROUGHOUT CHURCH HISTORY

Notes

Not only are dreams and visions prevalent in every dispensation of the Bible, they have also been a consistent part of Church history. In order to give you a clearer view of the Church's experience with dreams and visions throughout the last 2,000 years, I offer the following examples.

1. Augustine — Rather than ignoring dreams as the contemporary Church has done, Augustine took the entire Twelfth Book in his *De Genesi ad Litteram* to explain his understanding of dreams and visions.

2. Polycarp — The book *Martyrdom of Polycarp* tells of Polycarp praying not long before his martyrdom, and being informed of what was shortly to happen through a symbolic vision. He saw the pillow under his head catch fire and realized that this image of destruction signified his own impending capture and death.

3. Justin Martyr — In his writings, Martyr said that dreams are sent by spirits. He believed that dreams are sent by both evil spirits and God.

4. Irenaeus — As Irenaeus refuted gnostic speculation in his writings, he indicated his clear view concerning dreams and the life of the Christian. In his principal work, *Against Heresies*, Irenaeus commented appreciatively and intelligently on the dream of Peter in the tenth chapter of Acts; he believed that the dream itself was a proof of the authenticity of Peter's experience. Again, he stressed the legitimacy of Paul's dream at Troas. He also inferred from the dreams of Joseph in Matthew that Joseph's dreaming showed how close he was to the real God. In still another place, he explained that although God is Himself invisible to the eye directly, He gives us visions and dreams through which He conveys the likeness of His nature and glory.

5. Clement — In discussing the nature and meaning of sleep, Clement urged: "Let us not, then, who are sons of the true light, close the door against this light; but turning in on ourselves, illumining the eyes of the hidden man, and gazing on the truth itself, and receiving its streams, let us clearly and intelligibly reveal such dreams as are true.... Thus also such dreams as are true, in the view of him who reflects rightly, are the thoughts of a sober soul, undistracted for the time by the affections of the body, and counseling with itself in the best manner.... Wherefore always contemplating God, and by perpetual converse with Him inoculating the body with wakefulness, it raises man to equality with angelic grace, and from the practice of wakefulness it grasps the eternity of life" (*Stromata*, or *Miscellanies*).

6. Origen — In his great answer to the pagans, *Against Celsus*, Origen defended the visions of the Bible, saying: "...We, nevertheless, so far as we can, shall support our position, maintaining that, as it is a matter of belief that in a dream impressions have been brought before the minds of many, some relating to divine things, and others to future events of this life, and this either with clearness or in an enigmatic manner, a fact which is manifest to all who accept the doctrine of providence: so how is it absurd to say that the mind which could receive impressions in a dream should be impressed also in a waking vision, for the benefit either of him on whom the impressions are made, or of those who are to hear the account of them from him?"

Having satisfied his parallel between dreams and visions, Origen then went on to discuss the nature of dreams. In *Contra Celsus*, Origen further declared that many Christians had been converted from their pagan ways by this kind of direct breakthrough into their lives in waking visions and dreams of the night. He made it clear that many such instances of this sort of conversion were known.

7. Tertullian — Tertullian devoted eight chapters of his work *A Treatise on the Soul*, or *De Anima*, to his study of sleep and dreams. He believed that all dream, and evidenced it by the movement of sleeping infants. He believed that dreams occur from four sources: demons, God, natural dreams that the soul creates, and finally "the ecstatic state and its peculiar conditions" or, in other words, the unconscious. Furthermore he states, "And thus we — who both acknowledge and reverence, even as we do the prophecies, modern visions as equally promised to us, and consider the other powers of the Holy Spirit as an agency of the Church for which also He was sent, administering all gifts in all, even as the Lord distributed to every one...."

8. Thascius Cyprian, Bishop of Carthage in 250 A.D. — In a letter to Florentius Pupianus he said, "Although I know that to some men dreams seem ridiculous and visions foolish, yet assuredly it is to such as would rather believe in opposition to the priest, than believe the priest." In another letter he wrote that God guides the very councils of the Church by "many and manifest visions." He commended the reader, Celerinus, because his conversion to the Church had come through a vision of the night.

9. Lactantius, chosen by Constantine the Great to tutor his son. — In his *Divine Institutes*, he included a chapter, "The Use of Reason in Religion; and of Dreams, Auguries, Oracles, and Similar Portents," in which he cited examples to show that through dreams, a knowledge of the future is occasionally given to pagans as well as to Christians. His example of a logical fallacy is that of a man who has dreamed that he ought not believe in dreams.

10. Constantine — Lactantius writes of the heavenly vision that gave Constantine his great victory in 300 A.D. The story begins with Constantine being in desperate need and calling on God for help. "Accordingly he called on Him with earnest prayer and supplications that He would reveal to him Who He was, and stretch forth His right hand to help him in his present difficulties. And while he was thus praying with fervent entreaty, a most marvelous sign appeared to him from heaven, the account of which it might have been hard to believe had it been related by any other person. But since the victorious emperor himself long afterward declared it to the writer of this history, when he was honored with his acquaintance and society, and confirmed his statement by an oath, who could hesitate to accredit the relation especially since the testimony of after-time has established its truth? He said that about noon, when the day was already beginning to decline, he saw with his own eyes the trophy of a cross of light in the heavens, above the sun, and bearing the inscription, CONQUER BY THIS. At this sight he himself was struck with amazement, and his whole army also, which followed him on this expedition, and witnessed the miracle.

"He said, moreover, that he doubted within himself what the import of this apparition could be. And while he continued to ponder the reason on its meaning, night suddenly came on; then in his sleep the Christ of God appeared to him with the same sign which he had seen in the heavens, and commanded him to make a likeness of that sign which he had seen in the heavens, and to use it as a safeguard in all engagements with his enemies.

At dawn of day he arose, and communicated the marvel to his friends: and then, calling together the workers in gold and precious stones, he sat in the midst of them, and described to them the figure of the sign he had seen, bidding them represent it in gold and precious stones. And this representation I myself have had an opportunity of seeing" (*The Life of Constantine I*, 28-30).

11. Socrates — One dream Socrates mentioned was that of Ignatius of Antioch. Ignatius had a vision of angels who sang hymns in alternate chants, and so introduced the mode of antiphonal singing (*Ecclesiastical History*, Vol. 35 and 36, by Theodoret).

12. Athanasius, Bishop of Alexandria from 328 to 373 — In his great masterpiece of Christian apology, Against the Heathen, he wrote: "Often when the body is quiet, and at rest and asleep, man moves inwardly, and beholds what is outside himself, traveling to other countries, walking about, meeting his acquaintances, and often by these means divining and forecasting the actions of the day. But to what can this be due save to the rational soul, in which man thinks of and perceives things beyond himself?

"…For if even when united and coupled with the body it is not shut in or commensurate with the small dimensions of the body, but often, when the body lies in bed, not moving, but in death-like sleep, the soul keeps awake by virtue of its own power, and transcends the natural power of the body, and as though traveling away from the body while remaining in it, imagines and beholds things above the earth, and often even holds converse with the saints and angels who are above earthly and bodily existence, and approaches them in the confidence of the purity of its intelligence; shall it not all the more, when separated from the body at the time appointed by God Who coupled them together, have its knowledge of immortality more clear?" (II.31.5 and 33.3)

13. Gregory of Nyssa — In his major philosophical work, *On the Making of Man*, Gregory deals directly with the meaning and place of sleep and dreams in man's life. He believed that when man is asleep the senses and the reason rest, and the less rational parts of the soul appear to take over. Reason is not, however, extinguished, but smolders like a fire "heaped with chaff" and then breaks forth with insights that modern dream research calls "secondary mentation."

He went on to say that "while all men are guided by their own minds, there are some few who are deemed worthy of evident Divine communication; so, while the imagination of sleep naturally occurs in a like and equivalent manner for all, some, not all, share by means of their dreams in some more Divine manifestation...." His reasoning was that there is a natural foreknowledge that comes in an unknown way through the nonrational part of the soul — the "unconscious," according to modern depth psychology — and it is through this part of the soul that God communicates Himself directly.

Gregory then enumerated the other meanings that dreams can have, offering quite a complete outline of the subject. He suggested that dreams can provide mere reminiscences of daily occupations and events. Or, they can reflect the condition of the body, its hunger or thirst, or the emotional condition of the personality. Dreams can also be understood in medical practice as giving clues to the sickness of the body. Indeed, far from stating a superstitious belief, Gregory laid out quite well the principle upon which today's analytical study of dreams is based.

Gregory also told, in a sermon entitled "In Praise of the Forty Martyrs," of a dream that occurred while he was attending a celebration in honor of the soldiers who had been martyred. In the dream, the martyrs challenged Gregory for his Christian lethargy, and it had a profound effect upon his life.

It is clear that philosophically, practically and personally, Gregory of Nyssa believed the dream could be a revelation of depths beyond the human ego.

14. Basil the Great — In his commentary on Isaiah, Basil states, "The enigmas in dreams have a close affinity to those things which are signified in an allegoric or hidden sense in the Scriptures. Thus both Joseph and Daniel, through the gift of prophecy, used to interpret dreams, since the force of reason by itself is not powerful enough for getting at truth" (S. Basilii Magni, *Commentarium in Isaiam Prophetam*, Prooemium 6f., J.-P. Migne, Patrologiae Graecae, Paris, 1880, Vol. 30, Col. 127-30).

That Basil believed in continuing to consider dreams is indicated by the letter he wrote to a woman in which he interpreted the dream she had sent him. He suggested to her that her dream meant she was to spend more time in "spiritual contemplation and cultivating that mental vision by which God is wont to be seen."

15. Gregory of Nazianzen — In his second book of poems, Gregory writes: "And God summoned me from boyhood in my nocturnal dreams, and I arrived at the very goals of wisdom" (S. Gregorii Theologi, *Carminum*, Liber II, 994-950). In another place he told that this nocturnal vision was the hidden spark that set his whole life aflame for God. In one of his poems, he spoke of the ability of demons to also speak through one's dreams. "Devote not your trust too much to the mockery of dreams, nor let yourself be terrified by everything; do not become inflated by joyful visions, For frequently a demon prepares these snares for you" (*Carminum*, Liber I, 608-9, lines 209-12).

16. St. John Chrysostom — In his commentary on Acts, volume one, he states, "To some the grace was imparted through dreams, to others it was openly poured forth. For indeed by dreams the prophets saw, and received revelations." According to Chrysostom, dreams are sent to those whose wills are compliant to God, for they do not need visions or the more startling divine manifestations, and he mentioned Joseph, the father of Jesus, and Peter and Paul as examples of this truth (*Homilies on Matthew*, IV. 10f., 18; v. 5).

17. Synesius of Cyrene — Synesius wrote an entire book on dreams. He said, "One man learns…while awake, another while asleep. But in the waking state man is the teacher, whereas it is God who makes the dreamer fruitful with His own courage, so that learning and attaining are one and the same. Now to make fruitful is even more than to teach" (Augustine Fitzgerald, *The Essays and Hymns of Synesius of Cyrene*, London, Oxford University Press, 1930, p. 332 [from *Concerning Dreams*]).

Synesius laid out a sound reason for discussing dreams and then enumerated the blessings to be gained from studying them. For the pure soul who receives impressions clearly, a proper study of dreams gives knowledge of the future with all that this implies. Important information is also provided about bodily malfunction and how it can be corrected. Far more important, this undertaking brings the soul to consider immaterial things and so, even though it was begun merely to provide knowledge of the future, it turns the soul to God and develops a love of Him. Synesius also told how dreams had helped him in his writings and in his other endeavors, and how they often gave hope to men who had been oppressed by the difficulties of life.

He made fun of people who relied on the popular dream books, insisting that only by constantly checking dreams with experience could they be understood. Their essential nature is personal, and they must be understood by the dreamer in terms of his own life. Some of them seem to be direct revelations of God, but there are also many dreams that are obscure and difficult to interpret. He suggested that anyone who is serious in studying them should keep a record so that he knows his sleeping life as well as his waking one.

He even saw the connection between mythology and dreams, and explained his belief that the myth is based upon the dream; a true interest in mythology helps a man find the more vital meaning in his own dreams. Finally, Synesius showed the reason for his belief that dreams give hints about eternal life. As the sleeping state is to the waking one, so the life of the soul after death is to the dream life, and thus this state gives some idea of the kind of life that is led by the soul after death.

18. Ambrose — In Ambrose's famous letter to Theodosius calling for his repentance, he declared that God in a dream forbade him to celebrate communion before the Emperor unless he repented. These are his dramatic words: "I am writing with my own hand that which you alone may read…. I have been warned, not by man, nor through man, but plainly by Himself that this is forbidden me. For when I was anxious, in the very night in which I was preparing to set out, you appeared to me in a dream to have come into the Church, and I was not permitted to offer the sacrifice…. Our God gives warnings in many ways, by heavenly signs, by the precepts of the prophets, by the visions even of sinners He wills that we should understand, that we should entreat Him to take away all disturbances…that the faith and peace of the Church…may continue" (St. Ambrose, Letter LI 14).

Augustine tells how God revealed to St. Ambrose in a dream the hidden location of two martyred saints, who were then retrieved and given a proper consecration (St. Ambrose, Letter XXII; St. Augustine, *The Confessions*, IX [VII] 16; *The City of God*, XXII 8).

In St. Ambrose's more theological writings, Ambrose showed that an angel who speaks through a dream is functioning at the direction of the Holy Spirit, since angelic powers are subject to and moved by the Spirit.

19. Augustine — As has already been mentioned in number one of this series, Augustine wrote widely concerning the place and understanding of dreams in the Christian's life. His study of perception was as sophisticated as any in the ancient world. He saw reality as consisting of outer objects to which we react with our bodies, and the impressions of this sense experience, impressions that are "mental" in nature. We then have the inner perception of this sense experience, and finally the mental species in its remembered form. It is the action of the ego that unites these perceptions to the object.

In one place, he calls the faculty of imagination the bridge that mediates the object to consciousness, thus presenting almost the same thinking as that worked out by Synesius of Cyrene. Augustine saw man as possessing an outward eye that receives and mediates sense impressions, and an inward eye that observes and deals with these collected and stored "mental" realities that are called "memory."

In addition to the realities that come from outer perception and from inner perception of "memories," autonomous spiritual realities (angels and demons) can present themselves directly to the inner eye. These are of the same nature as the stored "mental" or psychic realities that are perceived inwardly. Augustine writes that men in sleep or trance can experience contents that come from memory "or some other hidden force through certain spiritual commixtures of a similarly spiritual substance" (St. Augustine, *On the Trinity*, XI. 4.7).

These autonomous realities are nonphysical; yet they can either assume a corporeal appearance and be experienced through the outward eye, or they can be presented directly to the consciousness through the inner eye in dreams, visions and trances. Thus, through dreams, man is presented with a whole storehouse of unconscious memories and spontaneous contents; he is given access to a world that the fathers called "the realm of the spirit."

Just as angels have direct contact with man's psyche and present their messages before the inner eye, so also do demons. "They persuade [men], however, in marvelous and unseen ways, entering by means of that subtlety of their own bodies into the bodies of men who are unaware, and through certain imaginary visions mingling themselves with men's thoughts whether they are awake or asleep" (*The Divination of Demons*, V. 9, N.Y., Fathers of the Church, Inc., 1955, Vol. 27, p. 430).

In addition to presenting a theory of dreams and visions, Augustine also discussed many examples of providential dreams in the course of his writings. One of the most important of them was the famous dream of his mother Monica, in which she saw herself standing on a measuring device while a young man whose face shone with a smile approached her. She was crying, and when he asked why, she told of her sorrow that her son had turned away from Christ. He told her to look, and suddenly she saw Augustine standing on the same rule with her and she was comforted. Realizing the significance of the symbolism, she was able to go on praying for him with patience and hope; her dreams and visions are also mentioned in several other places in *The Confessions* (*The Confessions*, III. 19; V. 17; VI. 23; VIII. 30).

20. Jerome — In his early life, Jerome was torn between reading the classics and the Bible until he had this dream. "Suddenly I was caught up in the spirit and dragged before the judgment seat of the Judge; and here the light was so bright, and those who stood around were so radiant, that I cast myself upon the ground and did not dare to look up.

"Asked who and what I was I replied: 'I am a Christian.' But he who presided said: 'Thou liest, thou are a follower of Cicero and not of Christ. For "where thy treasure is, there will thy heart be also."' Instantly I became dumb, and amid the strokes of the lash — for He had ordered me to be scourged — I was tortured more severely still by the fire of conscience, considering with myself that verse, 'In the grave who shall give thee thanks?'

"Yet for all that I began to cry and to bewail myself, saying: 'Have mercy upon me, O Lord: have mercy upon me.' Amid the sound of the scourges this cry still made itself heard. At last the bystanders, falling down before the knees of Him who presided, prayed that He would have pity on my youth, and that He would give me space to repent of my error. He might still, they urged, inflict torture on me, should I ever again read the works of the Gentiles....

"Accordingly I made an oath and called upon His name, saying: 'Lord, if ever again I possess worldly books, or if ever again I read such, I have denied Thee.' Dismissed then, on taking this oath, I returned to the upper world, and to the surprise of all, I opened upon them eyes so drenched with tears that my distress served to convince even the incredulous. And that this was no sleep nor idle dreams, such as those by which we are often mocked, I call to witness the tribunal before which I lay, and the terrible judgment which I feared...I profess that my shoulders were black and blue, that I felt the bruises long after I awoke from my sleep, and that thenceforth I read the books of God with a zeal greater than I had previously given to the books of men" (St. Jerome, Letter XXII, *To Ekustochium*, 30).

Jerome's studies also gave him good reason to value dreams and visions. In commenting on Jeremiah 23:25ff, he shared Jeremiah's concern, indicating that dreaming is a kind of prophesying that God can use as one vehicle of revelation to a soul. It can be a valuable revelation from God if a man's life is turned toward Him. But dreams can become idolatrous when they are sought and interpreted for their own sake by one who is serving his own self-interest instead of God. The value of the dream depends upon the person who seeks it and the person who interprets it. Sometimes God sends dreams to the unrighteous, like those of Nebuchadnezzar and Pharaoh, so that the servants of God may manifest their wisdom. Thus it is the duty of those who have the word of the Lord to explain dreams (S. Eusebii Hieronymi, *Commentariorum in Jeremiam Prophetam*, IV. 23).

This word could not be sought, however, by pagan practices. In commenting on Isaiah 65:4, Jerome went along with the prophet and condemned people who "sit in the graves and the temples of idols where they are accustomed to stretch out on the skins of sacrificial animals in order to know the future by dream, abominations which are still practiced today in the temples of Aescylapius (*Commentariorum in Isaiam Prophetam*). Later, however, in the discussion of Galatians, he brought up specifically the dream in the sixteenth chapter of Acts in which Paul "was given the true light (*lucam vero*)" (*Commentariorum in Epistolam ad Galatos*, 11).

Jerome made no distinction at all between the vision and the dream. He clearly valued them both. Yet in the end, he fixed the ground firmly that would justify a growing fear of these experiences. In translating Leviticus 19:26 and Deuteronomy 18:10 with one word different from other passages, a direct mistranslation, Jerome turned the law: "You shall not practice augury or witchcraft [i.e. soothsaying]" into the prohibition: "You shall not practice augury nor observe dreams." Thus by the authority of the Vulgate, dreams were classed with soothsaying, and the practice of listening to them with other superstitious ideas.[1]

From here we enter the 1,000-year period known as the Dark Ages, and little more is said until the writings of Thomas Aquinas.

21. Thomas Aquinas — Aquinas was greatly influenced by Aristotle and sought to reduce Christianity into Aristotle's worldview. This worldview left no room for direct spiritual encounter. Therefore dreams and visions were played down, along with experiences of angels and demons, healing, tongue-speaking and miracles. In the end, Aquinas' life contradicted what he had written. He did come into direct relationship with God through a triple dream experience and ceased to write and dictate. When he was urged to go on, he replied: "I can do no more; such things have been revealed to me that all I have written seems as straw, and I now await the end of my life" (*Great Books of the Western World*, Vol. 19 [Thomas Aquinas], Chicago, Encyclopedia Britannica, Inc., 1952, p. vi).

This was the turning point for the Church's view of dreams and their ability to carry revelation from Almighty God into the believer's life. Although the Church has flip-flopped back and forth somewhat in its opinion of the value of dreams, the pervading view today is much in line with the rationalism of our day, and very much out of line with the teachings of Scripture and the early Church fathers. One appears strange if he believes that God would actually communicate today to His children through the medium of dreams and visions.

22. Abraham Lincoln — Abraham Lincoln dreamed about his impending death just days before his assassination.

There are many more modern examples that could be quoted, but that is not our purpose at this time. There are entire books on the market today giving a Christian philosophical and theological base for interpreting dreams. There also are testimonial books concerning the variety of dreams and visions being experienced in the Church today.

As we have seen over and over again, dreams and visions are considered interchangeable, and so, even though much of this research deals primarily with dreams, it should be viewed in a wider scope to include visions as well.

It is time for the Church to return to a biblical understanding of dreams and visions and revelation.

Endnote

1. The word *annan* occurs ten times in the Old Testament. In most cases in the current versions, it is simply translated "soothsayer" or "soothsaying."

Notes

NEW TESTAMENT CHRISTIANITY VS. THE NEW AGE MOVEMENT

Notes

It has been said that counterfeits are the unpaid bills of the Church. The New Age is a counterfeit to true Christian experience. One reason for its success is that hungry people seeking spiritual realities were only offered creeds by their religious establishments, and so they went to the New Age in hopes of finding what they were searching for.

The New Age

The "New Age Movement" appears to be a loosely knit group of individuals who believe that we have entered a new era called the Age of Aquarius. This period has allegedly replaced the Age of Pisces, which represents the Christian era (pisces = fish = a Christian symbol). The Age of Aquarius (water-bearer) is characterized by humanism (in a good sense), brotherhood, and love. It is to be a golden age. It began, depending upon whom you ask, in 1904, 1936, 1962 or later. I personally reject such nonsense and believe we are living in the Church Age in which we are to preach the Gospel of the Kingdom of our Lord and Savior Jesus Christ.

Before I began writing this section, I went to a local bookstore and purchased a 244-page reference manual entitled *The New Age Catalogue.* Broken into eight parts, it lists hundreds of books, authors, definitions, and magazine and video resources for those wanting to explore New Age teaching. I almost lost a trusted co-worker when she walked into my office and saw *The New Age Catalogue* sitting on my desk! She thought that if this was what I was into, it was time for her to step out. She was very relieved to discover I had only purchased the manual in order to have authoritative source material for this appendix!

Notes

The adjacent chart shows some of the basic distinctions between the New Age and New Testament Christianity.

By testing yourself or another using the nine basic distinctions listed, it should be quite easy to determine whether a person is a "New Ager" or a New Testament Christian. As you can see, there is a world of difference between the New Age and New Testament Christianity. There should be no need for confusion as to whether someone is one or the other. It should be obvious to all that just because a New Testament Christian is doing something that appears to be similar to the actions of a New Ager, those actions are no sign the Christian has been deceived by New Age methodology or teaching. Obviously satan is a counterfeiter. Therefore, things of the New Age are counterfeits of the truth of Christianity. As a result, there will be many similarities. Yet there will be many differences.

New Testament Christianity	New Age
Who Is God?	
Yahweh, the personal Creator	The Evocative Other
The Standard for Truth	
The Bible	Evolving, eclectic
Who Is Jesus Christ?	
The Son of God	An enlightened teacher
What About Salvation?	
Purchased by the blood of Jesus	No such thing; or the process of Integration
The Focus	
Christ centered	Man centered
The Power	
Through Christ	Through man
The Wisdom	
God's wisdom	Man's wisdom
The Next Age	
Brought about by God	Brought about by man
The Stance	
Man receiving from God	Man reaching to become god

Figure Apx H.1

Why Is the New Age So Attractive to a Growing Number of People?

The New Age offers creativity and life to its followers. For example, David Spangler, who has been lecturing and writing on the New Age for 25 years, defines New Age as "the condition that emerges when I live life in a creative, empowering, compassionate manner."[1] That's an attractive prospect and goal for both Christians and non-Christians. He goes on to state, "I understand the New Age as a metaphor for being in the world in a manner that opens us to the presence of God — the presence of love and possibility — in the midst of our ordinariness."[2]

The ideals of the New Age are high and lofty and, if they can be achieved in even a small way by the power of man, they are tremendously enticing to a growing number of people. Therefore people flock to read and study the literature put out by the New Age.

Why Is the New Age So Deceptive?

One reason the New Age is so deceptive is that it espouses ideals and values that are very similar to Christianity. This, of course, should be expected, considering the fact that satan is the great counterfeiter. For instance, listen again to David Spangler: "Inwardly, the New Age continues the historical effort of humanity to delve deeply into the mysteries of the nature of God, of ourselves, and of reality. In the midst of materialism, it is a rebirth of our sense of the sacred....The New Age is essentially a symbol representing the human heart and intellect in partnership with God building a better world that can celebrate values of community, wholeness and sacredness. It is a symbol for the emergence of social behavior based on a worldview that stimulates creativity, discipline, abundance and wholeness; it is a symbol for a more mature and unobstructed expression of the sacredness and love at the heart of life."[3]

After reading definitions like the above, many Christians would respond with a feeling that Christianity itself holds to many of these ideals. However, the New Age believes man can reach for these goals and achieve them through his own effort, or if he does seek spiritual assistance, it is not restricted to Jesus Christ or God, but to any "good" spiritual energies that are floating around. Remember, the New Age movement is eclectic, and therefore is willing to draw from anyone's experiences or insight. They do not have a written standard against which to test all their experiences and teachings, as Christians do. For example, the following are some of the books and authors recommended in the *New Age Catalogue: Channeling — Investigations On Receiving Information From Paranormal Sources; The Sleeping Prophet; Develop Your Psychic Skills*; and *Crystal Healing* by Edgar Cayce.

What Should Be the Church's Response to the New Age?

Obviously we recognize it as a continuation of the deception that began in the Garden of Eden: "Man can become like God." It is the age-old lie that we can strive to reach divinity ourselves. Instead, Christians have discovered the freedom simply to rest in the Vine, experiencing the flow of the river of life that wells up within them by the Holy Spirit as they cease from their own labors and simply attune themselves to God.

We respect the New Ager's desire to become loving, creative and fulfilled, and we point them to the only true Source of such a lifestyle, Jesus Christ. New birth is mandatory as they acknowledge Jesus Christ, the Son of God, as their Lord and Savior and receive by faith His atoning work at Calvary.

We recognize that because New Agers are part of the great counterfeit, they may use words, phrases and techniques that have been borrowed from Christianity or Christian traditions. **Yet, we will not give over either these words or these experiences to the satanic counterfeit, as they are God's forever.**

For example, New Agers have written on "the rainbow," which of course was part of God's covenant with Noah, and on "centering," which is a word and an experience that has been used for decades by the Quaker church. *The New Age Catalogue* even recommends the Christian book *Hinds Feet On High Places* by Hannah Hurnard (ibid. p. 89), published by Tyndale House Publishers, Inc.

Being eclectic, we should expect them to draw from Christianity as well as everyone else. That does not concern us. We have a standard, the Word of God, and our acceptance of a truth is not based on whether or not a counterfeit group has yet picked it up. We look to see if it is taught in Scripture; and surely such things as centering or quieting our souls before the Lord, as is practiced by the Quaker Church, is clearly taught and demonstrated by King David in the Psalms as he states, "My soul waits in silence for God only" (Ps. 62:1,5).

Therefore we will expect the New Age to blur the line between truth and error through their eclectic nature, but we will walk calmly according to the eternal truths and experiences taught in God's Word. We shall not concern ourselves with how many cults are also drawing upon biblical concepts. We shall only concern ourselves with encountering fully and completely the God of the Scriptures.

"One thing the New Age calls Christians to do is to enter fully into all of the dimensions of our relationship with Christ. The New Age has arisen to take the territory abandoned by the main-stream Christianity. Because Christianity (even most Charismatics) has neglected the intuitive and relational and has majored on the propositional and the analytical, a void has been left in the hearts of those who were seeking spiritual encounters. In the churches they met only doctrinal studies, so they sought for spiritual relationships within the occult and New Age teachings.

"The very best antidote for the New Age teachings is for Christians to enter into and live fully in the supernatural. This is certainly no time to draw back from supernatural living and retreat into a mere defense of orthodoxy. Because we have adopted this stance for the last half-century, we have opened the door for the New Age to fill the vacuum. There is a longing in the human heart for communication and a relationship with the Divine. Since the dawn of history, when God's people do not preach, proclaim and model the genuine article, men and women will wander into whatever appears to offer the fulfillment of their spiritual quest. We need to cast aside our hesitation and proceed strongly forward, the Word and the Spirit as our unfailing guide.

"The early Church made the tragic error (after about 150 A.D.) of majoring on defending orthodoxy in the face of the heresies of Gnosticism (which has recently arisen again as part of New Age teaching), Mystery Religions and State Paganism. While they were vigorously defending Christianity, formulating creeds (propositional statements of doctrine), and attempting to vanquish heresy by excommunicating heretics, somewhere along the line they forgot that Christianity is a relationship to be lived, not merely a theory to be proved.

"The rationalistic patterns of argument adopted from the Greek philosophers replaced the much more forceful arguments of a changed life and the miraculous interventions of Almighty God in the affairs of men. The Church largely lost the battle of ideas merely by conceding that the battle was confined to arguments over ideas. The Bible is 90 percent narratives of God working in lives. Demonstrating God in our lives in all of His dimensions is our best defense. The best defense is still a good offense!"[4]

Additional Distinctions Between Christianity and the New Age

Since the New Age is seeking wholeness, life, love and creativity, it will obviously be reaching toward some of the same goals that Christianity reaches toward. Since the New Age is eclectic, it will be using some of the same approaches that Christianity uses, with some very subtle differences. Listed in the chart on the following page are some of these comparisons and some of the differences.

I believe that the New Age movement is a reaction to what God is doing in the Church of Jesus Christ. In 1900, the Holy Spirit began to move in new and powerful ways upon the Church. In the relatively short time since then, we have seen over 400 million Charismatic and Pentecostal Christians worldwide swept into these new (or restored) moves of the Holy Spirit. C. Peter Wagner estimated that 1.1 billion Christians would be sensitized to the Holy Spirit's flow by 2000 A.D. (*Target Earth*, p. 166).

Gallop poll surveys have revealed that the individuals in this group that call itself charismatic spend more time each week on the average in Bible study, prayer and church attendance than other Christians do. This is quite interesting. Regardless of your theological persuasion, the Bible says you can test things by their fruit. This surely is good fruit.

Therefore, I believe the New Age is satan's reaction to the mighty outpouring of the Holy Spirit that we are seeing in this century. I do not see it as something to fear or to flee from. Since when does light fear darkness? No, I stand against it in the power of the Holy Spirit, in the power of Almighty God! Often God has allowed tests to emerge within a culture so He can prove His supremacy over all else. Elijah and Baal are a classic example of this as Elijah proposed a test to see who could call down fire from heaven. Whoever was successful was the one who served the true God.

New Testament Christianity   New Age Movement

Intuitive Development

The voice of God may flow through man's heart or spirit as intuitive thoughts, visions, burdens and impressions. Christians attempt to learn to discern God's voice, so they can hear and obey, thus experiencing abundant life.

Called intuition, New Agers recognize that as the voice of man's heart, it releases man's creativity, and thus they seek to cultivate it.

Contact with Spirit

Christians seek fellowship with the Holy Spirit. They may also encounter angels sent from God.

New Agers seek fellowship with any beings in the spirit world.

Method of Quieting Oneself

Christians often worship by fixing their eyes on Jesus, the Author and Perfecter of their faith.

New Agers use mantra.

Use of One's Visionary Abilities

Visionary abilities are presented before God so He may grant divine vision. They are recognized as a creative ability within man.

Visionary abilities are used by oneself to visualize one's goals. They are recognized as a creative ability within man.

Use of Writing in Spiritual Experiences

Journaling is a way of recording what one senses God is speaking within him. Impressions sensed in the heart are registered in the mind and recorded by the hand. It is similar to the Psalms except that one's journal never becomes Scripture. Rather it is tested by Scripture.

Journaling is a way of recording what is flowing from the spirit world. One's hand hangs limp, and a force takes it over and guides it. The heart or mind of man is not involved nor is it submitted to Scripture. This is called "automatic writing."

The Planet Today

Our world is being redeemed by the working of God through His Spirit, His angels and His Church.

Our world is becoming better through man's efforts.

The Planet Ultimately

New Heavens and a New Earth will come through God's direct intervention.

A new age will come through man's accomplishments.

Figure Apx H.2

You notice it is not the Pharisees or the false prophets who propose such tests or act with such courage and boldness. It is the prophets on the front line who prove God in the midst of their generation. I suspect that the books being written today by the Church about the New Age movement are not being written by the prophets. The ones I have read encourage a spirit of fear that we will be consumed, rather than a spirit of faith that we will conquer in this particular test. I believe the spirit of fear originates in satan, and the spirit of faith originates in God. Therefore I am very careful not to feed on anything permeated with the spirit of fear.

Endnotes

1. "*The New Age Catalogue* by the Editors of *Body Mind Spirit* Magazine, published by Doubleday 1988. Introduction

2. Ibid. Introduction

3. Ibid. Introduction

4. "from a letter written by Rev. Maurice Fuller"

Notes

SELF-CHECK TEST ON PHARISEEISM

Circle "yes" if you generally do or believe the following statement.

Circle "no" if you generally do not believe or do the following statement.

1. I come alongside people who hold different positions than I do (John 16:7).

    yes   no

2. I come against people who disagree with me (Rev. 12:10).

    yes   no

3. When someone disagrees with me, I seek to discover the truth in what they are saying (Acts 17:11).

    yes   no

4. When someone disagrees with me, I seek to prove that they are wrong (Acts 17:11).

    yes   no

5. I find it easy to accuse and put people down (Rev. 12:10).

    yes   no

6. I look for ways to build people up and encourage them (1 Cor. 14:3).

    yes   no

7. When I go to the Scriptures, I try to find verses that prove a person is right (Acts 17:11).

    yes   no

8. When I go to the Scriptures, I try to find verses that prove a person is wrong (Acts 17:11).

    yes   no

285   HOW TO HEAR GOD'S VOICE

9.   I use the Scriptures to encourage people and build their hope in who Christ is in them (Rom. 15:4; Phil. 4:13).

yes   no

10.   I enjoy debates where I can try to trap my opponent (Matt. 22:15-40).

yes   no

11.   I try to phrase questions in such a way that I might have grounds to accuse a person, based on his answer (Matt. 22:15-40).

yes   no

12.   I try to show people the ease of living out of divine grace (Matt. 23:4).

yes   no

13.   I help those who are burdened down (Matt. 23:4).

yes   no

14.   I like people to notice my religious deeds (Matt. 23:5).

yes   no

15.   I like to be honored by men (Matt. 23:6).

yes   no

16.   I like to be called by my full title (Matt. 23:7).

yes   no

17.   I instruct people in the many commandments that will help them become more holy (Matt. 23:3; Gal. 4:3).

yes   no

18.   I am precise and demanding when it comes to obeying the rules I have established (Matt. 23:23).

yes   no

19.   I emphasize love and mercy more than I emphasize justice and rightness (Micah 6:8).

yes   no

20.   I tend to overlook the little things while keeping my eyes fixed on the more important (Matt. 23:24).

yes   no

21. I tend to get caught up in the little things and overlook the big issues (Matt. 23:24).

        yes   no

22. I devote more time and care to inner attitudes than I do to outer appearance (Matt. 23:25).

        yes   no

23. I take more time and care on outer appearance than I do on caring for the condition of my heart (Matt. 23:25).

        yes   no

24. I think the harder I try to be good and right, the better I will become (Rom. 7).

        yes   no

25. I have discovered that when I stop striving and instead yield myself to the in-working power of Christ, He works more easily within me (Rom. 8).

        yes   no

26. I focus on containing the outside, yet my heart rages with evil within (Col. 2:20-23).

        yes   no

27. I see hypocrisy within myself (Matt. 23:29-31).

        yes   no

28. I tend to feel that life is found in the study of the Scriptures (John 5:39,40).

        yes   no

29. I feel that life is found in the experience of Christ (John 5:39,40).

        yes   no

30. I can see prophets in my community (John 6:42).

        yes   no

31. I seldom judge by outer actions alone. I try to look into the heart and perceive the heart motive behind the action (John 7:24).

        yes   no

32. I tend to judge by outer actions and appearances (John 7:24).

        yes   no

33.   I try to destroy people (either verbally or actually) rather than love them (John 8:37,40,44).

yes   no

34.   I live out of the voice and vision of God within me (John 5:19,20,30).

yes   no

35.   I live focused on the principles within Scripture (John 5:39,40; Heb. 12:2).

yes   no

36.   I trust the theology I have built (Gen. 2:16,17; Luke 24:21-32).

yes   no

37.   I trust the flow within me (John 7:37-39).

yes   no

38.   I tend to say that those who I disagree with have demonic influences in their lives (John 8:48; 10:20).

yes   no

39.   I find it difficult to be taught by those I view to be beneath me (John 9:34).

yes   no

40.   I tend to think that those of the persuasion of my particular church or group are the most right and most likely to make it to heaven (John 10:16).

yes   no

Non-pharisaical answers. Grade yourself. For every answer you have incorrect, place a "P" next to it. Then total the "P's" to find any tendencies of phariseeism within you. Look up the supporting verses, pray over them and ask the Holy Spirit to heal any such tendencies within you.

1. yes	2. no	3. yes
4. no	5. no	6. yes
7. yes	8. no	9. yes
10. no	11. no	12. yes
13. yes	14. no	15. no
16. no	17. no	18. no
19. yes	20. yes	21. no
22. yes	23. no	24. no
25. yes	26. no	27. yes
28. no	29. yes	30. yes
31. yes	32. no	33. no
34. yes	35. no	36. no
37. yes	38. no	39. no
40. no		

PRAYER THAT IS *LED* BY THE HOLY SPIRIT

All prayer is to be *led* by the Holy Spirit which means...

> *"...Pray at all times in the Spirit"* (Eph. 6:18, NASB)

> *"...We do not know how to pray as we should, but the Spirit Himself intercedes for us with groanings too deep for words."* (Rom. 8:26, NASB)

All our praying is to be *in* the Spirit (inspired, guided, energized and sustained by the Holy Spirit), otherwise, we are praying in the flesh (Eph. 6:18). Some of our praying is to be with the Spirit (1 Cor. 14:14,15) which is in tongues. So whether we are praying in tongues or in our native language, we are to be tuned to flow and allowing the Holy Spirit to pray through us (Eph. 6:18). Thus all our praying is in the Spirit, whether it is in our native language or it is in tongues.

The Goal of Spirit-led Prayer Is to Be Flooded With God's Love, Light and Power.

> *"But you, beloved, building yourselves up on your most holy faith, praying in the Holy Spirit, keep yourselves in the love of God, waiting anxiously for the mercy of our Lord Jesus Christ to eternal life."* (Jude 20,21, NASB)

Our Right and Our Access as We Approach God

*"Jesus said to him, 'I am the **way**, and the truth, and the life; no one comes to the Father but through Me.'"* (John 14:6 NASB, emphasis added)

*"For through Him we both have our **access** in one Spirit to the Father."* (Eph. 2:18 NASB, emphasis added)

We have a right to come before the throne of God because of what our Lord and Savior Jesus Christ accomplished for us at Calvary. However, it is the Holy Spirit Who takes us there. It is the Spirit Who gives us actual access. So in prayer I may say, "Father, thank You for making it possible for me to come before You through the shed blood of Your Son, Jesus Christ. Holy Spirit, thank You for providing me access into the throne room of Almighty God."

Our Weakness Is Perpetual, So We Simply Step from Self to Christ, Again and Again

"For He Himself knows our frame; He is mindful that we are but dust." (Ps. 103:14, NASU)

"…Christ Jesus… intercedes for us." (Rom. 8:34, NASB)

"In the same way the Spirit also helps our weakness" (Rom. 8:26, NASB)

The Lord must reveal to us that our weakness in praying is perpetual so that we might learn to be perpetually dependent on the Holy Spirit. We must learn to "rest" in our weakness, not "strive" in it. In other words, God is everything we need; we ask Him again and again for everything and we receive it in simple childlike faith.

When we are weak, tempted, or unable to focus, we ask for a flow of divine power through us to transform us. We tune to flow, God's power infuses us, and we are changed. It is a simple and beautiful transaction of stepping from the weakness of self into the fullness of Christ. We do this continuously.

Additional Reading: *Pray in the Spirit* by Arthur Wallis

Personal Journaling Response Concerning Spirit-led Prayer

Ask the Lord to speak to you about above truths. Fix your gaze upon Him. Experience Him in a comfortable setting. Tune to spontaneity and record what flows within. Don't test it as you are receiving it. Test it later. Write in simple childlike faith what is flowing within your heart. Thank You, Lord, for what You speak.

Praying in the Spirit

Stage	Scripture	Example
1. Relaxation — Become quiet, comfortable and relaxed physically so your mind is freed from thoughts of your body and can become totally immersed in the being of God and the person for whom you are praying.	Psalm 46:10	Sit comfortably, head at rest, hands folded in lap, spine relaxed, yet erect. Encourage (do not command) the different parts of your body to relax. Visualize them relaxing.
2. Contact God in your spirit by meditation upon the reality of God. Know and believe that He is at work in you.	His nearness: Acts 17:28 Philippians 2:13 Galatians 2:20 Psalm 123:1	We overcome ourselves (our worries, cares, thoughts, efforts) by opening our spirits to receive the flowing life of God within (using whatever means that make Him most real to us). Rather than rushing to Him with our petitions and clamoring, we quietly come into His presence using vision.
3. Unite with His indwelling life.	Luke 11:13 1 John 5:14,15	"Please increase my awareness of Your life-giving power in me, in Jesus' name." Unite your heart with His love by loving Him. See with your eye of faith the spiritual reality taking place.
4. Believe in faith that you have received His power and give thanks for it. Faith is the switch that turns on the power.	Mark 11:23,24	Do not keep saying, "Oh, please, Lord." Rather say, "Thank You, Lord, that Your power is making me well," as you look ahead with the eye of faith seeing that part of your body whole and functioning. Forget about everything else and think of God and Jesus Christ and His light flowing through you. Do not work too hard at it. Get comfortable and relax.

Figure Apx J.1

Exploring Additional Principles Concerning Prayer

When I first made the decision to allow my prayer times to be led by the Holy Spirit, I was wary because I did not know for sure where the boundaries were, and I did not want to fall into error. Therefore, I studied the biblical principles concerning prayer to give me an understanding of the kinds of prayer we can pray, the areas we are to pray in, the principles which are part of effective prayer, etc. I am listing these below along with Scripture verses supporting each. In the weeks that follow, I suggest you look up these verses, write them out, and meditate and journal about them, asking God what He wants to say to you concerning the application of each one to your life.

1. **Forgive everything against everyone** — Mark 11:25; John 15:9,12,13; 1 John 4:7,8,12,18-21; Matthew 6:12,14,15

   Following is a simple exercise to help you forgive from your heart: a) Use vision, seeing the person at the point they hurt you; b) Invite Jesus into the scene and ask Him to show you what He was doing and saying. Tune to spontaneous thoughts and pictures and write down what is flowing within you; c) In prayer, forgive the offender in the name of Jesus Christ; d) Like Job, pray God's blessing upon him (Job 42:10).

2. **Walk in holiness** — Psalm 66:18; Isaiah 59:1,2; Hebrews 5:7; 12:1; James 5:16

3. **Prayer must flow together with *rhema*** (*Rhema* gives **heart** faith, reveals God's will, and is to abide in you.) — Mark 11:22-24; Romans 10:10a,17; 1 John 5:14,15; John 15:7; Hebrews 11:1,6; James 1:6,7

4. **Pray fervently and earnestly with your whole heart** — James 5:17,18; 1 Kings 18:43 and context; 2 Chronicles 15:15b

5. **Pray in Jesus' name** — John 14:13; Mark 16:17

6. **Speak to the mountain** rather than simply praying to Jesus. Hold fast to your confession — Mark 11:23; Matthew 8:26; Hebrews 10:23

7. **See it done.** Believe that what you say is going to happen. Letting God show you a vision of the completed action will cause your heart to believe — Mark 11:23,24

8. **Pray until you praise.** A need is not prayed for until it has been overcome in prayer by the power and promises of God, and you have entered into peace — Philippians 4:6,7

9. **Pray persistently and exercise patience** — Luke 11:8-10; 18:1,7; Hebrews 6:12

10. **Fortify prayer with fasting** — Isaiah 58; Matthew 9:15; 17:21

11. **Pray with intensity**, with compassion and a sense of burden, with a broken heart, with agony, groaning and travail — Matthew 20:34; Psalm 34:18; 62:8; Hebrews 5:7; Luke 22:44; Romans 8:26

12. **Pray when you need God's strength.** Do not hide yourself in shame at your weakness — Hebrews 4:16; Psalm 50:15

13. **Pray in secret** — Matthew 6:6

14. **Pray specifically** — Acts 4:29-31

15. **Resist satan's attack by calling upon God.** Do not fight satan yourself. You will lose — 2 Corinthians 10:3-5; James 4:6-8; Ephesians 6:10-13

16. **Sow bountifully**, for in so doing, you will reap bountifully — 2 Corinthians 9:6-8 ; Philippians 4:16,17,19

17. **Avoid vain repetition** — Matthew 6:7; Luke 20:47

18. **Do not seek your own pleasure** — James 4:3

Notes

Notes

Areas of Prayer

As we examine the Lord's Prayer and other prayers in the Bible, we find that there are various areas of prayer in which we can engage. Seven of these areas are listed below. They will not all be found in every prayer session, nor will they follow a legalistic order or a rigid time slot. They are to flow **as directed by the Holy Spirit**. We are always to "pray in the Spirit" (Eph. 6:18), meaning that all our prayers are to be inspired, guided, energized and sustained by the Holy Spirit. Through *Logos*, we find what these seven prayer areas can encompass; through *rhema*, we find daily direction for our prayers.

As you pray, cultivate a constant openness to seeing and sensing the spiritual realm. Through dream, vision and imagery, you are able to see with the eye of faith what God is doing just as Jesus did (John 5:19-21; 8:38). Through sensing peace, burdens and other movings in your spirit, you are able to feel those things which God is feeling and impressing. By so doing, your prayer life will ascend above dry rationalism into the beauty and power of spiritual experiences. For prayer to be meaningful, it must be more than simple rationalism. Write out and prayerfully ponder the verses below.

1. **Confession of Sin** — 1 John 1:7-10; Psalm 139:23,24

2. **Praying with the Spirit** — 1 Corinthians 14:2,4a,14a,15,18

3. **Praise, Thanksgiving, Singing, Worship, Adoration** — Psalm 100:1-4; 1 Thessalonians 5:18

4. **Receiving: Waiting, Watching, Listening, Writing, Meditating** — Psalm 46:10a; Ecclesiastes 5:1,2; Habakkuk 1:1; 2:2

5. **Personal Petitions** — Matthew 6:11; 7:7; Psalm 50:15

6. **Intercession for Others** — 1 Timothy 2:1-4

7. **Speaking to the Mountain** — Mark 11:23

Personal Journaling Application

Prayer: "Lord, please speak to me about the balance between using a 'system' in prayer and flowing freely in prayer as You direct." Fix your eyes upon Jesus in some comfortable setting. Tune to spontaneity, ask the above question and record what comes bubbling back into your heart and mind.

Promises of Prayer

There are many promises concerning prayer. It is good to know them so they can be used as a source of encouragement. The following is a partial list. Once again, you will probably want to add other promises that the Lord reveals to you. Write out, meditate upon and journal about the verses below.

2 Chronicles 16:9a
John 11:40
John 14:21
John 15:7,8
John 16:12,13
Hebrews 6:14,15

Prayer and Action

Fitting prayer and work together in proper understanding and balance can be trying at times. The following are four truths about the combination of prayer and action.

1. Prayer must precede action in order to have Spirit-born action.

Prayer paves the highway of accomplishment. Increasing work and decreasing prayer equals meaningless endeavor. It is the doing that flows out of prayer that is the mightiest in touching human hearts. "Unless the Lord builds the house, they labor in vain who build it" (Ps. 127:1). "That which is born of the flesh is flesh; and that which is born of the Spirit is spirit" (Jn. 3:6).

If you do not want action of the flesh (i.e., a dead work — Heb. 6:1), then you must pray and find what action the Spirit wants and move in that. How easy it is to decide what we will do and then pray and ask God to bless it. Later, we may wonder why the results were not what we had hoped. God wants us to come to Him first for direction. Then, He will pour out His blessing upon "our projects," for they will truly be "His work."

2. Prayer is to lead to action.

Write out James 2:17,22,26.

When we have finished praying, we most likely will have received specific instructions that we are to obey. We may act and speak with **confidence**, knowing that God is performing the work according to the word that has been spoken.

3. Pray without ceasing while working at different tasks.

While working, your mind will often be attuned to the task before you. Your spirit (heart), however, is to remain open to being moved upon by God. Our work is not to enter our spirit. Only God is to be there. Anything else is idolatry. By keeping our spirits open, relaxed and attuned to God, we are praying without ceasing (1 Thess. 5:17).

4. Separate yourself unto God so you can bring life to the world.

We can be totally immersed in God all the time, living in our little utopia, and not even be aware of the misery of the world around us. On the other hand, we can be overcome by the woes of the world and feel there is no hope for it. We must again achieve the balance of Jesus of Nazareth, who spent enough time with God receiving His power that when He went to the world, He was able to overcome its darkness with His light.

That is precisely what we are to do. We are to spend enough time with God in prayer that we are charged with His love and power; and then, guided and directed by the Holy Spirit, we are to go to a needy world and minister His grace. We flow with His power, not ours. We minister His thoughts, not ours. We are directed by our spirits rather than our own reasoning. When we feel the power and life of God diminishing within us, we must again go to our quiet place of prayer to renew God's life within us.

Personal Journaling Application

Ask the Lord to speak to you about the balance of prayer and work in your life. Fix your eyes upon Him. Tune to spontaneity. Record below the flow that issues forth from your heart.

Ways to Pray

There are many ways to pray for other people. Following are seven of them. Write in the verses and meditate and journal about them, asking God to reveal to you what He wants about each verse.

1. Bind Evil Powers and Cast Them Down — Mark 3:27; Ephesians 6:12

2. Loose the Holy Spirit to Move in Hearts — Matthew 16:19; Romans 2:4

3. Build a Hedge of Thorns — Hosea 2:6,7

4. Pray That God Will Turn Hearts — Proverbs 21:1

5. Pray That God Will Direct Mouths — Proverbs 16:1

6. Pray for a Spirit of Revelation — Ephesians 1:17,18

7. Intercede — 1 Timothy 5:5; Luke 2:36-38; Genesis 18:32; Isaiah 59:16a; Ezekiel 22:30,31

Personal Application

Spend some time in prayer. Ask the Lord to burden you with the way(s) you should pray for any situations that He presents before you. Pray in these different ways.

I have wondered whether I should use a prayer list. For me it was the problem of *rhema* versus legalism. Each one will have to solve this question in the way that is best for them. I would recommend that if you decide to keep a prayer list, try not to be married to it in a legalistic sense.

When I first began to pray, I carefully followed a prayer list. I found it deadening. After coming to an understanding of *paga*, I rejected all prayer lists. I then found there were things I wished I had prayed for more diligently, but I would forget about them for periods of time. I currently use a prayer list for prompting, but do not require slavish obedience to it, or guilt and condemnation when I fail to perfectly keep it. I seek to pray for those things the Spirit wants prayed for that day. Each of you will have to establish your own balance.

From My Journal

"Lord, what about prayer…?"

"Pray for those I lay on your heart."

On another day, from my journal:

Having just finished studying the ways of praying, and the principles and areas of prayer, I felt like prayer had become a cumbersome burden.

6/17/80: "Good morning, Lord. I love You. I give You this day. I place it in Your hands. Are there things You would like to say to me?"

"Yes. Remember how simple it has been to come to Me? It still is. Do not make it difficult. I am here. I desire to answer you. The things you are learning are good and helpful, but do not let them become obstructive and block the simplicity of our relationship together. If you let Me help you keep them in proper perspective, they will be a real help and blessing. If they get out of balance, they will become meaningless legalism and bondage. I will help you keep them in proper balance. Just come to Me.

"Also, do not forget the specific actions that can be worked out through prayer. As one learns to come to Me, specifically in times of need, I am there to give the specific help they need — whether it be a word of wisdom or knowledge or discernment for the casting out of demons. All power and ability will flow out of our relationship, and that is the order. First, a love relationship. Out of that, the meeting of specific needs.

"I love you, Mark. Keep tuned to My Spirit."

"Thank You, Lord …"

This reminded me of Psalm 105:4a: "Seek the Lord and His strength." It is so easy to overbalance one or the other, or to reverse the order altogether. But as we come to Him, He will help us keep it straight.

Personal Journaling Application

Ask the Lord whether He wants you to use a prayer list or not. Fix your eyes upon Him. You may want to begin with a time of praise and worship until you are caught up in His presence. Then tune to spontaneity and ask Him the question suggested above. Record in your journal or on your computer the effortless flow of thoughts within your heart.

Notes

WORKING DEFINITIONS
CONCERNING SPIRITUAL REALITIES

Precise workable definitions help us accomplish purposes swiftly, easily and continuously. Because science has defined "gravity," they can also define "air pressure" and "lift." They can do this so precisely that airplanes can take off and land <u>effortlessly and with great regularity</u>. <u>I want the same clarity and consistency for my spiritual life</u>. I want "Spirit-anointed lift" on a daily, ongoing basis.

These definitions help me achieve this by teaching me to stay away from rationalism, humanism, man's reason and dead works. I enjoy instead God's voice, His vision, and the anointing which comes through the Holy Spirit.

When I began my walk in the Spirit many years ago, and I asked others who had gone before me for working definitions, I received little help. When I asked what God's voice sounded like, they responded, "You know that you know that you know." Obviously this is totally worthless if you don't know, and I didn't.

When I wanted to walk in the Spirit and I wanted to know what my spirit felt like, they said it was the innermost part of me. Of course that is not what it feels like, that is where it is located. Then they told me that it was the part of me that contacted God. That is not what it feels like, that is what it does. So no one could even give me a definition of what my spirit feels like. How could I possibly "walk in the Spirit"? I didn't even have a clear understanding of what the experience was.

Well, it is pretty hard to live a life in the Spirit with no solid working definitions to build upon. The assortment of definitions below will get you started in this pursuit. Some come from this book and some from other books we have written. Below we simply state the definition without all the supporting Scripture which is in our various books. May this understanding assist you as you build your life in the Holy Spirit!

God's voice — sounds like spontaneous thoughts which light upon your mind.

HOW TO HEAR GOD'S VOICE

Man's spirit — is sensed as underlying attitudes, underlying motivations and underlying character traits. For example, we could tune to God with an **attitude** of reverence, awe and respect, a **motivation** of seeking Him diligently, and a **character trait** of humility and dependence upon Him.

Man's spirit or heart — largely interchangeable words

The Function of the Human Spirit

- To be joined to the Holy Spirit (1 Cor. 6:17)

- To receive and transmit the life of the Holy Spirit to man through the fruits and gifts

Five faculties of man's spirit/heart

- **Ears of my heart** (John 5:30) — where I hear spontaneous thoughts from the spirit world.

- **Eyes of my heart** (Rev. 4:1) — where I see spontaneous pictures from the spirit world.

- **Mind of my heart** (Luke 2:19) — where I ponder, meditate and muse

- **Will of my heart** (Acts 19:21) — where I establish convictions which I live out of

- **Emotions of my heart** (1 Kings 21:2-5) — deep underlying emotions which affect my behavior; we can pick up God's emotions or demons' emotions

Language of the mind — Man's analytical reason, which is rebuked by Jesus four times in the Gospels, and never encouraged in the Scriptures. Left-brainers must be instructed to turn away from this or they will naturally do it when they seek to come into the Lord's presence. Sometimes right-brainers, after hearing from God, will add to that word with left-brain thinking and will believe they are still in the right brain and still hearing from God. Both left-brainers and right-brainers must learn to distinguish what is from the Spirit and what is from their own minds.

Language of the heart — is flowing thoughts (John 7:38), flowing pictures (Acts 2:17), flowing emotions (Gal. 5:22,23), pondering and meditation (Ps. 77:6). Sensing God's movement in our hearts can be called illumination, revelation, revelation knowledge, perception, discernment, word of wisdom, word of knowledge or prophecy.

Western study — man using his reasoning capacity

Biblical meditation — the Holy Spirit using all faculties in man's heart and mind

Proper fuel for our hearts — Faith, hope and love (1 Cor. 13:13). If you journal, God will automatically fill you up on this fuel so you will run well for the day.

Four Keys to Hearing God's Voice:

Key # 1 — Recognize God's voice as spontaneous thoughts which light upon your mind.

Key # 2 — Quiet yourself so you can hear God's voice.

Key # 3 — Look for vision as you pray.

Key # 4 — Write down the flow of thoughts and pictures that come to you.

Four words which summarize the four keys to hearing God's voice:
Stillness — Vision — Spontaneity — Journaling

Hearing God's voice is as simple as quieting yourself down, fixing your eyes on Jesus, tuning to spontaneity, and writing. (MEMORIZE AND SHARE THIS!)

As exemplified in Habakkuk 2:1,2	Key Succinctly Stated
I will stand on my guard post	Quiet yourself down by…
And I will keep watch to see	Fixing your eyes on Jesus.
What He will speak to me	Tune to spontaneity.
Then the Lord will answer me…and said, "Record the vision."	Write down the flow of thoughts and pictures.

The heart posture that ensures the flow within will be the Holy Spirit!

Biblical Statement (John 7:37-39)	Key Confession
If any one is thirsty	Lord, I am **thirsty** for You
Let him come to Me	Lord, I **fix my heart upon You**
And drink	I **tune to flow**
He who believes in Me	I **believe** the flow within me is You!

The Leader's Paradigm — a broad-based system for discovering truth based on six ways God communicates with us: illumined thoughts in our minds, peace versus unrest in our hearts, illumined Scriptures, illumined counsel of others, illumined understanding of life's fruit, and direct revelation through dreams, visions, journaling, and prophecy. A consensus of all six is sought, especially when making major decisions.

Spiritual advisors — people who are alongside you or ahead of you in an area and whom you seek out for spiritual advice; who are willing to seek God with you and share with you, for your prayerful consideration, what they sense in their hearts.

Notes

Submission — openness to the Spirit-led counsel and correction of several others, while keeping a sense of personal responsibility for our own discernment of God's voice within.

Sorting out three categories of thoughts

1. Spontaneous Positive Thoughts we will assume come from the Holy Spirit. They line up with the names/character of the Holy Spirit, including Edifier, Comforter, Teacher, Creator and Healer, Giver of Life.

2. Spontaneous Negative Thoughts we assume come from demons, and thus will line up with the names/character of satan, which include Accuser, Adversary, Liar, Destroyer, Condemner, Thief and Murderer.

3. Analytical Thoughts come from self, from our own reasoning process, and are sensed as cognitive, connected thoughts.

A dead work — Man doing things through his abilities (Heb. 6:1–to be repented of)

A live work — An activity birthed in the Holy Spirit (John 5:19,20,30)

Law of the Spirit of Life in Christ Jesus — the energizing we experience as we fix ourselves upon God and call for His life to flow out through our spirits (Rom. 8:2).

Know where the eyes of your heart are fixed at all times because:

- The intuitive/spontaneous flow comes from the vision being held before your eyes.

- Whatever you focus on grows within you and whatever grows within you, you become.

- We are transformed by what we look upon. We are to fix our eyes upon Jesus and be transformed into His likeness (2 Cor. 3:18; 4:18; Heb. 12:2). It is called "coming to the light."

- Looking at our sin and weakness and seeking to battle them really doesn't provide victory (called "stripping away"). Seeing and radiating Jesus is the only true approach to spiritual growth.

Philosophies:

- *Humanism* — puts human effort as the center of life

- *Rationalism* — puts man's reasoning process at the center of life

- *Christian Mysticism* — Puts releasing the Holy Spirit at the center of life (1 Cor. 2:9,10)

- *Satan's temptation* in the Garden of Eden was to step from direct spiritual encounter with God on a daily basis (mysticism), to rational humanism (YOU can be like God, KNOWING …) (Gen. 3:5).

Man's reasoning — man controlling his reasoning process — self in action

Spirit-led reasoning — allowing flowing pictures and words from the Holy Spirit to guide the reasoning process.

Demonically-led reasoning — allowing flowing pictures and words from demons to guide our reasoning process.

Vain imagination — man picturing what he wants (Rom. 1:21)

Evil imagination — man picturing demonic things (Jer. 16:12)

Godly imagination — Man picturing things from God (1 Chron. 29:18)

Dream and vision — Holy Spirit guiding the eyes of man's heart (Acts 2:17)

Christian maturity is defined as — living as Jesus did, naturally and comfortably out of the Father's initiative, doing what you hear and see the Father doing (John 5:19,20,30; 8:26,28,38). This is counter to the Western lifestyle which says we live out of reason (rationalism) and self-effort (humanism). So we step out of the Western worldview and step into God's anointing!

The Lord of All — Almighty God (trust Him, He even numbers the hairs on your head)

The defeated foe — satan (don't re-empower him by placing your faith in him)

Spiritual treason and spiritual adultery — where the King's engaged Bride, the Church, is infatuated with the belief that the King's archenemy, satan, whom the King Himself defeated at great cost will expand his rule and reign, and will ravish and humiliate the King's Betrothed.

New Age — People hungering for spiritual reality and not going through our Lord and Savior Jesus Christ to get it. Many of these people could not find spiritual reality in dead churches so they turned to the New Age. The Church should be offering them true spiritual encounters in the Holy Spirit.

Logos — the entire communication process; also, the Bible, the Word of God

Rhema — when words leave one's lips

Naba — the word for "true prophecy;" it means "bubbling up," so when I want to prophesy, I posture my heart properly before God and speak forth the thoughts and words that are bubbling up within me.

Paga — God's voice leading me in prayer. It is sensed as spontaneous thoughts which light upon my mind while I am praying. So I fix my eyes upon Jesus, and tune to flow and pray, being guided by the flow.

The Law:

- Teaches us that we can never be holy without Jesus' shed blood (Gal. 3:22)

- It **cannot** impart life/anointing to us (Gal. 3:21)

- Keeps us from destroying ourselves before we learn to walk in the Holy Spirit (Gal. 3:23)

- Is **not** the driving force of those who walk in the Spirit (Gal. 3:25; 5:18)

Workers of the Law — an attempt to become spiritual through our own efforts (Gal. 3:2,3)

Hearers with faith — believe you become spiritual by saying "yes" to what God has done (Gal. 3:2-8). You declare that everything was completed in Jesus, and now Jesus lives in you making you complete. Whenever you need anything, you ask for Christ to provide it through the indwelling Holy Spirit.

You tune to flowing thoughts, flowing pictures and flowing emotions, and because of the operation of the "Law of the Spirit of Life," you experience the Holy Spirit providing it. You thank Him for this wonderful provision. A miraculous transaction has taken place within you. You have stepped from your frame which is dust (Ps. 103:14), to the power of God in your spirit (2 Pet. 1:4). You see yourself as dust fused to glory. You may take this step, from weak dust to divine anointing, hundreds of times a day.

Living and walking by the Spirit — (Gal. 5:25) I live as Jesus, tuned to divine flow — flowing thoughts, flowing pictures, flowing emotions, and flowing power (anointing).

Ongoing warfare between workers of the Law and hearers with faith — Workers of the law are slaves. They persecute those who are free and who live by faith (Gal. 4:21-31). They generally take satan's stance (the accuser's stance — Rev. 12:10). So if you are living by faith, know that legalists will be persecuting you and calling you demonized just as they did Jesus (Matt. 12:24). They will have websites against you. They carry the spirit of murder with them (Jn. 8:44), so they will be trying to kill you. I guess we just agree with Jesus, that they are sons of the devil, thinking they are doing God a service as they kill the prophets (Acts 7:51-53).

God's exams — God tests us to see if there is faith in our hearts or if we are still grumblers (Deut. 8:2).

God's plan for our lives — to prosper us (Jer. 29:11,12)

Giving thanks always lets us pass God's tests — we are to give thanks *for* everything (Eph. 5:20) and *in* everything (1 Thess. 5:18).

Journaling/Prophecy reveals potential — A promise from God in your journal reveals what is available to you. It is stating your potential. If you go after it, you can possess it. If you don't, you are likely to never realize it.

Checklist for Tuning in to God   *Notes*

I Am Living the Tabernacle Experience

❑ **Altar** — I have laid down my own initiative, self-effort and strength.

❑ **Laver** — I cleanse myself regularly by meditating upon the Bible.

❑ **Shewbread** — I allow my will to be ground fine before God and I walk in fellowship with the Body of Christ.

❑ **Lampstand** — I have moved from my reasoning to Spirit-led reasoning.

❑ **Incense** — I am a continuous worshipper; in everything I give thanks.

❑ **Ark** — I wait before God in stillness to receive what He has for me.

I Am Applying the Tuning Dial of Habakkuk 2:1-3

❑ I am quieting myself down.

❑ I am fixing my eyes on Jesus.

❑ I am tuning to spontaneity.

❑ I am writing down the flow of thoughts and pictures that come to me.

I Am Applying the Fine-Tuning Dial of Hebrews 10:19-22

❑ My heart is true, honest and sincere.

❑ I have absolute faith that God's river is flowing within me.

❑ My conscience is completely clear through Christ's cleansing blood.

❑ I have been obedient to God's previous *rhema*.

I Am Confirming My Journaling Through Other Ways God Speaks

❑ My journaling lines up with Scripture and the character of God.

❑ My spiritual advisors confirm my journaling is from God.

Notes

STARTER QUESTIONS FOR BEGINNING JOURNALERS

Having coaches is always great, because they take you by the hand and get you doing an activity properly. The following questions can serve as a coach to you, helping you ask wise and effective questions of the Lord. It is recommended you work your way through these during the first six months of your journaling.

Begin journaling by quieting yourself down, perhaps with worship, and fixing your eyes on Jesus in a comfortable setting. Ask Jesus to speak to you, then tune to flowing thoughts and flowing pictures. Write down your questions and what the Lord says to you.

Make sure you share with your spiritual advisors any entries which (1) you are unsure came from God — so you can know for sure and (2) anything which would call for a major decision or major new direction.

General

Good morning, Lord. I love You and I give You this day. What would You like to speak to me?

How do You see me?

What do You want to say to me?

Do You love me?

What blocks keep me from moving forward in my relationship with You? How can these best be dealt with?

What wrong beliefs would You like me to repent of, and what godly beliefs would You like to replace them with?

Lord, are there any people whom I need to forgive and release to a greater extent than I have?

Notes

Marriage

What do You want to say to me about my marriage?

How do You see my marriage?

How do You want me to see my marriage?

What would You have me do to enhance my marriage?

How can I show greater love to my spouse?

Are there things You would have me do to show greater love, honor and respect toward my spouse?

Children

Tell me how You see each of my children.

Can You give me any special instructions about how we should raise these children? (Judg. 13:12)

What are the gifts and strengths You have given them that You want me to focus on and help them develop?

What are their weaknesses and how do You want me to come alongside to strengthen them?

What are their special needs that You would have me meet?

How would You have me enhance my relationship with each of my children?

Is there anything You would have me do to enrich my children's walk with You?

Are there things You would have me do to show greater love, honor and respect toward my children?

Work

Lord, what do You want to say about my work?

How do You see it?

How do You want me to see it?

Are there any attitudes I have about my work or my work companions that You would like to speak to me about?

Ministry

Lord, what is the primary ministry You would have me doing at this time?

What would You have me do to continue preparing myself for effectiveness in this ministry?

Bible Meditation

Read a Gospel story, and then picture the story with you being one of the characters. Watch the action, tune to flow and journal. Ask, "Lord, what do You want to say to me from this story?" Record in your journal what God says.

You can expand this by going to other sections of the Bible also, entering the stories and asking God what He wants to speak to you from them.

ADDITIONAL RESOURCES

Hear God's Voice—Guaranteed

Did you know that you can be totally confident in your ability to hear the voice of God? You don't have to settle for being unsure of what His will is for your life. You *can* take all of the guesswork out, and get to a place where you can say, for sure, "The Lord spoke to me."

> "My sheep hear My voice." John 10:27
> It's not our guarantee. It's God's.

This package of materials contains everything you will need. It includes a copy of *How to Hear God's Voice* for you to share and invest in the life of a friend or loved one. Your creative and intuitive side will love *Dialogue with God*, which is presented in an easy-to-read story format. *Learning to Communicate with God* will give teenagers these very same principles, bringing them into daily conversation with God. *Living with Jesus 3 — Talking and Listening* will even get your children hearing from Jesus. Is there any more valuable gift you could possibly give them?

For the ultimate in immersive mentorship, the complete course on video cassettes or the abbreviated weekend seminar audio CDs will draw you into a classroom experience with others who are learning to hear from God right alongside you. You are guaranteed to have a great time hearing about Mark's often hilarious experiences: the all-too-familiar trials, misconceptions and mistakes that are an integral part of the journey. A teacher's guide is also included, allowing you to help transform the lives of others by sharing the gift of God's voice.

> "I'm taking Communion With God. [Communion With God is the previous title of How to Hear God's Voice.] I am so blessed so far. My life is already completely transformed. I went from hearing God speak to me once in a while to hearing Him not just in my journaling times but even throughout the rest of the day. What a difference this has made."
>
> — Andrew Steck

Notes

311   HOW TO HEAR GOD'S VOICE

Notes

"*Dialogue with God* is worth a million dollars to any Christian who is serious about the issue of hearing the voice of God. Mark's teaching on this issue profoundly impacted my life."

— Rev. John Arnott
Senior Pastor of Toronto Airport Christian Fellowship

Hear God's Voice Guaranteed Package
How to Hear God's Voice
How to Hear God's Voice Teacher's Guide
How to Hear God's Voice CD Set
How to Hear God's Voice Videos
Dialogue with God
Learning to Communicate with God
Living with Jesus 3 — Talking and Listening

Invest in this package today!

Get current pricing and order your discounted package online at
www.cwgministries.org/voicepackage.htm
Or give us a call at 1-800-466-6961

Special Discount Coupon

$125 OFF the Christian Leadership University Course
REN103 Communion With God

Why would I want to enroll in this course?

You've already taken the first step by reading *How to Hear God's Voice*, but don't let your journey end there. What you've just learned requires a major shift in the way you live your life and experience your relationship with God. Don't risk missing out and falling back into your old patterns and habits. That still, small voice is too precious to let fade away.

When you meditate on revelation truths in the context of a CLU course, you are required to fully integrate the life-changing principles. Nothing is left to chance. You will learn what you are supposed to learn and your life will be transformed by the power of the Holy Spirit.

REN103 Communion With God — 3 credits (Reg. ~~$330~~*)
Graduate version REN503 — 4 credits (Reg. ~~$433~~*)

This is a thoroughly practical course on discerning God's voice. Biblical techniques of vision and journaling are combined to help you discern and clarify the spontaneous thoughts that come from God. *How to Hear God's Voice* is the primary text, and you will be immersed in the full classroom experience utilizing audio cassettes and a seminar workbook. *You will* hear God's voice and be equipped to train others to do the same.

Follow these simple steps to enroll today:

- Go online to www.cluonline.com/apply and complete the New Student Enrollment Form.

- At the end of this form you can order REN103 or REN503 by clicking on the appropriate box.

- In the note box at the end of this form, type in the following. "Please apply the $125 Coupon Discount Offer 777."

*Excludes Prior Purchases.
*Offer cannot be combined with any other discount.
*Prices approximate and subject to change without notice.

CREATE A LAMAD ENCOUNTER GROUP!

Lamad: Real life, biblically-grounded, revelation-based learning

Disciple your friends and earn a college education — www.cwgministries.org/LEGs

Purpose: To transform lives by bringing people into interaction with the Holy Spirit. Lamad learning groups begin with real life issues and add enlightenment from God which produces transformation through the power of the Holy Spirit. The Lamad Encounter Group member is required to interact with life, the Bible, and the Holy Spirit.

Main Activity: Family and friends gather in a home, a church, or other building for 12 weeks to discuss and practice the truths they are exploring through a Lamad learning experience.

L.E.G. Facilitator: Guides group discussion and learning experiences. See preparation requirements at www.cwgministries.org/LEGFacilitator.

L.E.G. Participant: Completes lamad book/course during the 12-week learning experience and participates in group discussions and activities.

CLU Audit/Credit Options: If four or more Encounter Group participants are enrolled in Christian Leadership University, taking the lamad course for credit from CLU, the course tuition for these students will be discounted $100 off the published price (does not apply to one-credit courses).

A Lamad Group participant may begin by auditing the CLU course ($25 plus cost of course materials), and then change to a full-credit CLU student anytime before the end of the course by simply notifying CLU, completing all course requirements, and paying the difference.

The Group Facilitator will receive $25 tuition credit toward the future purchase of a CLU course for each paid full-credit CLU student in his group. If the facilitator has previously completed the course with CLU, he will earn two extra CLU credits free of charge for leading the group. If he disciples 12, his next course could be completely paid for (12 x $25 = $300, which is the average cost of a CLU course). If he desires and is approved as a CLU adjunct faculty member (www.cluonline.com/AdjunctApplication), he may assist CLU in grading the coursework of L.E.G. participants, receiving an additional $25 gift of tuition credit for each CLU student graded.

All CLU students enroll directly with CLU at www.cluonline.com/apply, ordering their course materials from CLU. When registering for a CLU course and desiring a Lamad Group tuition discount, a "Lamad Encounter Group Order Form" must be completed. This is available at www.cwgministries.org/LEGOrderForm. If a total of four students do not enroll with CLU for full credit for the course, then the L.E.G. discount will not be extended to members of that group.

If videos are available for the course (see course materials list at www.cluonline.com/coursedetail.txt), you may choose to order them to watch as a group. In this case, be sure that when group members enroll for the course they state that they do not need the cassettes.

WHY CHRISTIAN LEADERSHIP UNIVERSITY IS THE RIGHT CHOICE FOR YOU...

"The classes have been beyond anything I had hoped for. This has been more like an adventure than school."

— Vanessa Tinsley-Stone

- You learn from home at 1/5 the cost of traditional college.
- You learn to hear the voice of God through the course "Communion With God."
- You grow in revelation knowledge by hearing God's voice in every course.
- You are trained for anointed leadership in the area that God has chosen for you.
- Curriculum is developed by *proven leaders* in each field.
- "Delight-centered learning" lets you follow your heart in course selection.
- "*Lamad Education*" provides real life, biblically-grounded, revelation-based learning.
- "*The Leader's Paradigm*" offers a broad-based system for discovering truth.
- Associate's, Bachelor's, Master's and Doctoral degrees available in 13 areas.
- Transcripts from other colleges and life experience credits are accepted.

*Raising up leaders by bringing
the voice of God to your learning experience*

www.cluonline.com
Complete catalog and online enrollment

Affiliated with the Apostolic Council for Educational Accountability

---

Visit Communion With God Ministries on the web:
www.cwgministries.org

Download **free books** and articles.

Sign up for a free monthly newsletter with examples of journaling and Christian dream interpretation, as well as exclusive **discounts** for subscribers.

Shop our complete catalog of 60 books, cassettes and videos by Mark and Patti Virkler.

HOW TO HEAR GOD'S VOICE